Jacky Newbrook   Judith Wilson

NEW first certificate

Gold

coursebook

Longman

Contents

Writing reference p.206   Vocabulary reference p.222

Exam information

The Cambridge First Certificate Examination in English is made up of five papers, each testing a different area of ability in English. Each paper is worth 20% of the total mark. There are five grades. A, B and C are pass grades; D and E are fail grades.

Paper 1 Reading *(1 hour 15 minutes)*

The Reading paper has four parts. Each part tests a different reading skill or skills. There are 35 questions altogether. You write your answers on an answer sheet during the exam.

Part 1 Multiple matching
Focus: Finding the main points of the paragraphs in a text
Task: You match headings or summary sentences to each paragraph of a text. There are six or seven paragraphs and seven or eight headings or sentences, so there is one extra heading or sentence that you do not need to use.
▶ **Exam focus** p.160

Part 2 Multiple-choice questions
Focus: Understanding detail, gist and opinion, and deducing meaning of words
Task: There are seven or eight four-option multiple-choice questions. You have to choose the correct option (A, B, C or D) based on the information in the text.
▶ **Exam focus** p.44

Part 3 Gapped text
Focus: Understanding text structure and organisation
Task: You read a text from which seven or eight paragraphs or sentences have been removed and placed in jumbled order after the text. You have to decide where they fit in the text. There is one extra paragraph or sentence that you do not need to use.
▶ **Exam focus** p.148

Part 4 Multiple matching
Focus: Finding specific information and detail
Task: You read 13–15 questions or statements about a text which has been divided into sections, or several short texts. You have to decide which section or text contains the information relating to each question or statement.
▶ **Exam focus** p.24

Paper 2 Writing *(1 hour 30 minutes)*

The Writing paper is divided into two parts, and you have to complete one task from each part. You have to write 120–180 words for each answer. Each answer carries equal marks, so you should not spend longer on one than another.

Part 1 is compulsory, and there is no choice of questions. You have to write a transactional letter based on given information and prompts. The letter may be informal or formal. ▶ Unit 1 p.16, Unit 2 p.28

Part 2 has four tasks to choose from. The first three options may include any three of the following:
- a non-transactional letter ▶ Unit 11 p.140
- an article ▶ Unit 4 p.52
- a report ▶ Unit 6 p.78
- a discursive composition ▶ Unit 7 p.50
- a story ▶ Unit 3 p.40

The fourth option has a choice of two tasks based on one of five background reading texts. The task could be any one of the following: a letter, an article, a report, a composition.

The background reading texts change regularly, so you should check the current regulations to find out what the texts are. ▶ **Writing reference** p.206

Paper 3 Use of English *(1 hour 15 minutes)*

There are five parts in the Use of English paper, with 65 questions altogether. You write your answers on an answer sheet during the exam. There is always an example at the beginning of each task to help you.

Part 1 Multiple-choice cloze
Focus: Vocabulary
Task: You read a text with 15 gaps. You choose the best word to fit each gap from a choice of four options (A, B, C or D). ▶ **Exam focus** p.157

Part 2 Open cloze
Focus: Grammar and vocabulary
Task: You read a text with 15 gaps. You have to think of the most appropriate word to fill the gaps. You must use one word only. No options are provided.
▶ **Exam focus** p.83

Part 3 Key word transformations

Focus: Grammar and vocabulary
Task: There are ten items. You are given a sentence and a 'key word'. You have to complete a second, gapped sentence using the given word. The second sentence has a different grammatical structure but must have a similar meaning to the original. ▶ **Exam focus** p.61

Part 4 Error correction

Focus: Grammar
Task: You read a text with 17 lines. Some lines are correct and some have an extra word which should not be there. You have to identify the extra word in the incorrect lines. Up to five lines may be correct.
▶ **Exam focus** p.36

Part 5 Word formation

Focus: Vocabulary
Task: You read a text with ten gaps, one in each line. You are given the stem of the missing word in capitals at the end of the line. You have to change the form of this word to fit the context. ▶ **Exam focus** p.110

Paper 4 Listening *(approximately 40 minutes)*

There are four parts in the Listening paper, with a total of 30 questions. You write your answers on the question paper and then you have five minutes at the end of the exam to transfer them to an answer sheet. In each part you will hear the text(s) twice. The texts may be monologues or exchanges between interacting speakers. There will be a variety of accents.

Part 1 Extracts with multiple-choice questions

Focus: Each extract will have a different focus, which could be: main point, detail, purpose or location of speech, relationship between the speakers, intention, mood or opinion of the speakers
Task: You hear eight short, unrelated extracts of about 30 seconds each. They may be monologues or conversations. You have to answer one three-option multiple-choice question (A, B or C) for each extract.
▶ **Exam focus** p.88

Part 2 Sentence or note completion

Focus: Specific information
Task: You hear a monologue or conversation lasting about three minutes. You complete sentences or notes with words from the text. ▶ **Exam focus** p.98

Part 3 Multiple matching

Focus: As for Part 1
Task: You hear a series of five monologues or exchanges, lasting about 30 seconds each. The speaker/s in each extract are different, but the situations or topics are all related to each other. You have to match each speaker to one of six statements or questions (A–F). There is one extra option that you do not need to use.
▶ **Exam focus** p.131

Part 4 Selection from two or three possible answers

Focus: Specific information, opinion and feeling
Task: You hear a monologue or conversation which lasts about three minutes. You have to select answers from two or three choices such as true/false, yes/no, three-option multiple choice. ▶ **Exam focus** p.109

Paper 5 Speaking *(approximately 14 minutes)*

You take the Speaking test with a partner. There are two examiners. One is the 'interlocutor', who speaks to you, and the other is the 'assessor', who just listens. There are four different parts in the test.

Part 1 Interview *(3 minutes)*

Focus: Giving personal information
Task: The interlocutor asks each of you to say a little about yourself, such as where you come from, what you do in your free time. ▶ **Exam focus** p.15

Part 2 Individual long turn *(4 minutes)*

Focus: Organising your ideas, giving information, expressing opinions
Task: The interlocutor gives you a pair of photographs to compare and contrast, and to give a personal reaction to. You speak by yourself for about a minute while your partner listens. Then the interlocutor asks your partner a question about what you have said. Only a short answer is expected. You then change roles. ▶ **Exam focus** p.77

Part 3 Collaborative task *(3 minutes)*

Focus: Interacting with your partner, agreeing and disagreeing, speculating, making suggestions
Task: You are given a task to discuss together, based on a set of pictures. You should try to reach a conclusion together, but there is no right or wrong answer to the task, and you don't have to agree with each other. It is the interaction between you that is important.
▶ **Exam focus** p.126

Part 4 Discussion *(4 minutes)*

Focus: Exchanging information and opinions, etc.
Task: The interlocutor asks you both general questions related to the topic of Part 3, and gives you the chance to give your opinions on other aspects of the same topic.
▶ **Exam focus** p.126

UNIT
1 What's on?

Speaking 1

1 Look at the film stills and discuss the questions.

1 Can you name the films?
2 What kind of films are they? Choose from the words in the box.
3 What type of film do you like best? Why?

action animation/cartoon comedy horror
musical romance science fiction/fantasy
Western thriller

2 Think of the film you have seen most recently.

1 What was it called?
2 Who was in it?
3 Where was it set?
4 What was it about?
5 How many stars would you give it?

* * * * *	outstanding
* * * *	good
* * *	all right
* *	not very good
*	terrible

6 Why did you give the film this rating? Explain, using words and expressions from the boxes.

The plot was ...	exciting realistic terrible
The setting was ...	frightening unusual
The acting was ...	boring sad funny
	excellent average

Example:

*I gave it three stars – I thought it was all right.
The plot was quite exciting, but the setting wasn't
very realistic, and the acting was only average.*

3 Imagine you are a film producer.
Answer these questions and give your reasons.

1 What kind of film would you like to make?
2 Where will it be set?
3 Who will you choose to star in it?

Listening 1: note completion

1 You will hear a radio interview about a survey of popular films. First, read through the notes below. The results of the survey covered five main areas. What were they? Can you predict what any of the answers might be?

Film survey

Date of survey: (1) ....
Number of people responding: (2) ....

Results of survey

Most popular type of film: (3) ....
e.g. 'The Godfather'

Best plots: two popular themes:
(4) .... and good versus evil.
(NB can have a (5) .... of both themes
e.g. in 'Star Wars')

Most popular settings:
<u>place</u> (6) .... locations (e.g. deserts, jungles)
<u>time</u> the (7) ....

Most popular stars:
<u>male</u> Robert de Niro, Harrison Ford, Humphrey Bogart
<u>female</u> Diane Keaton, Jodie Foster, Marilyn Monroe, Carrie Fisher
(NB pop. female stars had (8) .... + glamour)

Titles of the most popular films:
often consisted of (9) .... and included name of a place or (10) ....

2

🎧 **1** Now listen and complete the notes. Write a word or short phrase for each answer. (In this exercise there is a separate line for each word.)

> **TIP!** Complete the gaps with the exact words used in the recording – don't try to use your own words.

🎧 **2** Listen again to check and complete your answers.

3

1 Carry out a similar survey to find out what your class thinks are the best films of the 21st century so far. Work in groups. Ask and answer questions about:

- types of films (with examples)
- best plots (with examples)
- most popular settings (place and time)
- most popular actors (male and female)
- most popular titles.

2 Find out the results of the other groups.

3 Write an email that could be sent to the presenter of the radio programme summarising the findings of your class.

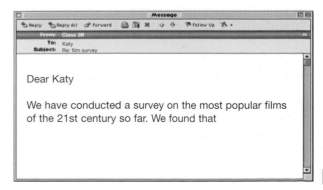

Vocabulary 1: recording vocabulary

1   Read the statements below. Which ones do you agree with?

1   I like sitting right in the front row at the cinema.
2   I prefer films that have a happy ending.
3   I think the special effects in modern films are much better than in older ones.
4   I admire film stars who do their own stunts instead of getting someone else to do them.
5   I find films with lots of flashbacks very confusing – it's hard to follow the plot.
6   I prefer films to plays because you can have close-up shots of the actors.
7   I think Steven Spielberg is the greatest director alive today.

2   It will help you to remember new words if you review and record them after each lesson.

A mind map is one way to record words related to the same topic. Look at the example below and add the highlighted words from Exercise 1. Then think of one more word to add to each part of the mind map.

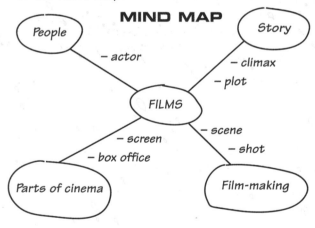

MIND MAP

People — actor

FILMS

Story — climax — plot

— screen — box office

— scene — shot

Parts of cinema

Film-making

3   The following extract from a student's vocabulary notebook shows another way of recording vocabulary.

1   Add the translation of the word in your own language.

2   Which line points to
   a) an example sentence?
   b) the pronunciation?
   c) related words?
   d) the definition?

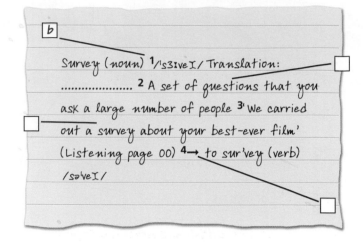

b

Survey (noun) ¹/'sɜːveɪ/ Translation:
.... ² A set of questions that you
ask a large number of people ³' We carried
out a survey about your best-ever film'
(Listening page 00) ⁴→ to sur'vey (verb)
/səˈveɪ/

4   Discuss.

1   What other ways of recording vocabulary have you used?
2   Which have you found most effective?

5   Look back at the first two pages of the unit. Are there any other words you would like to record?

Grammar 1: revision of simple tenses

1

1   Some of the following sentences have mistakes in the use of the verb forms. Correct those you think are wrong, using present simple, past simple or present perfect forms. Use the highlighted time expressions to help you.

Example: All my life, I loved going to the cinema. *Wrong. All my life, I've loved going to the cinema.*

1   I've met Carrie fifteen years ago.
2   I usually sit in the back row when I go to the cinema with my friends.
3   I've belonged to this club from 2001 to 2003.
4   I've already seen that film – let's go to something different.
5   He goes to the cinema at least twice every weekend. I haven't understood how he can do that!
6   I saw the video of *The Godfather* six times so far.
7   Have you ever been on television?
8   Have you seen Steven Spielberg's latest film yet?
9   When I was young, I've been to see my grandmother nearly every day.
10   That's the best film I've seen for a long time.

(handwritten: have / has, past, present, -ed)

2 Complete the table using the highlighted time expressions from Exercise 1.1.

Tense	Time expressions
present simple	always *usually*
present perfect	since *for*
past simple	

— Watch Out! *British and American English* ◄—

1 I didn't have breakfast yet this morning.
2 I haven't had breakfast yet this morning.

The first sentence is acceptable in American English, but might sound strange to a British person. True or false?

► Grammar reference p.203 (19)

2 Complete the following pairs of sentences using words from the box. Each pair of sentences should have a similar meaning.

ago before ever for never since when

Example:
a) Ever ..*since*.. I was six years old, I have been afraid of spiders.
b) I started being afraid of spiders ..*when*.. I was six years old.

1 a) My father last went on holiday ten years ....
b) It's been ten years .... my father last went on holiday.

2 a) I've had this car .... I passed my driving test.
b) I bought this car .... I passed my driving test.

3 a) I've known Steve .... four years.
b) I first met Steve four years ....

4 a) It's the first time I've .... been to an English-speaking country.
b) I've .... been to an English-speaking country before.

5 a) I've been friends with Jenny .... as long as I can remember.
b) I can't remember .... I started being friends with Jenny.

6 a) He's never appeared in a film ....
b) This is the first time he's .... appeared in a film.

3 Complete the following extracts using the verbs in brackets. Use the present simple, past simple or present perfect simple tenses.

AMERICAN ACTOR IS NEW LONDON THEATRE BOSS

Actor Kevin Spacey (1) .... (*just/become*) the new director of London's famous Old Vic theatre. He (2) .... (*promise*) to appear on stage himself and bring in big-name talent in his new role.
'I love making movies, but I (3) .... (*always/love*) the stage as well. This job is something that I (4) .... (*think*) about a lot and I am looking forward to the challenge,' he (5) ...*says*....... (*say*).
Spacey, who (6) .... (*win*) Oscars for *The Usual Suspects* and *American Beauty*, (7) .... (*fall*) in love with the Old Vic after visiting it as a child.

MOVIE MAGAZINE DATELINE 10 February 2003

First Oscars for black actors

Actress Halle Berry (1) ...*become*.. (*become*) the first black woman to win an Oscar for her part in the film *Monster's Ball*. She (2) .... (*make*) an emotional speech when she (3) .... (*accept*) the award at yesterday's Oscar ceremony in Hollywood. Berry (4) .... (*also/appear*) in the popular James Bond movie, *Die Another Day*. Another black actor, Denzel Washington, also (5) .... (*win*) the Oscar for best male actor for his role in *Training Day*.

MOVIE MAGAZINE DATELINE 25 March 2002

4

1 Make questions from these prompts. How many can you answer?

1 How many times / Brad Pitt / marry?
2 Who / direct / *Titanic*?
3 Which football team / win / World Cup / five times?
4 In which country / *Lord of the Rings* / film?
5 Mel Gibson / ever win / an Oscar?
6 Can you name any musicals / win Oscars / last ten years?
7 Which famous English footballer / call / child / Romeo?
8 Who / usually present / evening news programme / television / your country?

2 Now ask your questions to another student. Which of you can answer most questions?

Reading: multiple matching
(Part 4)

1   Look at the description below. Have you seen any television programmes like this?

Reality TV is a term for television shows based on a group of real people who are put in an unusual or dangerous situation, or given the chance to achieve an ambition. Their experiences are shown live on television as entertainment. Reality TV often takes the form of a game, in which the viewers vote for people to leave the show until there is only one left. This person is the winner and receives a prize.

2   You are going to read a magazine article about four ordinary people who have taken part in Reality TV programmes. Look through the article quickly and decide which person:

1   had to overcome a physical problem.
2   lived on an island.
3   won a singing competition.
4   used to be a builder.

Reality TV -

A **Ron Copsey** was one of a group of contestants who agreed to live for a year on a desert island, with cameras following their attempts to survive together. He left the island after
5   five months, and later accused the producers of the show of misrepresenting him, claiming they had edited the film to make it look as if he was throwing a chair in the face of one of the women. 'I'm not an argumentative, aggressive, **¹**_nasty_
10 _piece of work_. It was shocking,' he told a journalist later. 'The producers led the public to believe that the other contestants were glad to **²**_see the back of_ me but it wasn't true.' After returning home from the island, Mr Copsey said he was
15 unable to continue with his college course as other students wouldn't talk to him, and he had to take antidepressant pills. The television company has agreed to pay him £16,000 **³**_compensation_.

B **Craig Phillips** was the winner of one of the
20 first Reality TV programmes to be shown in England, called _Big Brother_. Craig was originally a builder, and comes from Liverpool. After the series ended he admitted:
'I don't know why I won – you'll have to ask all
25 those people that voted for me.' Craig **⁴**_donated_ his £70,000 prize money to teenage friend Jo Harris, to help pay for a heart and lung operation in America. 'She is a unique young lady and it is wonderful to be in the position to help her,' he
30 said at the time. Craig later had a five-album **⁵**_deal_ with a record company but he **⁶**_was dropped_ after his first single. However, he has continued to raise money for **⁷**_charities_ as well as appearing regularly on daytime television shows.

C **Denise Leigh** won joint first prize in a TV
35 contest called _Operatunity_, in which ordinary people had the chance to be transformed into opera singers. But there is nothing ordinary about Denise. She is a blind woman of amazing
40 determination who has succeeded **⁸**_against all the odds_.
She had always dreamed of a musical career, but this was prevented by the births of her children. Being a blind mother of three is a challenge. 'It's
45 the hardest job in the world,' she says. 'Keeping them safe is definitely more worrying than anything that can happen to you on stage.'
Now the children are all at school, she is free to

the road to success?

pursue her dreams, and after *Operatunity* she is
50 better placed than she could ever have hoped
for. 'Now I have sung on stage at the London
Coliseum I am a different person,' she said the
morning after her [9]*triumph*. 'Winning the contest
has changed my life.'

55 **D** **Will Young** shot to success when he won
the TV competition *Pop Idol* out of over a
thousand contenders, and was offered a contract
with a major record company. He is modest
about his success. 'I don't think it's me myself
60 they're voting for, it's the TV contestant, and in
that context I feel very [10]*flattered* by it all,' he
said. His first single, *Evergreen*, became the
fastest-selling single of all time. It sold over a
million copies in its first week. Will thinks that
65 being a pop idol isn't only a matter of having a
good voice – there are generally other [11]*factors*
involved. 'Performers over the ages have always
given off a kind of energy. I think it's about a
whole image – the look, the clothes, the music –
70 which puts a distance between you and other
people.'

3   Look at the questions below. For each
question, you have to choose one of the people
A–D. The first one has been done as an
example.

> **TIP!** Before you start, highlight the key words
> in each question. Then read quickly through
> the texts for words or phrases with a similar
> meaning.

To help you, the 'parallel expressions' have
been highlighted for the first five questions.

Which person

0   is doing something they always wanted to do?
   C
1   gave away the money they won on the show?
2   received money to make up for the harm done by
   the programme?
3   shared the first place in the competition with
   another person?
4   was immediately successful in their career after
   the programme?
5   does not understand the reasons for their
   success?

6   says the programme gave an untrue picture of
   them?
7   found their personal relationships were badly
   affected by the programme?
8   feels their success is not just due to personal
   qualities?
9   had a musical career that turned out to be
   disappointing?
10   feels they are different from the general public?
11   finds family life more stressful than giving a
   public performance?
12   feels the other participants were sorry they left?

4   Discuss.

Thousands of people apply to go on these shows.
Would you apply to go on a Reality TV programme of
any sort? Why?/Why not?

5   Find the numbered words and phrases 1–11
in the text. Look at the context, then choose the
correct meaning a) or b).

1   a) someone who is likely to cause trouble
    b) something very unpleasant
    CLUE: *This is a colloquial expression. Look back at
    the subject of the sentence to find who or what it
    refers to.*

2   a) meet me
    b) see me leave
    CLUE: *Another colloquial expression. In which
    situation would you see someone's* **back**?

3   a) payment for work
    b) payment for something that went wrong
    CLUE: *Does the previous sentence refer to work or
    to a problem?*

4   a) gave   b) took away
5   a) contract   b) present
6   a) fell down   b) was no longer used
7   a) big companies   b) voluntary organisations
8   a) easily   b) in spite of difficulties
9   a) success   b) failure
10 a) pleased   b) worried
11 a) voices   b) things

Grammar 2: present perfect simple and continuous

1 Look at the pairs of sentences below. What is the difference in meaning between a) and b) in each case?

Example:

a) He's run the marathon for charity.
b) He's been running the marathon for charity.
In a) he ran the marathon at some time in the past. In b) he has just finished running the marathon and you can still see the effects – he is out of breath.

1   a) He's appeared on a daytime television show.
    b) He's been appearing on daytime television shows.
2   a) They've lived on the island all their lives.
    b) They've been living on the island for the last six months.
3   a) I've sent 20 emails this morning.
    b) I've been sending emails all morning.
4   a) She's read *Lord of the Rings* and says it's very good.
    b) She's been reading *Lord of the Rings* and says it's very good.

— Watch Out! *stative and dynamic verbs* ◀

Which sentence is NOT possible? Why not?

1   I've been knowing him for years.
2   I've known him for years.

▶ Grammar reference p.203 (19.3–4)

2 Choose the best form of the verb in the following extract from a health and fitness magazine. Both forms may be possible in some cases.

Last month actress Stella Glass gave birth to her second child – yet now she is back on screen and looks more attractive than ever. Many people (1) *have wondered / have been wondering* about her secret and how she (2) *has got back / has been getting* back her near perfect figure so quickly. She claims that the secret is a mixture of diet and exercise. 'I (3) *have never smoked / have never been smoking* and I (4) *have gone / have been going* to the gym regularly for years. To lose weight I (5) *have had / have been having* five portions of fresh fruit and vegetables every day and I (6) *have eaten / have been eating* popcorn as it's low in calories. Recently I (7) *have also drunk / have also been drinking* a lot of mineral water. My appearance has always been important to me – I (8) *have always wanted / have always been wanting* to look my best. '

3 The following dialogues contain examples of the present perfect simple. Which of them should be changed to the present perfect continuous so the dialogues sound more natural?

Example:
                                              been waiting
    A: Where have you been? I've ~~waited~~ for ages.
    B: It's not my fault. I've been stuck in a traffic jam for the last two hours.

1   A: Have you got these headaches regularly?
    B: Yes – I've had three in the last week.
2   A: Where's Carrie? Have you seen her today?
    B: Yes, she's worked in her office all day.
3   A: How long have you shared the flat with Lucy?
    B: A month. But we've known one another for years.
4   A: Have you spoken to Mrs Craven yet about the meeting?
    B: No. I've tried to contact her for ages, but she's never in when I phone.
5   A: Laurie has just gone to spend six months travelling in Canada.
    B: Yes, I know. He's saved up to go there for years.
6   A: Haven't you finished that book yet? You've read it for ages.
    B: I know. But I keep forgetting what's happened, then I have to go back to the beginning.

4 You bump into a friend who you haven't seen for six weeks. Role-play the conversation you have.

Student A look at page 187.
Student B look at page 188.

Begin like this:

A: Hi! I haven't seen you for ages.
B: No – what have you been doing?
A: I've just come back …

Use of English: key word transformations (Part 3)

Complete the second sentence so that it has a similar meaning to the first sentence, using the word given. Do not change the word given. You must use between two and five words, including the word given. The task below only tests the grammar you have studied in this unit. Here is an example (0).

Example:

0 I can't remember the plot at all.
forgotten
I ..... *have forgotten* ..... what the plot is about.

1 I don't know who the winner of the competition is.   **has**
I don't know who .... the competition.

2 I'm afraid I've lost the tickets.   **find**
I'm afraid .... the tickets.

3 She planted some flowers in the garden, but they are nearly all dead now.   **have**
The flowers she planted in the garden .... now.

4 I was talking to her mother a moment ago.   **been**
I .... to her mother.

5 It's been three years since I started to work here.   **working**
I .... three years.

6 It is Miranda's first visit to Scotland.
never
Miranda .... to Scotland before.

7 It's over a year since I last saw him.
seen
I .... over a year.

8 They don't know what the problem is.   **found**
They .... what the problem is.

9 She hasn't got any money left.
run
She .... money.

Vocabulary 2: word formation

1   The following words come from the text on pages 10–11. Underline the suffix of each word. Which group of words are all a) nouns b) adverbs c) adjectives?

1 shock<u>ing</u>   different   flattered
2 competition   performer   determination   contestant
3 regularly   generally

2

1 Complete boxes 1–10 in the following table with the correct forms of the words.

Noun	Verb	Adjective	Adverb
1	2	confusing/confused	confusingly
3	4	performing	
5	6	original	7 ....
8	9	flattering/flattered	10 ....

2 Now choose three more words from this unit and complete as many boxes as possible in the last three rows.

3   Complete these sentences using the correct form of the word in capitals.

1 The show was really ....   **ENJOY**
2 The winner gave an excellent ....   **PERFORM**
3 It was a big .... to me that I couldn't accept the invitation.   **DISAPPOINT**
4 I have to do a lot of .... for my exam.   **PREPARE**
5 The actress gave a long .... of all the problems she'd had to face.   **EXPLAIN**
6 The volunteers had to live on a desert island as a test of ....   **SURVIVE**
7 The winner gave a big .... to charity.   **DONATE**
8 Many of the contestants have built on their fame .... , and become very rich.   **FINANCE**

4   Answer these questions. Explain your answers.

1 Which lesson do/did you do most preparation for at school?
2 Are there any rules and regulations in your school, college or workplace that you think are unnecessary?
3 Have you ever given a public performance?
4 Have you ever won a prize in a competition?

Listening 2: extracts (Part 1)

You will hear people talking in six different situations. For questions 1–6, choose the best answer, A, B or C. You will hear each extract twice.

> **TIP!** The information in the recording is not always given in the same order as the options.

1 You hear a man talking about a film.
  What does he say about the film?
  A The story is difficult to follow.
  B The film is better than the book.
  C The setting is unusual.
  *CLUE: You will hear his opinion about the setting first (**C**), then the story (**A**), then the comparison with the book (**B**).*

2 You overhear two people talking in the street. What are they talking about?
  A a play at the theatre
  B a concert
  C a film on TV
  CLUE: Listen for information about the setting and the ending.

3 You hear an actress being interviewed on the radio. What is the actress doing?
  A giving an explanation
  B making a comparison
  C offering advice
  CLUE: In this type of question, you have to think about the main point of what the speaker says.

4 You turn on the radio in the middle of a programme.
  What is the relationship between the speakers?
  A mother and son
  B boss and employee
  C teacher and pupil
  CLUE: Listen carefully to what the woman says towards the end of the conversation.

5 You hear a woman on a phone-in radio programme complaining about a problem.
  Who is responsible for her problem?
  A some workmen
  B the local town council
  C a mobile phone company
  CLUE: At the end, the woman says,:'That's not right'. What is she referring to?

6 You overhear two people talking in a café. What has the man just taken part in?
  A a competition on the radio
  B an oral examination
  C a job interview
  CLUE: All three answers may involve answering questions and feeling nervous. Listen for additional information to give you the correct answer.

Vocabulary 3: entertainment

1 Complete these sentences with an appropriate word. You have been given the first part of each word and the number of letters.

1 It's the first Shakespeare p_ _ _ I have seen in the t_ _ _ _ _ _ .

2 There were a lot of critics from the newspapers at the theatre. I want to read their r_ _ _ _ _ _ to see what they thought of it.

3 The play was excellent and the au_ _ _ _ _ _ app_ _ _ _ _ _ very enthusiastically at the end.

4 I thought I didn't like o_ _ _ _ , but then I saw a wonderful p_ _ _ _ _ _ _ _ _ of Carmen and I changed my mind.

5 There was a c_ _ _ _ _ _ last week which included a new sym_ _ _ _ _ by a young Italian com_ _ _ _ _ . It was almost s_ _ _ o_ _ so I was lucky to get a seat!

6 It must be very difficult to con_ _ _ _ an orc_ _ _ _ _ _ ; there are so many different in_ _ _ _ _ _ _ _ _ being played by so many different mus_ _ _ _ _ _ !

7 I enjoy po_ m_ _ _ _ as well, and I listen to different si_ _ _ _ _ and gr_ _ _ _ . I've got a big collection of CDs.

8 On Saturday evenings I like going to ni_ _ _ cl_ _ _ and di_ _ _ _ with my friends.

2 What kind of entertainment do you enjoy most? Put these in order from 1–7 and discuss your preferences with a partner.

- ☐ pop concerts
- ☐ theatre
- ☐ opera
- ☐ television
- ☐ cinema
- ☐ comedy
- ☐ classical concerts

3 Read this extract from an informal letter, describing a musical. Have you heard of this show? Would you like to see it?

Last night I went to a musical called 'Les Miserables'. I thought the main stars sang and danced brilliantly and the costumes were superb. The story was very moving and there were some wonderful songs. It's one of the best shows I've ever seen.

It's set in 19th century France and it's based on a story by the writer Victor Hugo. It tells the story of Jean Valjean, who was sent to prison for 19 years just for stealing a loaf of bread. When he gets out of prison, Jean tries to make a new life for himself but he finds it vey difficult as an ex-convict, so he breaks his parole. Eventually, Police Inspector Javert finds him and ... well, I won't tell you the ending.

4 Now write a description of a show, concert or play you have been to recently. What was it like? Did you enjoy it? Why?/Why not?

Exam focus
Paper 5 Speaking: introduction (Part 1)

About the exam: Part 1 of the Speaking test lasts for three minutes. The examiner will ask you and the other candidate some questions about yourselves. You may have to answer questions about:

- the place where you live
- your family
- your work or studies
- what you do in your free time
- your future plans.

This part of the test gives the examiners their first impression of you, so it's important to answer the questions clearly, accurately and with enough detail.

DO speak clearly so the examiners can hear you.
DO try to make your answers interesting and personal.
DON'T give one-word responses, e.g. *Yes* or *No*. Add some details.
DON'T learn long speeches by heart before you do the exam. You probably won't give appropriate answers to the actual questions.

1

1 Each of the following answers has two mistakes in grammar or word order. Find the mistakes and correct them. Then match each answer to one of the topics above.

1 I am having two brothers. One is older than me; he has twenty-one years old. The other is younger – he's just twelve. So I'm in the middle.
2 I live in Milan. It's a very big city, with lots of traffic. Just now I stay in a hostel but I want have my own apartment one day.
3 I like very much playing computer games and doing sport, especially swim.
4 I have been studying English since five years, and I enjoy it very much. But I never been to England.
5 In ten years' time I hope I'll be a doctor. I want travel abroad, and maybe I married.

2 Now listen and check your answers.

2 Listen to some students doing Part 1 of the exam. How good do you think their answers are? Choose A, B, C or D for each speaker.

A A good answer.
B Not good – makes a lot of mistakes.
C Not good – does not answer the question.
D Not good – does not say enough.

1 Joanna ......
2 Karl ......
3 Katerina ......
4 Jorge ......

3 Work with a partner. You are going to practise asking and answering questions. Remember to add some detail to each of the answers.

Student A look at page 180.
Student B look at page 184.

Writing: informal letter (Part 1)

1 Look at the writing task below and answer the following questions.

1 Who are you writing to?
2 Why are you writing?
3 What information must you include in your reply? Underline the important parts.

You have been working hard but now you want to go out to the theatre for the evening with some friends. Read the letter extract, the advertisement and the email. Then, using the information in your notes, write a reply to Jack's letter. (120–180 words)

> ... Anyway, how are you doing? Still working for your exams? It would be great to get together if you have time. Let me know if you have any ideas.
>
> All the best
> Jack

Alhambra Theatre

King for a Night

MURDER MYSTERY

Last performance Saturday 8.00

'A masterpiece'
Daily Times

Excellent reviews!

'Don't miss it!'
Theatre news

Message
Reply Reply All Forward ✉ 🗑 ✖ ↑ ↓ Follow Up A ▾
From: Sue and Milo
To:
Subject: Saturday

Yes, we're both free on Saturday and would love to go to the theatre. How about going for something to eat afterwards – do you know anywhere good?

Best wishes
Sue and Milo

- Thanks for letter
- Explain about play – when? what? reviews
- Invite Jack
- Explain about Sue + Milo – meal
- Suggest restaurant (Gino's Pizzas?)

2

1 Read the sample answer below and put the paragraphs in the right order.

2 Look back at the task. Check that the writer has included all the information.

3 The writer has made four mistakes with verb forms, which are marked. Correct the mistakes.

> ☐1 Dear Jack

> ☐ Hope to see you on Saturday.

> ☐ Would you like to come along? I (have emailed) Sue and Milo yesterday to see if they can come, and they say they can, so it should be a good evening. They suggested (to go) for something to eat together after the show – I know you like Italian food so we could all go to Gino's Pizzas. I (never went) before but everyone says it's very good.

> ☐ Give me a ring if you're free and would like to come, then I'll book the tickets.

> ☐ I (work) really long hours recently preparing for my exams but now I'm planning to take a break and go out to the theatre next Saturday to see 'King for a Night'. It's on at the Alhambra. The reviews are excellent – and it's the last night.

> ☐ Thanks for your letter. It was very good to hear from you again after all this time.

> ☐ Best wishes
> Pedro

3 Now write a similar letter to a friend inviting him/her to a concert or a film with you. Give details of the time and place, and say who else is coming and where you could go afterwards. Write 120–180 words.

> **TIP!** You don't need to include postal addresses in any letters for Paper 2 of the FCE exam.

4 When you have finished, check your work. Use the checklist in the Writing reference.

▶ Writing reference pp.206, 209

1

1 Put the words in the right order to make questions.

1 long is since English started it studying how you ?
2 you have when last a did holiday ?
3 many have lived town years this you how in ?
4 book you long had how for have this ?
5 leave home did this you morning when ?
6 have films month seen how you this many ?

2 Ask and answer four of the questions above with a partner.

2

1 For 1–6 below, think of the word which is being defined. The words are all connected with the cinema or television.

1 the character that an actor plays in a play or film
2 the large white surface that pictures are shown on in the cinema
3 the place in a cinema where tickets are sold
4 the place or time where a film or television programme is shot
5 the story of a film or book
6 the technique of starting a story in the present, then moving to the past

2 Choose five more words connected with this topic from the unit and write a definition for each. Then see if your partner can guess what they are.

3 Choose the correct alternative in each of these sentences.

1 *Have you run / Have you been running?* You look hot.
2 *Did you ever go / Have you ever been* to Milan?
3 *I've had / I've been having* a TV in my bedroom ever since I was small.
4 *I have never seen / I never saw* an opera before.
5 *She has done / She has been doing* her homework for the last two hours.
6 *I have known / I have been knowing* him for three years.
7 Tom asked me for your email address, but *I haven't known / I didn't know* it.

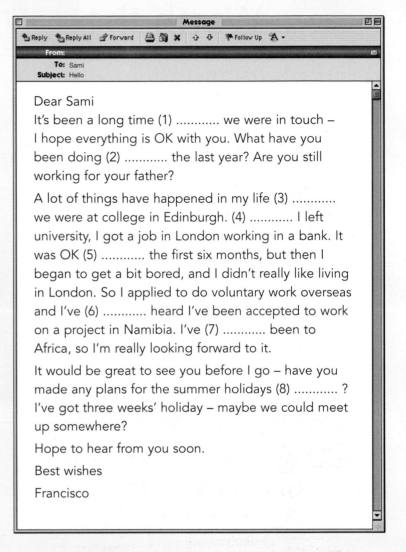

Dear Sami

It's been a long time (1) .... we were in touch – I hope everything is OK with you. What have you been doing (2) .... the last year? Are you still working for your father?

A lot of things have happened in my life (3) .... we were at college in Edinburgh. (4) .... I left university, I got a job in London working in a bank. It was OK (5) .... the first six months, but then I began to get a bit bored, and I didn't really like living in London. So I applied to do voluntary work overseas and I've (6) .... heard I've been accepted to work on a project in Namibia. I've (7) .... been to Africa, so I'm really looking forward to it.

It would be great to see you before I go – have you made any plans for the summer holidays (8) .... ? I've got three weeks' holiday – maybe we could meet up somewhere?

Hope to hear from you soon.

Best wishes

Francisco

4 Complete the email above using appropriate time expressions.

5

1 Complete the highlighted expressions with a suitable preposition.

1 I think everyone should have a chance to vote ...... their favourite stars in the Oscars.
2 If I won a lot of money, I would donate at least half ...... charity.
3 I like watching films set ...... the future.
4 Being a film star isn't just a matter ...... looking good.
5 Appearing ...... stage is much more difficult than acting ...... a film.
6 I wouldn't want to take part ...... a Reality TV show.

2 Which sentences above do you agree with?

UNIT 2 Worth the risk?

Speaking 1

1 Look at the photo and discuss these questions.

1 The woman is 'free diving'. What do you think this involves?
2 Would you be prepared to try this? Why?/Why not?
3 What type of person do you think you need to be to do this?

2

1 Answer the following questions for yourself. Write:

always   often   occasionally   never

How adventurous are you?

1 Do you enjoy taking risks?

2 Do you always leave things until the last minute?

3 Would you make sure you had another job before giving up your old one?

4 When you buy something new, do you usually read the guarantee?

5 Would you like to drive a fast car?

6 Do you take chances even when you think you may not succeed?

7 Do you think about what might go wrong before you try anything new?

8 Do you check a map before you set off on a journey to a new place?

9 If someone dares you to do something, do you accept the dare?

10 Would you find life boring if there was no danger anywhere?

2 Explain your answers to a partner. Which of you is more adventurous?

3 Discuss these questions.

1 Is it always a good thing to take risks?
2 Why do you think some people might not approve of risk-takers?

18

Listening: true or false? (Part 4)

1 The woman in the photo opposite is Tanya Streeter, who broke a world record for free diving on 17 August, 2002. You will hear an interview with her.

> **TIP!** Before you listen, read through the sentences and highlight key words.

To help you, the key words have been highlighted for the first two questions.

When she was very young, Tanya was afraid of the water. `[  1  ]`

When she joined her first free diving class, Tanya found she could do some things better than any of the men there. `[  2  ]`

Tanya decided to try to break diving records in order to please her parents. `[  3  ]`

Once Tanya has gone as deep as she can on a dive, she has to return to the surface very gradually. `[  4  ]`

Tanya's heart beats more rapidly when she is deep underwater. `[  5  ]`

When Tanya dives, there are other people ready to help in case of emergency. `[  6  ]`

Tanya says her main reason for free diving is to explore what humans can do. `[  7  ]`

2 Listen to the interview. Decide whether the statements are True or False. Write T for True or F for False in the boxes provided.

3 Compare your answers with a partner, then listen again to check.

4 Discuss these questions.

1 Do you think that what Tanya does is worth the risk she is taking? Why?/Why not?
2 Describe to a partner the most dangerous and/or exciting thing you have ever done. Would your partner like to do the same thing?

Vocabulary 1: adjectives of feeling

1 Complete the adjectives in the following sentences by adding -ed or -ing.

Example: Tanya was amaz.ed and thrill.ed when she beat the world record.

1 A lot of people are excit.... by the idea of doing dangerous sports.
2 Top athletes must find all the media attention very flatter.... .
3 I think I'd find hang gliding rather frighten.... .
4 I'm really unfit! It's so depress....!
5 I can't understand why some people are interest.... in trying to beat records.
6 I thought the way the coach explained things was rather confus.... .
7 People who attempt to beat records often feel very frustrat.... when they fail.
8 My instructor was very encourag.... about my chances of winning.
9 I was annoy.... with myself when I lost the game.
10 Please stop whistling. It's really irritat.... .

▶ Grammar reference p.191 (1)

2 Complete the following sentences with a suitable adjective from Exercise 1 in the correct form.

Example: The programme wasn't very *interesting* so I switched off.

1 These instructions don't make any sense – I'm totally .... !
2 After failing his exams, Jamie felt very ....
3 It was a very .... match. The score was 2–2 until just before the end.
4 I was .... by all the compliments I received.
5 The first time I flew, I was very ....
6 There's nothing I can do to help – it's really ....

3

1 How would you feel if:

- your friend gave you an unexpected present?
- you thought a stranger was following you?
- your brother or sister borrowed your CD player without asking you?

2 Write some more questions like the ones above and ask a partner.

Reading 1: multiple-choice questions (Part 2)

1   You are going to read a magazine article about an unusual way of travelling. Look at the photo and the title of the text.

1 What is the young man doing?
2 Why do you think he is doing it?
3 What do you think the title means?

2   Look through the text quickly to find the answers to these questions.

1 Who is the young man in the photo?
2 What is the importance of the cable to
   a) the young man? b) the local schoolteacher?
   c) the village where the man lives?

The cable racer

Robinson Diaz lives in a small cottage high in the Andes Mountains of South America. Diaz is a 'cable racer', and every morning he faces the difficult task of taking the local teacher to her school.
5   To do this, he first walks for an hour up to a place the locals call *Los Pinos* (the Pine Trees), right at the edge of the 400-foot deep **¹***gorge* of the Negro valley. Here, one end of a thick metal cable has been fixed to a wooden post. The cable stretches right across the deep
10   valley to the other side, a kilometre away.

A metal hook is fixed to the cable, with leather straps hanging from **it**. Diaz fastens the straps around his shoulders and waist, does a quick safety check and then, without hesitating, throws himself off the edge of
15   the mountain. Attached to the cable by only the metal hook, he rapidly picks up speed and soon he is racing through the air. Crossing the valley by wire takes him 30 seconds, instead of the two hours it would take him to walk down through the **²***snake-infested* rain forest and
20   climb up the steep muddy slopes on the other side.

As Diaz begins his trip, Diana Rios, a 23-year-old elementary teacher, is waiting on the other side of the gorge for the moment when **he** will come racing through the **³***mist* towards her at 100 mph. She will then
25   return with him, hanging on to him as he goes back along the cable. Diana had no idea when she took the teaching job that just getting to work in the village school would be so dangerous. 'At first I wanted to cry,' she says, **⁴***clutching* her books as the metal cable starts
30   to **⁵***rattle* violently at Diaz's approach. 'But I soon got used to it.' She still prefers to go with Diaz, though, rather than making the frightening and hazardous crossing on her own.

For the inhabitants of *Los Pinos*, the wire cable is a
35   lifeline. For more than 50 years, it has served the community as a form of transport to and from the rest of the world. Everything that comes arrives via the cable – bricks and wood for building, sacks of rice and corn. Puppies are held between the knees of young men like
40   Diaz who act as 'cable-racers', and go flying over the gorge. Pregnant mothers, who must get to the nearest clinic, cross the wire during the darkness of the night, returning with their newborn babies. **It** is dangerous, but **they** have no choice.
45   This time Robinson Diaz makes a perfect landing on Diana's side of the gorge. For him, the dangers of his daily journey are **⁶***insignificant*. 'What I'm really scared of is snakes,' he says. 'This is nothing in comparison.' Then Diana straps herself into her harness and hooks
50   herself up to the wire behind Diaz, holding on to him tightly. He turns, **⁷***flashes* her a smile, releases the brake and kicks away. Within seconds, teacher and cable-racer have disappeared back into the mist.

Adapted from THE INDEPENDENT

3   Read the text again and choose the answer (A, B, C or D) which you think fits best according to the text. There are some clues to help you.

> **TIP!** You will find it easier to do this task if you read the questions first without reading all the options A–D. Then find the part of the text which the question relates to, and see if you can find the answer yourself. After this, go back and check your own answer with all the options. The questions are always in the same order as the information in the text.

1 Robinson Diaz has a difficult task every morning because he has to
   A climb a long way up a mountain.
   B get to the edge of a valley.
   C help someone get to work.
   D walk through a dangerous area.
   CLUE: *What is his main task?*

2 In the second paragraph, the writer suggests that Diaz is
   A confident about what he is doing.
   B unaware of the danger he faces.
   C neglectful of his own safety.
   D uncertain of what he is doing.
   CLUE: *Look for information about what Diaz does and how he does it.*

3 Diana Rios found out how she would travel to work
   A when she was a student.
   B when she saw the cable.
   C after she had met Diaz.
   D after she took the job.
   CLUE: *Look for a time expression in the text.*

4 What is Diana's opinion about the journey now?
   A She enjoys it.
   B She no longer finds it a problem.
   C It makes her feel very frightened.
   D It would be impossible without Diaz.
   CLUE: *Her opinion has changed – think about how she feels **now**.*

5 The cable is important to the people of *Los Pinos* because
   A it allows contact with other communities.
   B it provides entertainment for the young people.
   C it enables the doctor to visit the village.
   D it gives the inhabitants the chance to sell their produce.
   CLUE: *Think about the main purpose of the cable.*

6 What does Diaz say about using the cable?
   A He does not think there is any risk.
   B He is worried about the danger of snakes.
   C He is happy that he can help the teacher.
   D He does not find it as frightening as other things.
   CLUE: *You need to check what a pronoun in the last paragraph refers to.*

4   Find the numbered words and phrases in the text.

1 Look at each one in context and then choose the best meaning a) or b).

1 a) a deep river   b) a deep valley
2 a) full of snakes   b) without snakes
3 a) thick fog   b) light cloud
4 a) holding tightly   b) touching
5 a) break suddenly   b) shake noisily
6 a) important   b) not important
7 a) smiles quickly   b) smiles slowly

2 Choose two other words from the text that you don't know and try to work out their general meaning from the context.

5   Look at the following pronouns in the text and choose what each one refers to.

1 it (line 12)   a) the hook   b) the cable
2 he (line 23)   a) Diaz   b) the teacher
3 it (line 43)   a) the night   b) the crossing
4 they (line 44)   a) the cable racers b) the mothers

6   Discuss these questions.

1 How do you travel to school or work every day?
2 How enjoyable do you find the journey? Does it involve any problems?
3 Have you ever had to use a dangerous or risky form of transport while travelling? When? Why?

Grammar 1: making comparisons

1

1 Each of the following sentences has a mistake with comparisons. Find the mistakes and correct them.

Example:
    highest
The Andes Mountains are among the ~~most high~~ in the world.

1 Life in the country is not as busy than life in the city.
2 Transport is more easier for people who live in cities.
3 There are the most people living in the world today than ever before.
4 Teachers today are less stricter than they were in the past.
5 Antarctica is the less populated continent in the world.
6 I think windsurfing is the more exciting than sailing.
7 I am more good at sport than my brother.
8 I would rather to travel by car than by train.

2 Compare your answers with a partner.

▶ Grammar reference p.193,197 (8.6)

2

1 Match the sentences so that Ben always agrees with Alex.

Alex:

1 This rope doesn't seem nearly as strong as the old one we had. *e)*
2 I suppose it was a lot cheaper.
3 It's rather harder to hold on to though.
4 I suppose it's no worse than the old one.
5 Maybe the bottom of the mountain isn't quite as far as it looks.

Ben:

a) Mmm, perhaps it's a bit nearer.
b) Yes, it is slightly more difficult.
c) No, I expect it's just as good.
d) You're right, it was far less expensive.
e) No, it's much thinner.

▶ Grammar reference p.194 (4.8)

2 Now underline the intensifiers in Ben's sentences and complete the tables.

a lot / .... /	more expensive
rather	
a bit /	less expensive
	cheaper
no	

....	
almost / not quite	as expensive
(not) nearly	

3 Complete the second sentence so that it has a similar meaning to the first sentence, using the word given. Do not change the word given. You must use between two and five words, including the word given.

Example: Football is the most exciting sport to play.
    as
    No other sport *is as exciting* .... to play as football.

1 I've never seen such an amazing show. **the**
    This is .... that I've ever seen.
2 Sam isn't nearly as brave as Chloe. **lot**
    Chloe is .... Sam.
3 Last year the show wasn't quite as expensive as this year. **bit**
    Last year the show was .... expensive than this year.
4 I think playing tennis is a lot easier than golf. **far**
    I think it's .... tennis than golf.
5 Not many other cities are as large as Tokyo. **the**
    Tokyo is one .... in the world.
6 I prefer sightseeing to lying on the beach. **rather**
    I'd .... on the beach.

4 Work with a partner. Choose one of the following topics. Think of five names, write them in a circle and compare them using the adjectives given and intensifiers from Exercise 3.

Famous people: well-known, tall, intelligent, wealthy, old, fit, talented
Places: busy, quiet, exciting, crowded, old, modern
Films: frightening, funny, thrilling, boring, innovative
Cars: fast, sporty, practical, expensive, economical

Example:
Nicole Kidman is much better known than J K Rowling or Tanya Streeter.

Vocabulary 2: word formation
(negative prefixes)

1   Choose the correct alternative in each of the following sentences.

Example:

People who are *active* / *inactive* do not make good athletes.

1   You should *trust* / *distrust* anyone who says it's easy to have a career in sport.
2   Having skill and talent is *insufficient* / *sufficient* for a career in sport nowadays.
3   You need to be quite *unlucky* / *lucky* to succeed in such a competitive area.
4   Some people think that if you believe in yourself then it is *impossible* / *possible* to fail.
5   Because you are pushing your body so hard, a career in sport can actually be quite *healthy* / *unhealthy*, so you need to look after yourself.
6   Please don't *misunderstand* / *understand* me – I think it's a wonderful career!

2   Complete these sentences using the correct form of the word in capitals. Add a negative prefix where necessary. There are three sentences where you don't need to change the word.

1   Many people feel .... when they move to a new town and don't know anyone. **SECURE**
2   I think it's .... how brave she is. **CREDIBLE**
3   Anything is .... if you have a positive mental attitude. **POSSIBLE**
4   She spoke very quickly, so it's possible I .... what she said. **UNDERSTAND**
5   Most people are .... of learning several languages given the chance. **CAPABLE**
6   Steve was still .... even though he had hit his head as he fell. **CONSCIOUS**
7   The new player was very .... – he had never played at that level before. **EXPERIENCE**
8   I wanted to learn scuba diving, but .... there were no instructors available. **FORTUNATE**

3   Complete these sentences. Give true information.

1   I think it's incredible that …
2   I tend to distrust people who …
3   I'm incapable of …
4   I think it's unhealthy to …
5   It's impossible for me to …

Use of English: word formation
(Part 5)

1   Look at the title of the text below. What do you think the answer to the question might be?

2   Read the text through quickly to see if you were right.

3   Look at each sentence and think about the gap.

1   What part of speech is needed – noun, verb, adjective or adverb?
2   If the word is a noun, should it be singular or plural? Do you need to add a negative suffix?
3   If it is a verb, what ending does it need?

Example: 0 – *adjective*

4   Use the word given in capitals below the text to form a word that fits in the space in each line. There is an example at the beginning (0).

WHY DO PEOPLE TAKE RISKS?

Why are some people risk-takers? What makes them take part in **(0)** *dangerous* or even life-threatening activities? There are different **(1)** .... for this. Car racers love the **(2)** .... of speed, while climbers get their thrills from **(3)** .... the challenge of high mountains. Millions of years ago, when people faced danger daily, risk-taking was essential for **(4)** .... Although living in today's world is **(5)** .... than it was in those days, perhaps that **(6)** .... instinct still remains. However, taking risks can become a very **(7)** .... obsession. Some people can even become addicted to danger, and are unable to stop looking for it. It is also **(8)** .... that the majority of risk-takers seem to be men. Is this because men have more **(9)** .... ? Or do women think twice about taking risks because they are more **(10)** .... ?

0 DANGER	
1 EXPLAIN	6 BASE
2 EXCITE	7 HEALTH
3 FACE	8 INTEREST
4 SURVIVE	9 CURIOUS
5 EASE	10 SENSE

5   Do you think it is true that men take more risks than women? Give examples.

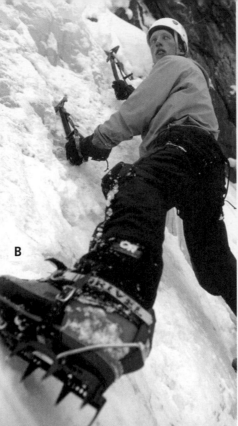

A

B

C

Exam focus

Paper 1 Reading: multiple matching (Part 4)

About the exam: In Part 4, you read several short texts, or one longer text divided into sections. The questions require you to locate specific information in the text. The answers can come from any part of the text; they do not follow the same order as the questions. If there are more than four texts, there may be more than one answer to some questions.

Procedure

1 Read the title of the text and any subheadings, and skim the text quickly. This will give you an idea of what the text is about. Don't read the whole text yet.
2 Read the questions carefully and underline key words.
3 Look through each section of the text to find the information. You don't need to read the text in detail. Look for words or expressions which mean the same as the words in the question. Underline possible answers in pencil. Be careful – there may be similar information in different sections.
4 Leave any questions that you are not sure of, and go back to them at the end. You should always choose an answer, as you will not lose any marks in the exam for a wrong answer.
5 When you have finished, transfer your answers to the answer sheet.

1 You are going to read a magazine article in which five people talk about their interest in outdoor activities. Look at the photos.

1 What outdoor activity does each photo show?
2 Match the photos to the appropriate texts.

2 For questions 1–15, choose from the people A–E. Some of the people may be chosen more than once. When more than one answer is required, these may be given in any order. There is an example at the beginning (0).

Which of the people

talks about being concerned about the environment?	**0** C
enjoyed being taught how to do their activity?	**1**
found out about their activity from another family member?	**2** **3**
was suddenly asked to do something new?	**4**
says that public interest in their activity is growing?	**5**
says that their activity has formed their character?	**6**
mentions an activity made more dangerous by the weather?	**7**
says they are different from most other people doing the activity?	**8** **9**
likes the way people of different abilities can take part together?	**10**
finds the danger involved in doing their activity exciting?	**11**
says it has become easier for others to take up their activity?	**12**
wants to be better than other competitors?	**13** **14**
does their activity less often than they used to?	**15**

The Great Outdoors

A Anna Collins

My twin sister, Lucy, and I have an identical interest in BMX racing. We got into riding competitions by accident really, when Lucy entered a cross-country cycle race and came second. She came home full of the thrill of it all,
5 and started going regularly. I was bored staying at home while she was getting all the excitement, so I decided to take it up too. It didn't take long before I found the speed and element of danger it involved as exciting as she did. There are only about twenty girls who race in the UK
10 compared to over 300 boys, but we like being treated the same as the boys. We're not stupid, but we do like taking risks – and we both want to be BMX champions one day!

B Jenny McCormack

In adventure racing, you're in a team covering vast distances out in the wild, doing different things –
15 swimming, canoeing, running and so on. I had a very lucky introduction to it – I was a last-minute replacement for someone in a team going to Nepal. I'd never been in an adventure race before, but I'd lived in Nepal for two years and done a lot of mountain climbing there as well
20 as mountain biking and white water rafting. In the race, we covered 900 km and the winning team finished in just under five days. Our team did it in seven, which wasn't bad, although of course it would have been great to come first. What I love about adventure racing is that you often
25 compete in exotic places that you might never get the chance to visit otherwise. I also love the fact that it is a very friendly world – even the top athletes mix with the beginners.

C David Bellamy

My lifelong addiction to walking began when I was a
30 child. I used to meet up with my friends and go on long walks. I remember standing in the country one day with everything covered in frost. Then the sun suddenly came out and all the frost melted off the trees in a matter of seconds. It was the sort of thing you'd never see from a
35 motor car. That kind of experience made me the person I am. I still walk whenever I can, although I'm often too busy for day-long walks now. My main concern now is encouraging people to take greater care of the world's most important and popular sites of natural beauty.

D Laura Jeans

My dad and I wanted to do something different one
40 weekend so we decided to try hang gliding, and my first lesson was brilliant! The more I did, the more I enjoyed it and I soon forgot to be scared. I started by taking off from small hills but now I can go as high as 100 metres and I'm getting more adventurous and confident all the time.
45 It's not as dangerous as people think and I've never hurt myself doing it. My friends think I'm crazy but I love the sense of freedom I get when I'm gliding up there in the air. Unfortunately, it isn't great for meeting people of my own age as most people I glide with are older than me, so
50 I wouldn't recommend it for anyone who wants to find a boyfriend!

E Peter Beaumont

My brother had started mountain climbing and when I heard about it from him it seemed to me that it was something I simply had to do. So he arranged to take me
55 when he next went climbing locally. It was raining, so we tried climbing in the rain, slipping about on wet, polished stone. It was hardly the best start, but I loved it. When the winter came, we went to the mountains in North Wales to try climbing on ice. I climbed by instinct, just picking it
60 up as I went along, but these days most people start safely indoors, and learn the basics there. You'll find a lot of sports centres nowadays have indoor climbing walls so newcomers can get a feel for the sport and build up their confidence before they tackle a real mountain. As a result,
65 climbing is becoming an increasingly popular activity – but it remains one of one of the most dramatic sports on the planet.

---

3 Discuss these questions.

1 Which person do you think seems to enjoy their activity the most?
2 Which of the activities would you prefer to do? Why?
3 Which would you like to do least? Why?

Grammar 2: articles

1   Some of the following sentences have mistakes with articles. Find and correct the mistakes.

1   I've never crossed the Atlantic Ocean in a ship.
2   I didn't go out yesterday because it was a terrible weather.
3   When he grows up, he wants to be footballer.
4   I can't get out because a front door's locked.
5   The London Marathon takes place every year near River Thames.
6   It's over 50 years since Hillary and Tensing climbed the Mount Everest.
7   I live at the home with my parents but I'm going to get my own place soon.
8   It happened by an accident – I didn't mean to do it.
9   We were almost home when the sun finally came out.
10   One day I'd really like to go mountain climbing in the Nepal.

▶ Grammar reference p.192 (3)

2   Complete the following sentences with *a, an, the* or (-) when no article is needed.

1   It is possible that .... whale might become extinct in the future.
2   People say that you always meet someone you know in the middle of .... Times Square in .... New York.
3   .... best way of carrying things when you're on .... walking holiday is in a rucksack.
4   .... Belgium is famous for its chocolate.
5   Eating .... bananas is a good way of getting energy quickly.
6   Some people wish that .... mobile phone had never been invented.
7   Why do you think .... Spanish are so good at football?
8   It is possible to go sailing on .... Lake Garda in the summer.
9   .... highest wind speeds officially recorded reached 370 kph.
10   Some of the most important scientific discoveries were made by .... chance.

3

1   Here is some information about a new sport. Look at the highlighted sections and make any necessary corrections with articles (*a/an/the* or zero article). Not all the highlighted sections are incorrect.

Zorbing
– the latest adventure experience

A *zorb* is (1) hollow plastic ball, about three metres in height. You climb into the ball and then roll down (2) the hill inside it. (3) A first zorb was built by (4) an organisation called (5) A Dangerous Sports Club. The idea was developed in (6) the New Zealand in (7) late 1990s, and is now spreading rapidly throughout (8) world.

There are two different types of zorb, a dry zorb and a wet zorb. With (9) the dry zorb, you are strapped into (10) the harness inside the ball. The zorb can reach speeds of 50 to 60 kph. The wet zorb is totally different. With this one, you are not strapped in and you are encouraged to stand up and try to run as (11) a ball rolls down the hill. (12) The challenge is to remain upright all the way to (13) bottom. This sounds easy, so to make things (14) a little harder, they throw some warm soapy water inside, so things get very slippery. People say it feels a bit like being in (15) washing machine!

2   Imagine that you have tried either the wet zorb or the dry zorb. Write a short email to a friend telling them what it was like and how you felt.

A

B

Speaking 2: comparing and contrasting (Part 2)

About the exam: In Paper 5, Part 2, you speak on your own for about a minute. You have to compare and contrast two photographs, and answer a further question about them. For this part, you need to use the language of comparison, and to link contrasting ideas together.

1 Look at the two photos. How are they similar? Choose a) or b).

a) Both photos show people trying to do something difficult.

b) The photos show people on the stage and in the air.

2

1 Read these sentences contrasting the photos, and underline the comparative structures.

1 The man looks much older than the woman.
2 There are fewer people in the first photo.
3 The woman's clothes are more brightly-coloured than the man's.
4 The man looks more nervous than the woman.
5 The man is taking a bigger physical risk.
6 The man seems to be enjoying himself more than the woman.

2 Some of the sentences give incorrect information about the photos. Find them and correct them.

younger

Example: The man looks much ~~older~~ than the woman.

3

1 Choose the correct linking expression in each of the following sentences.

1 *While / On the other hand* the first photo shows a man who's about to perform in public, the woman in the other photo is on her own.
2 The man is inside *but / also* the woman is out in the open air.
3 In the first photo, the man looks quite nervous, *whereas / although* in the other one the woman looks quite relaxed.
4 That's funny because the woman is taking a risk *in addition / while* the man is not in danger.
5 I think the woman has practised a lot and is an expert *and as well as this / but on the other hand* the man might be doing this for the first time.

🎧 **2** Listen and check your answers.

🎧 **3** Listen again and mark the stressed words. Practise saying the sentences with the same stress and intonation.

4

1 Compare and contrast the photos, using ideas from Exercises 1–3. Try to keep talking for about 40 seconds.

2 Briefly say which activity you think is the most difficult, and why (about 20 seconds).

5 Work with a partner.

Student A look at photo A above and at photo C on page 180.
Student B look at photo B above and at photo D on page 180.

The photos show people trying to do something difficult. Take turns to compare and contrast your photos and say which activity you think is the easiest to do.

Writing: formal letter (Part 1)

About the exam: Part 1 of Paper 2 is compulsory. You have to write a letter using information supplied. The letter may be formal or informal.

> **DO** read the question carefully.
> **DO** include all the necessary information.
> **DO** use an appropriate style for the reader.
> **DO** remember to use paragraphs.

1 Read the task below. Are these statements true or false?

1 You are writing to the competition organiser.
2 You have to choose one afternoon activity.
3 You have to write about 100 words.
4 You should write your letter in an informal style.

You have entered a competition and have just received this letter from the organiser. Read the letter, on which you have made some notes. Then, using the information in your notes, write a suitable reply.

Congratulations! You have won first prize in our competition – two weeks on the English Adventure Course in Australia! This includes your air ticket, your accommodation and all expenses. To help us make the arrangements for your trip, please could you give us the following information:

We have courses in August and September. Which month is better for you? ——————— *August (say why)*

You will have English classes in the morning. You can join a grammar and vocabulary class, or a speaking and listening class.
Which would you prefer? ——————— *say which and why*

There is a choice of activities in the afternoon. Please choose **two** from the list and tell us why you would like to do them.
• making a radio programme
• making a class website ——————— *tell them!*
• learning to play a musical instrument
• doing a scuba diving course
• visiting an Australian secondary school

Please let us know if you need any further information.

accommodation? clothes?

Yours sincerely

Tom Spiller

Tom Spiller
Competition organiser

Write a **letter** of between **120** and **180** words in an appropriate style. Do not write any postal addresses.

2 Your letter could have five paragraphs. Number the following paragraph outlines in the best order.

Paragraph …   preferences for morning classes and afternoon activities
Paragraph …   closing remark
Paragraph …   request for further information
Paragraph .1.   thanks for letter and general remark
Paragraph …   which month you want to travel

3 In your letter, you have to expand the notes in the task into sentences and add your own ideas. Complete the following sentences.

1 I would like to do the course in August because …
2 In the morning, I would like to join a grammar and vocabulary class because …
3 In the afternoon, I would like to try … because …
4 I would also be interested in trying … because …
5 Could you tell me what type of … is provided and what kind of … I should bring with me?

4 Write your letter. The first paragraph and closing remark have been done for you.

> **TIP!** In formal letters, use the full forms (*I am, I have*) rather than contracted forms (*I'm, I've*).

Dear Mr Spiller

Thank you very much for your letter informing me that I have won first prize in the competition. I am looking forward to going to Australia and attending the course.

I look forward to hearing from you.

Yours sincerely

5 When you have finished, check your work.

▶ Writing reference pp. 206–207

1

1 Choose two adjectives from the box below to describe your feelings about each of these sports. Don't use any adjective more than once.

cycling / football / free diving / windsurfing / walking

boring   challenging   dangerous   difficult   easy
enjoyable   exciting   frightening   frustrating
healthy   relaxing   risky   thrilling   tiring   unsafe

2 Tell your partner the adjectives you have chosen. Can he/she guess the sports?

Example: *It's difficult and dangerous.*

2

1 Decide what the missing word is in each of the following sentences.

1 I don't think mountain climbing is dangerous as diving.
2 Deep sea diving is most dangerous sport I've ever done.
3 Hang gliding is lot more popular than fishing.
4 Adam isn't nearly strong as his brother is.
5 Most people I know are more interested in sport I am.
6 I rather walk in the mountains than lie on the beach.

2 Do you agree or disagree with the sentences above?

3 Choose the best alternative to complete the following sentences.

1 It's not a good idea to .... unnecessary risks when you are doing dangerous sports.
   A make   **B** have   **C** take   **D** give
2 When Irene was injured, Janet was chosen as a last-minute .... for the hockey team.
   A preference   **B** change   **C** alternative   **D** replacement
3 The Boston Marathon .... every year.
   A gets on   **B** takes place   **C** goes through
   D takes part
4 A prize of $25,000 is offered to whoever .... the one-hour cycling record of 90 kilometres.
   A breaks   **B** tears   **C** rips   **D** splits
5 If someone wants to do something dangerous, I always advise them to think ...... !
   A once   **B** twice   **C** often   **D** double

6 I .... cycling by accident, but once I had started, I loved it.
   A got by   **B** got over   **C** got through   **D** got into
7 You can get a much better .... for a new town if you explore it on foot.
   A way   **B** understanding   **C** knowledge   **D** feel
8 When you're riding on the back of a motorbike, you need to .... tightly.
   A stick down   **B** hang on   **C** hold up   **D** sit up

4 Correct the mistakes with the use of articles in the following sentences.

1 A next bus to a country doesn't leave for six more hours.
2 I met my English teacher in Andes Mountains.
3 Best way of carrying your things is in the rucksack.
4 I'm planning to visit the Nepal in a June.
5 He said that he wanted to do a course in the diving.
6 I think that a activity like mountain biking is healthy and fun.
7 Why do you think Italians are so good at the football?
8 Some people are afraid of taking the risks in life.

5 Complete the following sentences, using the correct form of the word in capitals.

1 The English footballer David Beckham became famous for his goal-kicking .... **ABLE**
2 The record of 47 hours for watching TV without stopping was set last year and is still .... **BREAK**
3 The David Coulthard victory over Michael Schumacher in the Australian Grand Prix was .... **EXPECT**
4 That bridge looks rather .... ; I don't think we should drive the car across. **SAFE**
5 I found the drive over the mountains very .... **FRIGHT**
6 Although I was .... in the competition, I was still glad I'd taken part. **SUCCESS**
7 I thought it would be .... for me to climb that mountain, but somehow I managed it. **POSSIBLE**
8 People say that you need to take regular exercise in order to be .... **HEALTH**
9 I can swim, but I don't have much .... in the water. **CONFIDENT**
10 I'm really rather .... – I'm happiest just staying at home with a good book. **ADVENTURE**

6 Write a paragraph about a sport that you would like to be good at, explaining why.

Fact or fiction?

Reading: gapped text (Part 3)

1 You are going to read an extract from a story.

1 Look at the picture and the title of the text and discuss these questions.

1 Who is the young man?
2 Where is he?
3 How did he get there?

2 Think of some more questions of your own and suggest possible answers.

2 Read through the main part of the text. Does it answer your questions in Exercise 1?

3 What sort of story do you think the extract comes from?

a) a thriller
b) a science fiction story
c) a travel story

4 Eight sentences have been removed from the text. You have to choose from the sentences A–I the one which fits each gap 1–7.

> **TIP!** To do this type of task, you often need to check links between pronouns (e.g. *some*, *this*, *she*) and nouns.

1 Look at the example sentence **I**. Which of the three highlighted nouns in the first paragraph of the text does *its* relate to?

2 Do the task. There is one extra sentence which you do not need to use. To help you, key words in the sentences have been highlighted. As you do the task, check what these words refer to.

3 When you have finished, read the whole text again with your answers to check it makes sense.

Strange landings

The force of his landing made Julian gasp. He lay stunned and **1***disoriented* for a long moment, then rose **2***unsteadily* to his feet. 'This is not at all right,' he thought. There was no sign of the lecture room, the college, the whole part of North London that he had just been in. In fact, there was no feature he could recognise at all in the landscape before him. **0** **I**

He remained perfectly still for a moment, gazing around. His surroundings seemed strange, almost dreamlike. Then he turned in a slow circle, trying to catch a glimpse of anything familiar. **1** In the distance ahead of him, the land rose up steeply towards something that made a straight horizontal line. A road, perhaps? He decided that, dream or not, there was no point in staying where he was. He would walk to the top of the hill.

He picked up the bag of books he had dropped when he hit the ground and started to make his way through the tall grass. **2** Halfway up, he paused to take his jacket off. In London it had been winter, but here it felt like May or June. He looked behind him. Here and there were other lone figures moving about, leaving **3***trails* of flattened grass like his own behind them as they walked. 'What's happening?' Julian wondered. 'It looks as if we all just dropped out of somewhere. But never mind right now. Just get up the hill, and take it from there.'

He finally reached the top of the slope, and pulling himself up the last few feet, found that he had been right. **3** It stretched straight before him, leading as far as he could see into the distance. There was no sign of any traffic.

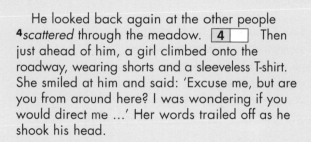

He looked back again at the other people **4**_scattered_ through the meadow. [4   ] Then just ahead of him, a girl climbed onto the roadway, wearing shorts and a sleeveless T-shirt. She smiled at him and said: 'Excuse me, but are you from around here? I was wondering if you would direct me ...' Her words trailed off as he shook his head.

'Sorry. I came from out there, too.' He pointed at the field behind her. [5   ] 'Where did they all come from?' she **5**_murmured_ softly. Julian realised that she had an American accent. He shrugged. 'No idea. I know as much as you. I was just coming out of a lecture. I tripped over something and landed here.'
'I was out jogging. I slipped and fell.'

[6   ] 'Where exactly were you?' he asked.
'In Irvine. Just outside Los Angeles,' she said.
'I was in London. It was snowing.'
'In August?'
'No. January. You were in August?' He thought about this. 'What year?'
'1999. You?'
'2010.'
She stared at him, then looked away. 'It must be a dream,' she said. 'Maybe I hit my head when I fell. I expect I'll wake up in a minute with a splitting headache.' [7   ] He didn't know how or why they were here, but the reality was starting to sink in.

A   They looked at each other and he pointed at their different clothes, his thick jacket, her T-shirt and shorts.

B   Most were moving towards the road, but some were wandering about in seemingly random directions.

C   But Julian shook his head, knowing that this was not the explanation.

D   He could not see where it was coming from.

E   She turned, and seemed to realise the situation for the first time as she saw the other people.

F   He was standing on a road – a flat, black surface with the familiar white lines down the middle.

G   It reached almost to his shoulders and left seeds sticking to his clothes.

H   But there was nothing – only a seemingly endless field of grass, tall, yellowing and waving gently in the warm breeze.

I   Even its shape was wrong.

🎧 **5**   Listen to the story and check your answers.

6   Discuss these questions.

1   What do you think is at the end of the road?
2   How do you think the story continues? Will Julian and the girl return to their own times and places?

7   Find the numbered words 1–5 in the text. With a partner, try to work out their meaning. Think about:

- the word class (noun, verb, adjective, etc.)
- the form: is the word formed from one you know?
- clues from the context.

Check your ideas with a dictionary.

Vocabulary 1: using a dictionary

About the exam: Papers 2, 3 and 5 test your active knowledge of vocabulary. To expand your vocabulary during your course, it's a good idea to record and learn any useful new words you meet in Reading, Listening and Paper 3 texts. Use a dictionary to help you understand the meaning and grammar of the new vocabulary, and make sure you review it regularly.

1   Paper 3, Part 1 may test your knowledge of words with similar meanings. Read these sentences from the text on pages 30–31. The words in **bold** all refer to different ways of looking.

- *He remained perfectly still for a moment, **gazing** around.*
- *He turned in a slow circle, trying to **catch a glimpse of** anything familiar.*
- *She **stared at** him, then looked away.*

Now look at the entries for these words from the Longman *Active Study* Dictionary. Decide whether statements 1–8 below are true (T) or false (F).

> **gaze** /geɪz/ *v* [I] to look at someone or something for a long time: **+ at/into** etc *She sat gazing out of the window.* **– gaze** *n* [singular] *Judith tried to avoid his gaze.*

> **glimpse**[1] /glɪmps/ *n* [C] **1** when you see someone or something very quickly for a short time: **get/catch a glimpse of** *Dad only caught a glimpse of the guy who stole our car.* **2** a short experience of something that helps you to understand it: *a glimpse into the future*
> **glimpse**[2] *v* [T] to see someone or something very quickly for a short time: *For a second I glimpsed her face, then she was gone.*

> **stare** /steə‖ster/ *v* [I] to look at someone or something for a long time without moving your eyes: **+ at** *Stop staring at me!* **– stare** *n* [C] *She gave him a long hard stare.*

1 *Glimpse, gaze* and *stare* can all be used as either nouns or verbs. *T*
2 The noun forms of all three words are countable.
3 The vowel *a* is pronounced the same in *gaze* and *stare*.
4 The *p* in *glimpse* is silent.
5 The verbs *gaze* and *stare* can both be followed by the preposition *at*.

6 *Gaze* and *stare* mean exactly the same thing.
7 The noun *glimpse* is often used with the verbs *get* or *catch*.
8 You can have an object after the verbs *stare* and *gaze*.

2   The following sentences have mistakes in the use of vocabulary. Find the mistakes and explain why each is wrong, using the dictionary extracts above to help you. Then correct the sentences.

Example: The hunter glimpsed at the tiger in the long grass.
Wrong – we use an object after 'glimpse', not a preposition.
It should be 'The hunter glimpsed the tiger in the long grass.'

1 I saw a glimpse of them as they escaped.
2 I stared her for a long time.
3 She gave him a quick gaze.
4 I made her a stare and she looked away.
5 He was unaware of her gazes.
6 Why does that man keep staring at me?

3   Paper 3, Part 3 tests vocabulary as well as grammar. One area tested is phrasal verbs. The Longman *Active Study* Dictionary gives you example sentences which show the meanings of phrasal verbs in context.

> **look after** sb/sth *phr v* [T] to take care of someone or something: *We look after Rodney's kids until he gets home from work.*

1 Complete the second sentence so that it has a similar meaning to the first sentence, using the word given. Do not change the word given. You must use between two and five words, including the word given. All the sentences require a phrasal verb with *look*.

1 The authorities are investigating the cause of the fire.   **into**
The authorities are .... the cause of the fire.

2 I just can't wait to go on holiday!   **forward**
I'm really .... on holiday.

3 If you don't know the word, check it in a
  dictionary. **it**
  If you don't know the word, ... in
  a dictionary.
4 He had a lot of respect for his grandfather. **to**
  He really .... his grandfather.
5 You should keep your eyes open for Steve at the
  dance. **out**
  You should .... Steve at the dance.
6 Keith thinks he is much better than everyone else.
  down
  Keith .... everyone else.

2 Check your answers in your dictionary.

Grammar 1: *like, as, as if/though*

1 Choose the correct alternative in each of
these sentences.

1 You look just *like / as* your brother.
2 *What's / How's* the food like? Is it OK?
3 That man *seems like / seems* very familiar – I
  wonder if I've met him before.
4 You should do *as / like* your parents say.
5 My cousin started *like / as* a secretary, and now
  she's the manager.
6 That sounds *as / like* the train coming now.
7 You look *as though / like* you're worried.
8 A: Do you feel *like / as* going for a swim?
  B: No, it looks *like / as* if it's going to rain.
9 Let's meet at 7 o'clock, *like / as* we agreed.
10 I've always regarded Sue *as / like* my best friend.
11 Let's do something fun, *as if / like* throwing a
  party.

▶ Grammar reference p.205 (20.1-3)

2 Make questions for the following answers
using *like* or *as*.

Example: *What's the weather going to be like
tomorrow?*
The forecast said it's going to be hot and sunny.

1 My mother's very funny, but my father is a bit strict.
2 No, he's got dark hair, but I'm fair-haired.
3 Yes, why not, but I'm not very good at dancing!
4 It's quite small. There isn't much to do in the
  evenings. But the people are friendly.
5 Yes, I do. The best thing about a pool attendant's
  job is that you meet lots of people.

3

1 Look at the picture and complete the text
using *like/as/as if/as though*.

AIRLOCK 01

There's a man standing next to an insect which is
almost as big (1) .... he is. The man has one eye
which looks (2) .... an insect's. Maybe he uses it
(3) .... a sort of magnifying glass to improve his
vision. We can only see his right hand – it's a
mechanical hand, rather (4) .... a robot's hand. It
seems (5) .... the insect may be under his power.
Or maybe the insect is acting (6) .... his protector
or helper. In the background there are curved black
lines. They look a bit (7) .... the lines on a record
or CD. Further away there are some buildings – it
looks (8) .... there's a big city there.

2 Do you agree with the description of the
picture?

4 Work with a partner.

1 **Student A** look at the picture on page 187.
Student B look at the picture on page 189.

Describe your picture to your partner. Use
expressions from Exercises 1 and 2.

2 Look at each other's pictures. Were they the
same as you imagined them from your
partner's description? If not, how were they
different?

Listening 1: multiple matching (Part 3)

1   Discuss these questions.

1   What kind of things do you like to read?
2   What was the last thing you read for pleasure?

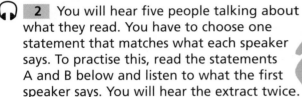   **2**   You will hear five people talking about what they read. You have to choose one statement that matches what each speaker says. To practise this, read the statements A and B below and listen to what the first speaker says. You will hear the extract twice.

1   Which statement, A or B, accurately reflects what the speaker says?
2   Which phrases in the extract tell you?

A I try not to be put off by books that seem hard to read.
B I think that some of what I read is a waste of time.

   3

1   Read through the statements below and listen to the whole recording. Choose from the list A–F what each speaker says. Use the letters only once. There is one extra letter which you do not need to use.

> **TIP!** The statements are not in the same order as the information you hear. As you listen, you need to check all six statements.

A I am prepared to try reading books that seem difficult.
B I think that some of what I read is a waste of time.
C I like reading books that are part of a series.
D I find that reading is a way of relaxing.
E I enjoy reading books that have been made into films.
F I choose books connected with the career I want to follow.

Speaker 1	1
Speaker 2	2
Speaker 3	3
Speaker 4	4
Speaker 5	5

2   Listen again to check your answers.

4   Which speakers' views do you agree with?

Speaking: asking for and reacting to opinions (Parts 3 and 4)

1   Look at the pictures above, which show people reading in various situations. Think about:

1   what each person is reading and why
2   how useful or important it is to be able to read in these situations.

2

1   Listen to two students discussing two of the pictures.

1   Which two pictures do they talk about?
2   How do they answer question 2 in Exercise 1?

2   Listen again. Tick the phrases the students use to interact with each other.

> That's right.   What do you think?
> I'm not sure.   Yes, I agree …   Sure, but …
> But on the other hand …   I suppose so.
> Right.   Well, yes, but …   Don't you think so?
> And another advantage is that …   OK, but …
> Yes, and as well as that …   Yes, that's true.

3   Practise saying the phrases with the same intonation as the recording.

3 Work with a partner. First, talk to each other about how useful or important reading is in each of the situations in the pictures. Then decide which type of reading is most important for you. Try to keep talking for about three minutes. Remember to listen and react to each other.

4 Discuss the following questions, which extend the topic you have discussed in Exercise 3. Try to use some of the phrases from Exercise 2.

1 Do you often read articles or emails on a computer?
2 Do you use the Internet to find information for your studies or work?
3 How far do you think television and the Internet have changed people's reading habits?
4 Do you think that people will still read books in thirty years' time? Why?/Why not?

Grammar 2: adverbs

1

1 Read these sentences. Underline the adverbs/adverbial phrases and circle the adjectives.

Example: I read the book <u>quickly</u> because it was so ⟨interesting⟩.

1 The exam was harder than we expected. I did badly, but my brother did worse.
2 If you want to do well and get good grades, you'll have to study more.
3 Please don't drive so fast on this dangerous road.
4 Why was he behaving in that silly, unfriendly way?
5 Stand still and look straight at the camera.
6 She works harder than anyone I know.
7 If you order a new book over the Internet, they send you a receipt automatically.
8 We'll have to make an early start if we want to get there by lunchtime. We don't want to arrive late.

2 Make a table like this one with words in Exercise 1.1.

Adjective	Adverb	Adverbial phrase
quick	quickly	–
hard	hard	–
silly	–	in a silly way

▶ Grammar reference p.191 (2.1)

2 Choose the correct form of the adverb in each pair of sentences.

1 a) No matter how *hard / hardly* she tried, she couldn't find the answer.
   b) She had *hard / hardly* noticed him in the crowd until he came up to her.
2 a) I haven't seen you *late / lately* – have you been ill?
   b) I have to work *late / lately* tonight so I won't be able to go out with you.
3 a) His teacher speaks very *high / highly* of his abilities.
   b) He kicked the ball *high / highly* up into the air.
4 a) I didn't pay for the concert – I managed to get in *free / freely*.
   b) Wear loose, comfortable clothes for yoga so that you can move *free / freely*.

▶ Grammar reference p.191 (2.1)

3 Put the adverb in brackets in the best place in each sentence.

Example: I *always* buy something to read if I'm going on a journey. (*always*)

1 Does she get the bus to college? (*usually*)
2 He's not late. (*often*)
3 She's been happy there. (*never*)
4 You'd better go to the house. (*straight*)
5 I'll be seeing her tomorrow. (*certainly*)
6 I didn't make it on time. (*nearly*)
7 She's missed her flight. (*perhaps*)
8 I managed to get his number from Judy. (*luckily*)
9 You are right. (*probably*)
10 I'm not free next weekend. (*definitely*)

▶ Grammar reference p.191 (2.4–5)

Exam focus

Paper 3 Use of English: error correction (Part 4)

About the exam: In Paper 3, Part 4, you read a text containing errors. Some lines of the text are correct. Other lines contain an extra, incorrect word which must be identified. These are usually grammatical words e.g.: articles (*a*, *the*), determiners (*some*, *much*, etc.), prepositions (*in*, *on*, *at*, etc.), pronouns (*he*, *she*, etc.), auxiliary verbs (*do*, *will*, *am*, etc.), adverbs, etc. Three to five lines of the text will be correct.

Procedure

1 Read the title, then read the text once to get a general idea of what it's about.
2 Read each sentence carefully – not just each line.
3 Now read each line and mark any extra, incorrect words. Be careful. This word must be definitely wrong.
4 Read each sentence without the word to check it makes sense.
5 Tick the correct sentences. If there is an extra, incorrect word, write it at the end of the line.
6 In the exam, you will transfer your answers to the separate answer sheet.

DON'T write more than one word in your answer.
DON'T leave blanks to indicate correct answers. Always put a tick.

1 The following text is about a writer's experience with a computer. Read through the text quickly. How did the writer feel about his computer?

a) impatient, because it didn't work properly
b) frustrated, because it didn't follow his instructions
c) grateful, because he thought it had helped him

2 Read the text again and look carefully at each line. Some of the lines are correct, and some have a word which should not be there. If a line is correct, put a tick (✓) at the end of the line. If a line has a word which should not be there, write the word at the end of the line. There are two examples at the beginning (0 and 00).

Examples:

0	✓
00	*was*

A STRANGE TALE

0 A writer of science fiction bought a new computer that behaved in a very
00 peculiar way. It was displayed strange characters on the screen instead
1 of normal words and numbers. Eventually he lost the patience with it,
2 and phoned up the manufacturer, asking of them to take it away. He
3 unplugged the computer and left it on his desk ready for to be collected.
4 Then something even stranger started to happen. Although the machine
5 was not plugged in it, words began to appear on the screen. The writer
6 watched in fascination. 'Long ago, on another planet,' he read, 'there
7 were people like to you. They sent messages into space but ...' Then the
8 screen went blank. The writer waited, but nothing had happened. Then
9 he plugged it in again, and started to write. This time the computer
10 behaved normally, and he wrote all night, feeling like inspired by the
11 a few words he had read. He knew that the story was different
12 from anything he had ever been written before. Eventually it was
13 published, and became as a huge best seller. Everyone said it was the
14 very most original thing he had ever written. But the writer always
15 would suspected that the new computer had something to do with it.

3 In Brendon's story, what was special about the music he chose to play?
A It was written for trumpet only.
B It was by a little-known composer.
C It was very difficult to play.

4 How was Brendon feeling when he arrived at the concert hall?
A nervous about the competition
B stressed because he'd been delayed
C ill because the journey had been uncomfortable

5 Where did Brendon find a copy of the music he needed?
A in a waste paper basket
B in another bag
C in a cupboard

6 In the story about the baby, Anna is unsure
A how the baby was saved.
B where the baby fell from.
C whether the baby was hurt or not.

7 Brendon thinks that the second time the baby fell, Mr Figlock was lucky because
A he didn't drop the baby.
B he was ready to catch the baby.
C he wasn't hurt by the baby.

Listening 2: multiple-choice questions
(Part 4)

1   You will hear two friends, Anna and Brendon, talking about coincidences. First, read through the questions in Exercise 2 (not the options) and match each story to one of the pictures above.

> **TIP!** Before you listen, look through the questions or sentence openings only, not the options. These will give you a general idea of what the recording is about. Then read through the options.

2   Read through the options for each question. Then listen and choose the best answer, A, B or C.

1 Why did Anna's Aunt Carrie go to Paris?
A for a special holiday
B to do some shopping
C to meet her husband

2 How did Aunt Carrie feel about the book she found?
A surprised someone had put her name in it
B curious about how it had got to Paris
C confused because she had one the same at home

3   Listen again and check your answers.

4   Think about the task you have just done.

1 Were the questions in the same order as the information on the recording?
2 Were the options (**A, B, C**) in the same order as the related information on the recording?
3 What should you do if you don't hear the answer to a question?
   a) Keep looking at that question in case it comes later.
   b) Look at the next question.

5   Discuss these questions.

1 Which of the stories you have just heard do you think is most/least believable?
2 Have you heard any other stories of strange coincidences like this?

Vocabulary 2: modifiers/ intensifiers

1 Adverbs are often used to intensify the meaning of adjectives. In each of the following sentences, two adverbs are possible and one is incorrect. Cross out the incorrect adverb.

Example: I've just heard *an absolutely* / *a very* / *a really* amazing story.

1 We had *a very* / *an extremely* / *an absolutely* narrow escape.
2 The film of *Wuthering Heights* was *absolutely* / *quite* / *fairly* good, but the book was better.
3 It must be *pretty* / *utterly* / *fairly* hard to write a book.
4 I think time travel is *extremely* / *absolutely* / *completely* impossible.
5 The special effects in the film were *totally* / *utterly* / *terribly* amazing.
6 I went to a concert last weekend. I found it *a bit* / *rather* / *completely* boring but my friend enjoyed it.
7 Your English is *absolutely* / *fairly* / *just* fantastic! You must have lived in an English-speaking country.
8 The match on TV this afternoon was *incredibly* / *very* / *totally* good.

▶ Grammar reference p.201 (15)

2

1 Respond to the following statements using an intensifier from the box and the adjective in brackets. Put the stress on the important words, as in the example.

extremely   absolutely   totally   really   utterly

Example: I thought the film was quite good. (*brilliant*)
Did you? I thought it was absolutely brilliant!
1 I thought the book was all right. (*wonderful*)
2 I thought the grammar was fairly easy. (*difficult*)
3 David said the film was quite good. (*superb*)
4 I think it's pretty cool outside today. (*freezing*)
5 I think John's ideas are absolutely right. (*wrong*)
6 She said the concert was quite impressive. (*great*)

2 Listen and compare your answers.

3 Which of the following things would you find:

a) really easy?
b) rather difficult?
c) totally impossible?

Example: raising one eyebrow
I can raise one eyebrow – it's really easy. Look!
1 standing on one leg with your eyes closed
2 walking on your hands
3 separating the white of an egg from the yolk
4 counting from 20 to 1 backwards in English
5 reading a whole book in one day (in your own language)
6 having a telephone conversation in English

4

1 Think about a really good time you had recently with your friends or family. Make a note of some key points, for example where you went, what you did, and why it was so good.

2 Tell a partner about it. Be very enthusiastic, and use some of the intensifiers and adjectives from Exercises 1 and 2.

Example:
Last month, I went away for the weekend with my friends. We had a really fantastic time ...

Grammar 3: narrative tenses

1

1 Read the first paragraph of the following story and answer these questions.

1 When and where does the story begin?
2 What was the writer doing when she decided to take Perky outside?
3 Why didn't she think Perky would fly away?
4 What happened when the writer got outside with Perky?

Blue Skies

When I was a child, I lived in Arizona. One day in 1956, I was walking around the house with my sister Kathy's new parakeet, Perky, on my finger. Suddenly, I had the idea of showing Perky what the sky looked like. His wings had been clipped, so I felt it was safe to take him outside. I took him into the garden, and then, to my horror, Perky suddenly flew off. One minute he was there, and the next minute he was gone, clipped wings and all.

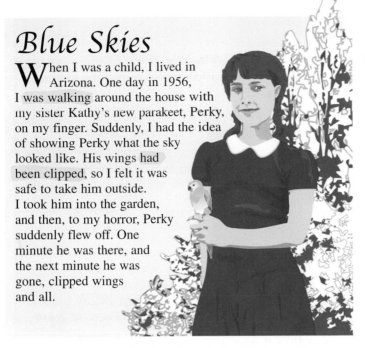

2 Look at the highlighted verbs in the text above.

1 What tense are they in?
2 Which tense form
a) refers to something that had already happened to the bird before this story began?
b) sets the scene for the story?

▶ Grammar reference p.204 (19.6–7)

2

1 Read the next part of the story. Did the writer find the parrot again?

Kathy managed to forgive me, and told me that Perky had certainly found a new home, but I did not believe her. For a long time, I was inconsolable. Time passed, however, and eventually my guilt lessened and we all grew up.

2 Discuss these questions.

1 Does the paragraph describe a short or long period of time?
2 What tense are the highlighted verbs? Do they describe events in the same order they happened, or a different order?
3 Find one more verb and underline it. What tense is it? What time does it refer to?
a) before the beginning of the story
b) before the other events described in this paragraph

▶ Grammar reference p.204 (19.5, 19.7)

3

1 Read the end of the story, and complete the text with the verbs in brackets in the correct form: past simple, past continuous or past perfect. Don't use the past perfect unless it is absolutely necessary to make the order of events clear.

Many years later I was living with my own family in a different city. My husband and I had become very friendly with another family who had children of the same age as ours. One summer evening, we (1) .... (*sit*) together in the garden telling stories about pets we (2) .... (*have*) in the past. Then Barry, the father of the other family, (3) .... (*announce*) that the Greatest Pet of All Time was his blue parakeet, Sweetie Pie.

'The best thing about Sweetie Pie,' he (4) .... (*explain*), 'was the way we got him. One day, when I was about eight, I (5) .... (*stand*) outside my house. Then, out of a clear blue sky, a little blue parakeet just (6) .... (*fly*) down and (7) .... (*land*) on my finger.'

I was astounded. When I was finally able to speak, we (8) .... (*examine*) the evidence. The dates and the locations and the description of the bird all (9) .... (*match*) up. Apparently forty years before we had actually met, our two families (10) .... (*be*) linked by Perky.

That night I (11) .... (*phone*) my sister and said to her, 'You were right! Perky did find a new home!'

From TRUE TALES OF AMERICAN LIFE

2 Answer these questions.

1 What were the two families doing in the garden?
2 How had Barry found Sweetie Pie?
3 How did they know that Sweetie Pie was the same bird as Perky?

4

1 Work with a partner. Look at the picture on page 188. Make up a story to explain the events that led up to the situation shown in the picture.

2 Compare your story with the class.

Writing: story (Part 2)

About the exam: In Paper 2 of the exam you may be asked to write a short story. You may be given the first or last sentence.

A story should have:
- a good plot, with a dramatic, funny or unexpected ending
- linking words and time markers to show the order of events
- correct use of narrative tenses.

1 Complete the story below using sequencing expressions from the box. There are two expressions you do not need to use.

after   as soon as   at first   before
after a while   eventually   finally   later
secondly   then   while

I waited outside the house, feeling very nervous.
(1) ...., a red car drew up in front of the house. (2) .... no one got out, but (3) .... the driver's door opened and a woman stepped out onto the road. (4) ....
I saw her, I remembered her. She had been in the restaurant where I had last seen James three months (5) ....
The woman walked up to the front door of the house, making no attempt to hide. I thought about following her, but I decided that it would be better not to confront her. (6) .... she had gone into the house nothing happened for a few minutes, then I heard a shot and someone screamed.
I got out my mobile and phoned the police. (7) .... I was waiting for them to arrive, I watched the house, but no one entered or left it. (8) .... the police arrived and went into the house. They searched all over and (9) .... found James tied up in the cellar, alive and well. There was no trace of the woman.

2 A story should have three or four paragraphs and include the following four stages.

- ☐ background information
- ☐ first events and/or a problem
- ☐ final outcome
- ☐ later actions or results

Read the story again and number the stages in order.

3 Read the task below. Think of some ideas for the story. Ask and answer questions like these.

1 Who is Emma?   3 Where is she?
2 What can she see?   4 What did she do?

You have been asked to write a story for your student magazine. The story must begin with the following words.

Emma could not believe what she saw in front of her.

4

1 Read the first part of a student's story below. Which of the four stages from Exercise 2 are included here?

Emma could not believe what she saw in front of her. She had been sitting in the classroom for the last two hours, not thinking about anything except finishing her history exam. Then suddenly, feeling that something in her surroundings was not right, she had raised her eyes from the exam paper. The classroom had completely disappeared ...

2 Discuss how the story could continue.

3 Which of these would be the best ending for the story? Why?

A

Emma left the classroom with her friends, went home and told her mother about the day.

B

Emma knew that after what she had been through, her life would never be the same again.

C

Two weeks later, Emma heard that she had passed her history exam and she felt very pleased with herself.

5 Now write your own story beginning with the same sentence. You should write between 120–180 words.

6 When you have finished, check your work.

▶ Writing reference pp.206, 208, 215

1 Answer the following questions using a word you have learned in Unit 3.

1 What verb means to *see someone or something very quickly*?
2 Which phrasal verb means *to continue to do something*?
3 What is the noun from *nervous*?
4 What is the adverb that means *not in a steady way*?
5 What adjective beginning with *s* is used to describe a headache that is very bad?
6 What verb has the same meaning as *to look into the cause of something*?
7 What verb is used in the phrase *to ... someone a stare*?
8 What verb means *to fall over something*?

2 Complete the second sentence so that it has a similar meaning to the first sentence, using no more than five words, including the word given.

1 I found an old photograph of my sister the other day.
   across
   The other day .... an old photograph of my sister.
2 There's no point in going to Pete's house – he won't be in.
   waste
   It's .... going to Pete's house – he won't be in.
3 I couldn't see the car anywhere.
   sign
   There was .... the car.
4 It's very noisy – what's happening in here ?
   on
   It's very noisy – what's .... in here?
5 I never discovered who had written the book.
   out
   I never .... who had written the book.
6 Mrs Stevens went up the path to the front door of the house.
   made
   Mrs Stevens .... up the path to the front door of the house.

3

1 Complete the following text. You have been given the first letter of each word.

A dictionary will give you information about how to write a word down – the (1) s .... – and how to say it – the (2) p .... It tells you whether the word is a (3) n .... , a (4) v .... or an adjective, and may also give you information about common (5) p .... that the word appears in. And, of course, it also tells you what the word (6) m ....

2 Look back through Unit 3 and choose three words that you didn't know before. Look them up in a dictionary and find out the information above.

4 Each of the following sentences has a mistake with grammar or vocabulary. Find the mistakes and correct them.

1 My brother has the same colour hair like me.
2 You look like unhappy – what's the matter?
3 How's the weather like where you are? Is it raining?
4 That outfit suits you – you look as a model or a film star!
5 I'm studying very hardly for the exams.
6 She spoke to him friendlily, and he felt better at once.
7 It was very freezing on the mountain top.
8 Your exam result was absolutely good.

5 Replace the incorrect linking expression in italics with a correct one.

1 He felt much better *while* he had solved the problem.
2 The weeks went by and *as soon as* I started to feel better.
3 He put down his suitcase for a minute and *secondly* he picked it up again and walked on.
4 *While* I phoned my sister, she was having a shower.
5 *Eventually* you get there, please phone and let me know.
6 I used my dictionary a lot *later* but now I try to guess what the words mean.
7 *At last* I got home, I found my friends had arrived.
8 *During* you were sleeping, something really exciting happened.

UNIT 4 Food for thought

Vocabulary 1: food

1 How much do you know about the food you eat? Match the sentence halves.

1 Milk and cheese   *f)*
2 Potatoes, carrots and beetroot
3 Cheese, butter and oil
4 Fresh fruit and vegetables
5 Eggs and red meat
6 Rice, potatoes and bread
7 Nuts and dried beans
8 Proteins, fats and carbohydrates

a) are rich in vitamin C.
b) are high in cholesterol.
c) are root vegetables.
d) are good sources of protein for vegetarians.
e) are all high in carbohydrates.
f) are dairy products.
g) are needed in a balanced diet.
h) have a high proportion of fat.

2

1 Match the people to the speech bubbles.

> I mostly eat fruit and raw vegetables. I don't touch meat or dairy products, and I only drink water – and champagne.

> I eat lots of protein and carbohydrates to give me the strength and energy I need.

2 What sort of food should the following people eat? What should they avoid? Why?

a) a pregnant woman
b) an Arctic explorer
c) someone with a cold
d) a model

3 Is there any sort of food you don't like much, but eat because it is good for you?

Listening: sentence completion
(Part 2)

1 Look at the photos and discuss these questions.

1 What job do you think the man does?
2 What can you guess about his lifestyle?

2   You will hear part of a radio programme about a young man who has become a celebrity because of his job.

1   First, look through the following gapped sentences to get a general idea of what the programme is about. What topics do you think will be discussed?

The well-known chef, Jamie Oliver, was brought up in **(1)** .... in the country.

Jamie started to help prepare meals at the age of **(2)** ....

In London, Jamie met his future wife, Jools, who was working as a **(3)** ....

Jamie appeared briefly in a **(4)** .... about The River Café in London where he was working.

The recipes in Jamie's first TV series were **(5)** .... but used good ingredients.

Jamie's food was popular because it matched the **(6)** .... of his trendy young audience.

Both Jamie's TV series and his **(7)** .... were very successful.

Jamie helped to prepare the food for the guests at his **(8)** ....

Jamie then opened his own restaurant and trained **(9)** .... and inexperienced teenagers.

Apart from cooking, Jamie enjoys playing the **(10)** .... in a band with his old schoolfriends.

2   Now look at the gaps in each sentence. Which gap(s) could be filled by:

a) a number?
b) a noun describing a place?
c) a noun describing a job?
d) an adjective describing food?
e) the name of a musical instrument?

3

1   Listen and complete the sentences, using a word or short phrase.

2   Listen again to check and complete your answers.

TIP! You should write no more than 1–3 words for each answer. Write exactly what you hear: don't change the word/s in any way.

4   Discuss these questions.

1   Do you enjoy cooking? What can you cook?
2   Are cookery programmes popular in your country? With what age groups?
3   What types of foreign food are popular in your country? What types do you like best?
4   In many countries, the way people eat is changing. Why do you think this is happening? Is this true in your country?

Vocabulary 2: prepositions

1   Complete the following sentences using the correct preposition.

for   to   in   on   as   of

1   Jamie Oliver was responsible .... training a group of young teenagers.
2   He's particularly interested .... helping disadvantaged young people.
3   Jamie has made many appearances .... TV.
4   He's still very close .... his parents and childhood friends.
5   I don't know if I'd like to train .... a chef.
6   Work .... the catering industry is hard and involves long hours.
7   Success depends .... luck as well as talent.
8   You need a talent .... cooking and a real interest .... good food.
9   The idea of running a coffee bar or café quite appeals .... me.
10   It would be hard work, but I'm not afraid .... that.

2   Tell a partner about:

1   an activity that you
   • have a talent for
   • have lost interest in
   • doesn't appeal to you
   • never find time for.

2   a job or profession that you would like to work in.

3   someone you
   • are close to
   • are dependent on.

4   something that you
   • are afraid of doing
   • are responsible for
   • takes up a lot of your time.

5   a TV programme you would like to appear on.

Exam focus

Paper 1 Reading: multiple-choice questions (Part 2)

About the exam: In Paper 1, Part 2, you read a text and then answer seven or eight four-option multiple-choice questions. These questions may test the main ideas, details, or the writer's opinion. For each question, you choose the correct answer, A, B, C or D.

Procedure

1 Read the introduction to the task. It will tell you where the text comes from and may say something about the main topic.
2 Read the title of the text and any subheading, and skim the text quickly. This will give you a general idea of what it is about.
3 Look at each question but NOT the options and mark the part of the text it relates to.
4 Now read the text carefully. When you reach a part you have marked, look at the question **and** the options, and decide on the correct answer. Make sure you have checked ALL the options before you make your decision.
5 Mark your answer on the question paper.
6 When you have completed all the questions, transfer your answers to the answer sheet.

1 You are going to read a magazine article about a man who studies the eating of insects. Follow step 2 of the suggested procedure.

1 Why does Peter think eating insects is a good thing?
2 How does his wife feel about it?

Tickle your taste buds

Peter Menzel thinks we are ignoring a tasty and nutritious source of food – insects.

First, take 30 to 40 live scorpions. Stir-fry in hot oil for 20 seconds. Add pork, ginger, salt and pepper. Cook gently for 40 minutes … Not your average take-away, but a traditional dish in some parts of the world and one of
5 the unusual recipes collected by photographer Peter Menzel and his wife, Faith, during a nine-year study of entomophagy, the eating of insects, which has taken them all over the globe.

'I remember as a child hearing a radio programme about
10 people eating live grasshoppers,' says Peter, talking from their home in California. 'At the time I thought it was just unbelievable that people could actually eat things like that. But then I came across a magazine called the *Food Insect Newsletter* and I just became fascinated with insect
15 eating and decided to find out more about it.'

He vividly remembers the first time he actually ate insects himself. 'It was in a village in a very remote region. There were all these people on top of a mountain who were hunting stink bugs. I walked up to a group of
20 women who were mashing them up ready to cook them – but some of the women were eating them live, and they offered me one. I knew that I couldn't refuse, or they would have been terribly offended. But it was revolting. First it tried to crawl across my tongue and out of my
25 mouth, so I had to crunch down on it so it didn't get

away, and it exploded. The taste made me feel sick but there were all these people watching me so I had to swallow it.'

After that **it** got easier and Peter gradually became a *line 29*
30 connoisseur. One dish he recommends from personal experience is roast tarantula spider. 'It's the world's largest spider, it's bigger than your hand. You roast it, and it has juicy white meat inside, like a crab. And there's actually very little difference between them,
35 except one of them lives in water and one on land.'

2 Look at the questions and follow steps 3–5 of the suggested procedure. Choose the answer (A, B, C or D) which you think fits best according to the text.

1 Peter and Faith have travelled round the world in order to
A do research into people's eating habits.
B learn how to cook scorpions.
C take photographs of unusual insects.
D write a book of traditional recipes.

2 When Peter read about insect eating, he decided the idea sounded
A shocking.
B strange.
C interesting.
D unpleasant.

His wife, Faith, is still far from happy about insect eating. 'I'm the reluctant bug-eater here,' she says. 'I know it makes sense in environmental terms, but I just don't like the thought of it. I suppose here in the USA
40 we've stopped thinking about where our food actually comes from – we just go along to the supermarket and buy something in a packet.'

'People have asked me why I do this,' says Peter. 'Well, the food we eat is a very basic part of our
45 culture, and when we share others' food I think we gain more understanding of their culture. But as well as that, it helps us to examine our own attitudes towards what we eat. In fact, many species of insects are lower in fat, and higher in protein than beef or
50 chicken. And raising insects is environmentally friendly – you don't need to destroy any wildlife habitat to do it.'

So what's on the menu for lunch today for Peter and Faith? 'Well, I've got a couple of kilos of dried
55 worms,' says Peter. 'We could make a nice little casserole with spices and onions.' 'Oh no,' says Faith, interrupting. 'I'll tell you exactly what we're having. We're going to have a very nice pasta with sun-dried tomatoes and a fresh salad – and no bugs in it.'

Adapted from THE INDEPENDENT

stink bug: *an insect which gives off a strong and unpleasant smell*

3 Why did Peter accept a stink bug from the women on the mountain?
A He did not want to be impolite.
B He did not realise they wanted him to eat it.
C He thought it had been cooked.
D He did not know what it was.

4 Peter bit into the stink bug because he wanted to
A stop it stinging him.
B prevent it from escaping.
C swallow it.
D taste it.

5 What does 'it' refer to in line 29?
A biting stink bugs
B enjoying stink bugs
C eating insects
D cooking insects

6 Peter says that the tarantula spider is
A similar in taste to a type of seafood.
B the most delicious insect he has eaten.
C not very different in taste from other types of insect.
D only good to eat if it is carefully cooked.

7 Faith says that although she isn't enthusiastic about eating insects, she
A is prepared to try anything to protect the environment.
B is aware that there are good reasons for eating them.
C will eat them if she knows where they come from.
D would buy them if she saw them in the supermarket.

8 Peter says that one advantage of his work is that he has
A become more aware of environmental problems.
B learned more about what makes food healthy.
C discovered new sources of food.
D found out about other ways of life.

3 Which of the following statements do you agree or disagree with? Give reasons and examples.

1 I would definitely eat insects if I was very hungry.
2 People have a lot of unreasonable prejudices about food.
3 If we thought about where some of our food came from, we might not want to eat it.

Grammar 1: countable and uncountable nouns

1 Put the nouns below into four groups:

a) countable b) uncountable c) countable or uncountable d) always plural

accommodation   advice   aerobics   book
chocolate   clothes   food   fruit
information   knife   luggage   maths
meal   news   plate   police
potato   progress   scissors   series
spider   traffic   transport   trousers

2 Read the following pairs of sentences. Which of the highlighted nouns are countable and which are uncountable? What is the meaning in each case?

1 a) I've got a stone in my shoe – I'll have to stop.
   b) Our house is built of local stone.
2 a) She's had her hair dyed bright pink.
   b) Look! I've found a hair in my coffee.
3 a) I don't really like living in the country.
   b) I'd like to try living in another country.
4 a) There's not much space in the boot.
   b) There's a space between those two cars to park.
5 a) I forgot to buy a paper today – I'll have to watch the news on TV.
   b) Have you got any paper to write on?
6 a) Spinach is full of iron.
   b) Have you got an iron so I can iron my shirt?

3 Find the mistakes in the following sentences and correct them.

1 Please leave your luggages at Reception.
2 This scissor isn't very sharp.
3 The police has been informed about the break-in.
4 Maths are my least favourite subject.
5 The trouser I bought last week doesn't fit.
6 Can you give me some informations about train times?
7 The news about the election aren't very good.
8 I need an advice about how to cook rice.
9 Traffics in the city have increased a lot.
10 They made several series of *Friends* but the very first series were the best.

▶ Grammar reference p.195

4 Complete the table below using the highlighted expressions of quantity in these sentences.

1 I didn't do much homework last night.
2 I have lots of aunts and uncles.
3 No members of my family are teachers.
4 I drink very little coffee.
5 I have hardly seen any films this year.
6 I did some shopping last week.
7 I have a little money in my pocket.

+ uncountable nouns	+ plural countable nouns
a lot of/lots of/much	a lot of/................/many
....	a few
....	some
....	not many
....	very few
hardly any	....
not any/no	not any/................

▶ Grammar reference p.196 (6.7)

5

1 Tick any sentences in Exercise 4.1 that are true for you. If a sentence is not true, make it true by using another expression from the table.

2 Compare your answers with a partner. Stress any information that you change.

Example: *Number one isn't true for me – I did a lot of homework last night. How about you?*

Watch Out! *few and little* ◄

Match the sentence halves.

1 He knew very few people in the room
   He knew a few people in the room
   a) so he felt all right.   b) so he felt a bit nervous.
2 We've got very little money left
   I've got a little money left
   c) so let's have a meal.   d) so we can't afford a meal.

What is the difference in meaning between *few/a few* and *little/a little*?

Use of English: open cloze
(Part 2)

1 Discuss these questions.

1 How many people in the class have a bottle of water with them now?
2 Why do people buy bottled water?

2 Read the title and the text below to get a general idea of what it is about. How does it answer question 2 above?

DESIGNER WATER
– The New Accessory

Many tourists nowadays walk around carrying plastic bottles **(0)** ...*of*.... water, even in cities. The bottles seem to **(1)** .... become an important fashion accessory, and not **(2)** .... for tourists. In fact, nowadays everyone seems to carry a bottle of water with **(3)** .... wherever they go. This fashion for being seen with bottled water, sometimes called 'designer water', **(4)** .... led to a massive increase **(5)** .... sales over the past few years. There are now **(6)** .... many different brand names available in the shops that it is hard to choose.

But **(7)** .... do some people prefer their water from a bottle rather than a tap? To start with, water forms **(8)** .... vital part of a healthy lifestyle. We **(9)** .... now advised to drink two litres of water daily, as **(10)** .... as eating large quantities of fruit and vegetables. In addition **(11)** .... this, designer water offers the promise of purity. **(12)** .... is advertised as clean and natural, while tap water may be viewed **(13)** .... suspicion.

But is there really any difference **(14)** .... bottled and tap water? Surprisingly, in **(15)** .... USA it was found that bottled water was not always as pure as most ordinary tap water.

3 You have to complete the spaces in the text with one word. The words are usually grammatical. First, look at the following sets of words and match them with the grammatical labels a)–h) below.

Example: *Group 1 are all expressions of quantity.*

1 *any few little many no some*
2 *a an one the*
3 *it them they you*
4 *what where which who why*
5 *as less more than*
6 *anyone anything everything everywhere whatever whoever*
7 *am is are was were has have had being having*
8 *at for from in with of on to with*

a) articles/numbers
b) auxiliary verbs
c) comparatives
d) expressions of quantity
e) indefinite pronouns
f) personal pronouns
g) prepositions
h) relative pronouns/question words

> **TIP!** You will find it easier to do this task if you think about what type of word is missing.

4 Read the text again and think of the word which best fits each space. Use only one word in each space. There is an example at the beginning (0). You will find most of the words you need in Exercise 3.

Reading 2: gapped text
(Part 3)

1   You are going to read a magazine article about a 19-year-old girl called Daniela. Look at the title of the article and the photograph.

1   Where do you think Daniela is?
2   Why is she there?
3   How do you think she is feeling?

2   Now read the main part of the article to check your ideas.

3   Seven sentences have been removed from the article. Choose from the sentences A–H the one which fits each gap (1–6). There is one extra sentence which you do not need to use. There is an example at the beginning (0).

TIP! Read each paragraph carefully and try to predict what is missing in the gap. Look for topic and lexical links in the extracted sentences.

---

1   Look at gap 1. Then look through the sentences in the box. The highlighted phrases may:

• summarise information that has already been mentioned in the text **or**
• be linked to the topic of the paragraph they come from.

Which sentence fits gap 1?

2   Do the rest of the task, using the highlighted words to help you.

I can't go out

Two years ago, when I was 17, I started feeling dizzy all the time and getting red spots all over my body. **0** **H** Finally I saw a specialist, who explained that I was severely allergic to many of the chemicals found in everyday things like clothes, food and make-up. The only treatment was to cut these chemicals out of my life completely.

To do this, the specialist said I had to live in isolation in a special room until I got better. **1** My parents converted a small room for me at the top of our house, and I moved in straightaway. The room is very plain – I can't even have paint on the walls because the chemicals in it are too dangerous for me. **2** I sleep on two blankets made of special material which hasn't been treated with chemicals – I can't use a mattress or a proper bed.

I have to be careful about what I eat too. My diet now consists of cereal, cabbage and beetroot, all cooked for an hour to make sure they don't contain any harmful substances. The only thing I can drink is spring water. If I eat or drink anything else, I get terrible stomach cramps. I really miss things like pizza and pasta and chocolate.

There's not really a lot I can do to pass the time. I can't have a TV or a computer, or a radio. **3** I'm not supposed to use the telephone for the same reason, but that's one rule I do break. I wrap the phone in a thick towel so I'm not directly in contact with it, then I call my old school friends once a day for a chat. That way I can keep in touch with the outside world, the latest news, music and fashions. **4** But I do miss having someone I can hug and be close to.

I can have visitors, but it's a very complicated process. Anyone who visits me has to make sure that for three days before they come, they don't use any soap, shampoo, or perfume. When they get to my house, they have to put on special clothes made out of material that hasn't been treated with chemicals. **5**

I've been living like this for two years now. Sometimes it makes me feel depressed, but I just try to think about the future and living a normal life one day. Fortunately I finished my school examinations before I got ill. **6** I'd also like a husband and children. But first I have to get better – and I'm determined I'm going to!

Adapted from SUGAR magazine

A I talk to my ex-boyfriend too, and we're still really good friends even though our relationship had to change when I moved into isolation.

B This means that if I get better I can have a career one day, maybe as a teacher.

C The floor is covered with special tiles made of stone, which is one of the few materials my body can tolerate.

D I'm allergic to the plastic in electronic equipment like this, and even to the ink in books.

E I was horrified by the news, but I realised I loved life too much to give up.

F As well as this, I've always been interested in fashion; before I got ill, I even did some modelling.

G And even after all these precautions they can't stay for more than an hour because I start to get allergic to them if they're near me for too long.

H My doctor didn't know what was causing them, so I went to see another, then another.

4 What would you miss most if you were in Daniela's situation?

5 Imagine that a cure has been found for Daniela and she is able to leave her room. Make a plan for her first day out in the normal world. Think about:

• where you would take her
• the sort of food you would have
• what you would do together.

Grammar 2: future forms

1

1 Look at the following statements and underline the future forms. Which are made by the patient and which by the doctor?

Example: 1 – *patient*

1 By the end of this week, I'll have been in hospital for a month.
2 I'm going to get better – I'm determined!
3 I think this new type of treatment will cure you.
4 They told me about a new type of treatment. Immediately I said, 'I'll try it!'
5 I begin my treatment next Monday.
6 I think the treatment's going to work – you're looking better already.
7 I'm leaving hospital tomorrow.
8 I hope that by this time next year, I'll be living a completely normal life.

2 When do we use the different future forms?

▶ Grammar reference p.204 (19.8)

2 In each of the following sentences one future form is possible and one is not. Cross out the incorrect form.

1 This time next week *we'll just be arriving / we'll just arrive* in America!
2 Be careful or that glass *will break / is breaking*.
3 *I'm going to apply / I will apply* for an evening job as a waitress.
4 As you can see from the satellite pictures, *it will rain / it is raining* in all parts of the country later this afternoon.
5 OK, well if you're getting a pizza, *I'll have / I'll be having* one too.
6 When *are you finishing / will you have finished* on the computer? I want to use it.

3 Complete the following dialogues using only the future forms given in brackets. Then listen to check your answers.

1 (present continuous/*will*)

A: (1) .... (*you/go*) to the meeting in London tomorrow too?

B: Yes. How are you getting there?

A: By car. I (2) .... (*give*) you a lift, if you like. I (3) .... (*leave*) quite early though – at eight o'clock. Is that OK?

B: Yes, that's great. Thanks very much. I (4) .... (*be*) ready.

2 (*going to*/present simple)

A: What (1) .... (*you/do*) for your birthday? It (2) .... (*be*) a week this Saturday, isn't it?

B: Yes. Jack (3) .... (*be*) due back from L.A. that day – his plane (4) .... (*land*) at 6.00 p.m. so we (5) .... (*not/have*) a party, just a quiet meal together.

3 (future perfect/future continuous)

A: We need to talk tomorrow – but I (1) .... (*not go*) into the office at all. You'll have to call me on my mobile.

B: OK. How about twelve o'clock?

A: Let's see – I (2) .... (*do*) my factory tour by then but after that there's a meeting. I don't think (3) .... (*finish*) by 12. Better make it one o'clock.

B: (4) .... (*you/not have*) lunch then?

A: Probably, but it doesn't matter.

4

1 Draw five bubbles like the one below. In each bubble, write notes on one of the following.

- something you're definitely going to do some time this week
- something you're doing tonight
- something you'll probably have done by this time next year
- what you'll probably be doing this time tomorrow

Example:

learned to drive

2 Work with a partner. Try to guess what the notes in your partner's bubbles refer to.

Example:

A: *I think you'll probably have learned to drive by this time next year?*

B: *Right.*

Vocabulary 3: body and health

1 Add one letter to the beginning and end of each word below to make a part of the body.

1 ..hroa..
2 ..nkl..
3 ..ris..
4 ..hee..
5 ..tomac..
6 ..hig..
7 ..ear..
8 ..hum..
9 ..inge..
10 ..ne..
11 ..lbo..
12 ..orehea..
13 ..out..
14 ..yebro..
15 ..houlde..

2 Which of the parts of the body below can you:

1 bend   5 nod
2 cross   6 clench
3 raise   7 stretch
4 shrug

arms   back   eyebrows   feet   hands   head   legs   shoulders   teeth   fist

Example: *You can bend your arms and your legs.*

3 Which movement would you make in these situations?

1 when you wake up
2 when you're tired
3 when you're doing exercise
4 when you're angry
5 when someone's trying to shoot you
6 when you agree with someone
7 when you don't care
8 after you sit down
9 when you're gardening
10 when you don't believe something

Example: *When I wake up, I open my eyes and stretch my arms.*

4   Complete the following idioms with the correct part of the body. Discuss their meanings with a partner.

1   I didn't say that at all – *you're putting words in my* ....!

2   He always tries to do the best for others – *his* .... *is in the right place.*

3   I prefer chocolate and biscuits to fruit – *I've got a really sweet* ....

4   He gave up work last year so he has plenty of *time on his* ....

5   You should work harder – you really need to *put your* .... *into it!*

5   Choose the correct alternative in each set. Only one is correct.

1   The doctor gave me a *receipt / prescription / recipe* for some painkillers.

2   There were a lot of people waiting in the doctor's *surgery / ward / pharmacy.*

3   It's quite a deep cut, but if you keep it clean it should *heal / recover / cure* quickly.

4   You feel quite hot – I think I need to take your *fever / heat / temperature.*

5   If you go on holiday abroad, you may need to have some *injections / needles / incisions* before you go.

6   When you catch a cold, you often have a very *rough / sore / injured* throat.

7   I did a lot of exercise and afterwards I had a *hurt / pain / sore* in my leg.

8   If you exercise without warming up first, you can *damage / wound / hurt* yourself.

9   If you keep fit, then you can get *over / by / out* illness more quickly.

10 Fortunately, I didn't break any bones when I fell, but I was badly *banged / damaged / bruised.*

6   Discuss with a partner.

1   When was the last time you were ill or had an accident? What happened? How did you feel? How long did it take you to recover?

2   Think of a person you know who is very fit and healthy for their age. How do they manage to stay that way?

Speaking: advantages and disadvantages (Parts 3 and 4)

1

1   Someone has suggested that a coffee machine should be installed in your classroom. Listen to some students discussing the suggestion and complete the sentences.

1   I think it's a .... I like coffee.

2   But one .... is the cost. Coffee machines are expensive, aren't they?

3   And think about the mess, with paper cups everywhere. That might be a ....

4   But coffee wakes you up. So being able to get a coffee when you are tired is a big ....

5   And another .... is that it will make the classroom feel more sociable.

6   I think the main .... is that it would encourage people to drink too much coffee. That isn't good for you.

2   Now complete the table using the words you wrote.

Positive	Negative
a good idea	....
....	....
....	....

3   What is your opinion?

2   Work with a partner. Look at page 181 and do the Speaking task.

3   Compare your decision with the class. How many students chose the same idea?

4   Discuss the following questions, which extend the topic you discussed in Exercise 2.

1   Do you enjoy keeping fit? Why?/Why not?

2   What do you think is the best way to keep fit?

3   Do you think that people have become too lazy nowadays?

4   Do you think we rely too much on cars? What are the advantages and disadvantages of this?

5   How much do you think your health depends on the food you eat?

Writing: article (Part 2)

About the exam: In Paper 2, you may be asked to write an article. You will always be given information about who the article is for. This is important because it tells you what style of writing to use.

A good article should have:
- a title. You have to make this up. It should be interesting and catch the reader's attention. Do NOT just copy out the task.
- an introductory paragraph linked to the title. This should make the reader interested in the topic. One way to do this is to begin with a question.
- one (or two) central paragraph/s that develop your main points.
- a final paragraph that summarises the main points and gives your opinion.

1   Look at the writing task below. The key words have been underlined for you. Answer the following questions.

1   Who will be reading your article?
 a) older people b) doctors c) younger people
2   What style would be most suitable?
 a) very formal b) neutral c) informal

You have seen the following advertisement in <u>a young people's magazine</u>.

The <u>young people</u> of today are likely to <u>live</u> <u>longer</u> and be <u>healthier</u> than any other generation.

<u>Why</u> do you think that is?

Write us an article answering this question. The best article will be published next month.

Write your **article** in **120–180** words.

2   Read the first and last paragraphs of one student's article below. Then choose the best title from this list and write it above the first paragraph.

A   Young people today
B   Healthier than ever before!
C   How to be healthy

....

Why do the older generation complain that we young people eat the wrong food, take no exercise, and don't look after our bodies? In fact, nothing could be further from the truth.

Better education, more nourishing food, more intensive and varied exercise, medical advances – no wonder we're going to be the healthiest generation ever!

3

1   The last paragraph above summarises what the writer has discussed in the previous paragraph. The writer gives four reasons why young people are healthy. Write them here:

1   ....
2   ....
3   ....
4   ....

2   Why do these four things make people healthy? Discuss your ideas and make notes.

Example:

1   *better education – learn how body works in Biology lessons – can help us avoid illness*

4   Now write the whole article, using the first and last paragraphs given. Your middle paragraph or paragraphs should have 70–120 words.

5   When you have finished, check your work.

▶ Writing reference pp.206, 211

1 Complete the text below using words from the box in the correct form. Use each word once only. There are two extra words you do not need to use.

experts   transport   information   product
progress   research   traffic   produce
climate   health   book

Where does our food come from?

Nowadays you can buy tropical fruit like lychees and mangoes all over the world. Many recipe (1) .... give useful (2) .... on how to prepare and serve it. However, imported (3) .... is much more expensive than locally grown food due to the high cost of air (4) .... Now scientists are carrying out (5) .... to see if they can genetically modify tropical fruit so that it can grow in cooler (6) .... They have already made (7) .... towards achieving this. But some (8) .... think that genetically modified food could be dangerous to our (9) ....

2 Write a list of five of your favourite foods. Then compare your list with a partner and discuss these questions.

1 How many of these foods are grown or produced in your own country? Do you know which part of the country they come from?
2 How many of these foods are imported? Do you know which countries they come from?

3 Each of the following sentences has one incorrect extra word. Cross it out.

1 I don't like riding my bike when there is too much of heavy traffic.
2 When I am finish college, I'm going to apply for a job in a hospital.
3 That was a good advice you gave me about how to cook vegetables.
4 There were a lots of insects in the garden.
5 I'll be going graduating this time next year.
6 I'm meeting to my friend for lunch on Saturday.
7 They will have being arrived in Australia by midday tomorrow.
8 Not the many people know the answer to that question.
9 By next year I will to have finished my medical course.
10 When are you going to be finish the course?
11 We've got hardly any of food left.

4 Complete the word tree.

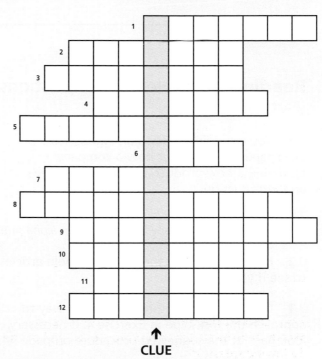

CLUE
This is found in bread, pasta and rice. It gives you energy.

1 This is the process of preparing food using heat.
2 Citrus fruits like oranges and lemons are good sources of .... C.
3 Some people are .... to the chemicals in our environment.
4 This is the natural environment where an animal or a plant lives.
5 You should chew your food thoroughly before you ....
6 Foods that are .... in cholesterol are bad for the heart.
7 Milk and cheese are examples of .... products.
8 The main .... of jam are fruit and sugar.
9 Insects are a highly .... source of food.
10 As a result of medical .... , many diseases are now curable.
11 This vegetable is used to make chips and crisps.
12 If you want to work in the .... industry, you have to be ready to put in very long hours.

UNIT
5 Material world

Reading: multiple-choice questions (Part 2)

1 You are going to read an extract from a newspaper article about how a company marketed a new product. First, read the title and introduction.

1 What do you think *alpha pups* are?

2 Why might the company be interested in *alpha pups*?

2 Now read quickly through the whole article to see if you were right.

3 Discuss what you think is the best way to approach the task type in Exercise 4. If necessary, look back at the suggested procedure on page 44.

HERE COME THE ALPHA PUPS

A company develops a video game about an alien virus. How do they make kids want it? The answer is easy: they give it to the coolest kids they can find and let them do the marketing.

Leading toy company Hasbro spent several years developing a new video game about an alien virus. The obvious way to market a game of this type would be to organise a huge advertising campaign. But Hasbro thought of another possibility: to give free copies of the game to the coolest kids they could find, and let them do the marketing instead.

So Hasbro's market researchers went into playgrounds across Chicago looking for what they call 'alpha pups', the young boys who set the trends in fashion among others of their age. They went up to boys between the ages of eight and thirteen and asked them all the same question: 'Who's the coolest kid you know?' They didn't bother to ask the girls, who seem to define coolness in a different way from the boys.

When the researchers were given a name, they would look for that boy and put the same question to him. Their goal was to go up the 'ladder of coolness', asking the same question again and again until

someone finally answered, 'Me'. **They** then had an alpha pup – the coolest kid in the school.   line 20

In a very short time, the researchers had questioned students in most of the schools in the city and identified the alpha pups among them. They then made them an offer that sounded too good to be true – the firm would pay them $30 to learn to play a new video game.

One of the alpha pups they chose was Angel Franco, an enthusiastic player of video games. He was invited to the Hasbro office building near the town centre, where he and several others were taken into a special conference room. Unknown to any of the boys, market researchers from Hasbro were sitting behind a one-way mirror in the next room, secretly watching their reactions.

The leader of the session, a casually dressed young man called Nino, introduced the game, explaining, 'We chose you because you're the coolest, funniest guys in your school. Raise your hands if you're cool.' Every hand shot up. Then Nino revealed what was special about the game – a radio transmitter which allowed a player to compete against any other player within 10 metres.

'Let's say you're at school waiting to go into class, and your friend has one,' Nino said. 'You could be in one room and he could be in another room and you could be battling … and no one else would know you were playing one another.'

The boys were immediately enthusiastic.
'This game is great!'
'This is the best game ever!'

50 The adults behind the mirror were excited too. 'Get the name of the kid who said it's the best game ever,' one publicist said to another.

After they had learned to play the game, Nino gave each alpha pup a backpack containing the radio

55 unit and ten copies of the game to pass on to his friends. Angel took four copies of the game into school the next day, and when he took them out in the cafeteria and handed them out to his friends, they – and the other less fortunate students – were

60 immediately impressed. They started playing straightaway without looking at the instructions – the classic boys' approach to video games and computers.

The manufacturers said the game was not meant

65 to be used at school, but unofficially, everyone knew better. Within a few weeks it was being played on the school bus, in the halls, and in class in 900 of the 1,400 schools in Chicago.

In the meantime, the search for the next great

70 game begins at Hasbro with a brainstorming session in which designers and marketers sit around a table and say repeatedly, 'Wouldn't it be cool if …'

Adapted from THE INDEPENDENT ON SUNDAY

4   Choose the answer (A, B, C or D) which you think fits best according to the text.

1   After developing a new video game, Hasbro needed to decide
   A   when the game should be put on the market.
   B   what sort of people the game would attract.
   C   who should design the advertising campaign.
   D   how they could interest young people in the game.

2   The Hasbro researchers were looking for boys who
   A   were born or living in a certain area.
   B   were successful in school lessons.
   C   were admired by their fellow students.
   D   were known by a lot of people.

3   'They' in line 20 refers to
   A   the alpha pups.
   B   the schools.
   C   the researchers.
   D   the students.

4   When they went to the Hasbro building, the boys
   A   were invited to meet the researchers.
   B   were not told they were being observed.
   C   were asked to choose someone as their leader.
   D   were not all allowed to play the game.

5   The boys were enthusiastic about the new game because they could
   A   use it while waiting to go into class.
   B   play against an opponent who was somewhere else.
   C   play and listen to the radio at the same time.
   D   attack an opponent unexpectedly.

6   During the session, the Hasbro researchers were pleased because the boys
   A   praised the game.
   B   finished the game quickly.
   C   said that the game was unusual.
   D   found the instructions easy to follow.

7   The boys were provided with copies of the video game
   A   to thank them for coming to the session.
   B   so that they could show the game to their teachers.
   C   so that they could give the game to other boys.
   D   to check that the instructions were clear.

5   Discuss these questions.

1   What are the advantages and disadvantages of this method of marketing a) for Angel and his friends? b) for the company?

2   Do you believe this kind of direct marketing to children is acceptable? Why?/Why not?

Speaking 1: advertising

1 Look at the pictures above. What different methods of advertising do they show? Which do you think is the most effective?

2 Discuss these questions.

1 How do you usually learn about new products and services?
2 What is your favourite advert at the moment? Why do you like it?
3 Can you think of an advert that you don't like?
4 Have you ever bought anything just because you saw an advert for it? Were you pleased with it or not?

Vocabulary 1: consumer society

1 Choose the correct alternative in each of the following sentences.

1 More and more people live in a *customer / consumer* society.
2 The streets of our cities are full of *advertisements / propaganda*.
3 Television programmes are regularly interrupted by *commercials / announcements*.
4 In some fashion magazines there is more *publicity / advertising* than there are articles.
5 A large company either has its own *marketing / selling* department or uses an advertising *agency / office*.
6 The *launch / take off* of an advertising *campaign / attack* for a new luxury product is often accompanied by massive *fame / publicity*.
7 Big stores often have special *promotions / publicity* or offer big *discounts / rebates* on certain products.
8 Products with well-known *logos / brands* are very popular.

2

1 Say the words in each set aloud and mark the stress. Then answer the question below.

Example: con<u>su</u>mer con<u>su</u>mption con<u>su</u>me
1 announcer announce announcement
2 advertiser advertising advertise advertisement
3 commerce commercial commercialisation
4 promoter promote promotion
5 publicity publicize
6 economics economy economical

In which sets of words does the stressed syllable change?

2 Listen and check your answers.

3 Complete the following sentences using words from Exercises 1 and 2 in the correct form.

1 The c........... of ready-prepared meals has increased dramatically in the UK.
2 Companies are always looking for new m........... for their products.
3 Large department stores often give away free samples when they are p........... a new range of make-up or toiletries.
4 The government has l........... a massive publicity c........... against smoking.
5 It is not permitted to a........... cigarettes on TV.
6 Many well-known celebrities have c........... against experiments on animals.

4 Discuss the advantages and disadvantages of the consumer society.

Example: *One advantage is that there is plenty of choice – for example, you can buy 20 different types of coffee in the shops.*

Use of English 1: multiple-choice cloze
(Part 1)

1   Read the text below quickly. Don't try to fill in the gaps yet. Is the text describing:

a) the dangers of brand names?
b) the good points about brand names?
c) both the dangers and the good points?

2   Read the text carefully and decide which answer (A, B, C or D) best fits each space. There is an example at the beginning (0).

ARE BRAND NAMES WORTH IT?

How do famous companies get people to spend a (0) ....A...... on brand names? To find the (1) .... to this question, just observe the children in any school playground.

Hannah is a (2) .... nine-year-old student at an English primary school. She's not quite sure what a brand (3) .... is, but she's sure of what she wants. As part of a new sales (4) .... , all the students in her class have been given a free bag with the Nike (5) .... on it. Hannah hasn't really (6) .... the connection yet, or asked for Nike trainers, but it's only a (7) .... of time before she does. But is it right that companies should (8) .... such young children for their promotional activities?

Brand names seem to have (9) .... over us because they allow us to (10) .... with a particular group of people. A brand name has a certain (11) .... It suggests that we're able to afford this product – and most of us like to (12) .... off what we can afford. Some people also believe that brand names provide a (13) .... of quality. So a brand has to provide this quality, (14) .... people will eventually stop buying it.

So only time will (15) .... whether it's really worthwhile paying extra money for a brand name. Meanwhile, Hannah is delighted with her free Nike bag.

0	A fortune	B treasure	C deal	D load
1	A reply	B response	C answer	D solution
2	A similar	B typical	C uniform	D regular
3	A certainly	B factually	C surely	D actually
4	A battle	B campaign	C attack	D propaganda
5	A diagram	B mark	C picture	D logo
6	A made	B taken	C done	D put
7	A situation	B problem	C question	D state
8	A target	B aim	C focus	D point
9	A rule	B meaning	C power	D force
10	A identify	B indicate	C sign	D point
11	A invention	B impression	C portrait	D image
12	A present	B show	C carry	D wear
13	A guarantee	B bond	C security	D receipt
14	A since	B otherwise	C but	D however
15	A say	B speak	C tell	D state

Listening 1: radio adverts

1   You will hear three radio adverts. Listen and tick which of these products each one is advertising.

a) shampoo and conditioner
b) penknife
c) make-up
d) digital camera
e) digital radio

2   Listen again and tick the things that are mentioned for each product.

	1	2	3
Who could use it			
What it can do			
Effect of the product			
Size			
Convenience			
Price			

3   Which advert did you think was the most effective? Which one would influence you the most? Why?

4   Listen again and tick the phrases used to persuade people to buy the products.

You'll never again be without something to …
It's the best one ever!
You'll wonder how you ever managed without it.
Take advantage of our special discount.
You've never seen anything like it!
This offer won't last long.
Why wait for that perfect appearance?
You won't regret it.
A price that suits your pocket.
Pop in to see our wide selection.

57

Listening 2: multiple matching
(Part 3)

1 Choose one of the following statements and complete it, giving two reasons.

a) I really enjoy shopping because … and …

b) I don't like shopping because … and …

2 You will hear five people talking about the shops and other facilities in a small town. Choose from the list A–F what each speaker says. Use the letters only once. There is one extra letter which you do not need to use.

> **TIP!** When you listen the first time, mark any possible answers in pencil. Listen the second time to confirm your ideas.

A The shop buildings are very picturesque.
B The shops are rather expensive.
C There are some good specialist shops.
D There is a good choice of cafés and snack bars.
E The town has been spoiled by tourism.
F There is a limited range of things to buy.

Speaker 1	1
Speaker 2	2
Speaker 3	3
Speaker 4	4
Speaker 5	5

3 How true is each statement in Exercise 2 about your town or city? Think of examples to support or oppose each statement.

Example: *Some of the shop buildings are really attractive in our town. For example, I really like the old shops round the main square.*

Grammar 2: reporting verbs

1

1 One of the options A, B or C in the following sentences is not possible. Cross out the incorrect word and explain why it is wrong.

Example:

My uncle .... to buy me a CD for my birthday.
A agreed   B promised   C ~~suggested~~
'Suggest' cannot be followed by the infinitive form.

1 He .... her to buy the red jacket.
A told   B advised   C offered
2 The shop assistant .... that I should try a smaller size.
A told   B recommended   C suggested
3 Maria .... us to stay to dinner.
A invited   B demanded   C persuaded
4 I complained about the service and they ....
to give me a refund.
A offered   B advised   C agreed
5 Did the man .... taking the money?
A remind   B admit   C deny
6 I think Robert .... that he was in the wrong.
A realised   B accepted   C accused
7 I .... him for breaking the glass.
A apologised   B forgave   C blamed
8 Peter .... us that he wouldn't be late!
A promised   B told   C explained

2 Put the verbs above into the table. Some verbs may go in more than one place.

verb + infinitive	verb + object + infinitive
verb + *that*	verb + object + *that*
verb + *-ing*	verb + object + preposition + *-ing*

Watch Out! *suggest*

Which pattern is NOT possible? Cross it out.
He suggested   a) paying her £20.
                b) that they paid her £20.
                c) that they should pay her £20.
                d) them to pay her £20.

▶ Grammar reference p.199 (12.4–7)

2 Rewrite the following sentences using the correct form of the verbs in brackets. Make any other necessary changes.

Example: 'You should go to the fish restaurant on the High Street – it's really good,' she said. (*recommend*)
She recommended (going to) the fish restaurant on the High Street.

1 'I won't go,' I said. (*refuse*)
2 'Don't forget to buy some bread on the way home, Jake,' he said. (*remind*)
3 'Well done Kerry, you passed your exam!' said Mum. (*congratulate*)
4 'I'm sorry I forgot your birthday, Sally,' Clare said. (*apologise*)
5 'Don't sit on that chair, Mary. It's broken!' I said. (*warn*)
6 'Maybe we could meet at the beach?' said Brad. (*suggest*)
7 'I'll give you a parking ticket if you don't move the car,' she said. (*threaten*)
8 'Would you like to come round for dinner on Saturday?' she asked me. (*invite*)

3

1 Recently you wanted to buy a new game. Summarise and report what the sales assistant said to you in each shop. Use indirect speech and some of the verbs in Exercises 1 and 2.

Example:

Right On: 'We don't have any games in stock at the moment. Why don't you try Wilkinson's down the street?'
In Right On they told me they didn't have any games in stock and suggested that I try Wilkinson's.

1 *Wilkinson's:* 'We've just sold our last copy. I'm very sorry. It's very popular, you see. But you might find one in GamesRUs, as it's a bigger shop.' (*tell/apologise/explain/say*)
2 *GamesRUs:* 'We're out of stock, but they're on order and we'll be getting some more in next week. I'll give you a ring when they come in, if you give me your name and a contact number.'
3 *VHM:* 'I'm not sure if we have any left. If you take a seat, I'll go and look in the stockroom for you … You're in luck. I've got one copy left! Do you want it?'

2 Have you had any similar experiences when you wanted to buy something?

Exam focus
Paper 3 Use of English: key word transformations (Part 3)

About the exam: In Paper 3, Part 3, you are given a sentence and asked to complete a second one using a 'key word'. The meaning of the second sentence must be similar to the first. This task tests a range of grammatical structures as well as vocabulary. Each item will probably be testing two things.

Procedure

1 Read the first sentence and look at the key word. Identify what the sentence is testing and work out possible answers.
2 When you are sure of the answer, write the missing words.
3 Check that you have not:
• changed the key word
• changed the meaning of the sentence
• written more than five words. Contractions (e.g. *don't*) count as two words.
• made any other unnecessary changes, e.g. to tenses
• made any spelling mistakes
4 Transfer your answers onto the answer sheet. Check the number of the question carefully to make sure that you write your answer in the right place.

For questions 1–10, complete the second sentence so that it has a similar meaning to the first sentence, using the word given. Do not change the word given. You must use between two and five words, including the word given. Here is an example (0).

Example:

0 'Who borrowed my book, Mary?' asked Andrew
   had
   Andrew *asked Mary who had borrowed* his book.
1 It was Susie's first visit to London.   **never**
   Susie .... to London before.
2 Chloe spent her childhood in the country with her grandparents.   **brought**
   Chloe .... her grandparents in the country.
3 James has been chosen for the main role because he is the best singer.   **as**
   No one else .... James does, so he has been chosen for the main role.
4 I'd like to go to India.   **appeals**
   The idea of .... me.

5 There's someone at the door – I think it's the postman. **sounds**

There's someone at the door – .... the postman.

6 'Do you want to have a drink, Peter?' asked Jane. **like**

Jane asked Peter .... have a drink.

7 They said they had found the directions he gave very confusing. **been**

They said they .... his directions.

8 There were students from ten different countries in the class. **up**

The class .... students from ten different countries.

9 Melissa has not appeared on television much recently. **made**

Melissa has .... on television recently.

10 You need both luck and talent to succeed. **well**

Success depends .... as talent.

Vocabulary 3: shopping and leisure facilities

1

1 Choose two of the words in brackets to complete the sentences.

1 I like shopping in the summer .... when there are good .... on everything! *(sales / bargains / reductions)*

2 Whenever you buy anything you should always keep the .... in case you want to .... it later. *(exchange / receipt / prescription)*

3 I never seem to be able to find a .... although my friend seems to get a .... on everything and never pays full price! *(discount / bargain / refund)*

4 Some people always pay .... when they go shopping, but I prefer to pay .... because I don't like carrying too much money. *(on credit / by cheque / in cash)*

5 I go shopping once a week – it's easier to .... that way so it's more .... *(economical / economic / budget)*

6 I hate waiting in a long .... at the .... in the supermarket. *(till / checkout / queue)*

2 Ask a partner these questions.

1 Do you like shopping in the sales?

2 Have you ever taken something back to the shop and exchanged it or asked for a credit note?

3 Are you good at finding bargains?

3 Now make more questions for Exercise 1.1, sentences 4, 5 and 6, and ask your partner.

2

1 Match the following descriptions to the leisure facilities below.

1 Large modern building with outdoor floodlit area, fitness room and snooker room. Wheelchair access to all areas.

2 Open 24-hours a day for a wide range of activities including skating lessons, ice hockey, public and disco skating sessions.

3 Includes displays of local history, archaeology, architecture and the environment.

4 A collection of books, videos, DVDs and CD Roms which can be borrowed by the general public. Reference and information services are also available.

5 Exhibitions by local painters and local contemporary craft, as well as a permanent display of British and international paintings.

6 An ongoing programme of day and evening classes including computer skills, dressmaking, First Aid and foreign languages.

a) art gallery   d) museum
b) ice rink   e) sports centre
c) library   f) Further Education college

2 Which of the facilities above does your town have? What other facilities are available?

3 Where would you go in your town or city:

1 to buy the trendiest clothes?
2 to buy the cheapest household goods?
3 to buy a really unusual present?
4 to listen to great music or dance till 2 a.m.?
5 to go for a relaxing walk?
6 to meet your friends for coffee?
7 to enrol for an evening class in pottery?
8 to get some serious exercise?

Speaking 3: expressing uncertainty (Part 2)

1 Match the words to the correct photos.

checkout   fitting room   cashier   shelves
trolley   shopping bag   rail   special offers
bargains   assistant
department store   advertisements

2 Work with a partner. Find two similarities and three differences between the photos.

Example: *Both photos show people shopping. The first photo is in a supermarket, but the second photo is in a department store.*

3 Listen to another student talking about the same photos. He is not always sure about what is happening in the pictures. Tick the phrases he uses.

I'm not sure, but (it/they) might be …
It's not very clear, but probably/I think …
(It) could be …   Maybe …   Perhaps …
It looks as if …   It seems as though …
They seem to be –ing …

4

1 Take it in turns with your partner to compare and contrast photos A and B. Try to keep talking for about 40 seconds.

2 Say which type of shopping seems to be the most enjoyable for the shoppers (about 20 seconds).

A

B

5 Work with another partner.

Student A look at photos C and D on page 182, which show different kinds of advertising. Compare and contrast the pictures and say in which place the advertising is probably most effective.

Student B look at photos E and F on page 182, which show people doing leisure activities. Compare and contrast the pictures and say which activity seems to be the most enjoyable.

Writing: letter of complaint (Part 1)

1 When you write a letter of complaint to someone, you usually need to do the following three things. Number them in the order you should deal with them in a letter.

☐ Say what you want the person to do.
☐ Say why you are writing.
☐ Explain the problem.

2 Look at the task below and answer these questions.

1 Who are you writing to?
2 Why are you writing?
3 How many problems will you describe?
4 What do you want the other person to do?
5 What style should you use, formal or informal?

You recently went to a special sale of CDs that was advertised in the local newspaper. You were very disappointed with the sale. Read the newspaper advertisement and the notes you have made. Then write a letter to the newspaper, complaining about the things that were wrong and asking them to withdraw the advertisement from the newspaper. (120–180 words)

CDs Incorporated Special Sale!

Want to buy the latest CD?
Check out our prices ⎯ *newest was 6 months old*

We sell the most up-to-date CDs and we stock albums by all the most popular singers ⎯ *none of my favourites* and bands available. ⎯

Prices start at £2, and there are *cheapest was £5* huge discounts available on ⎯ all our products for students. ⎯ *5% discount only*
⎯ *not all products*

One week only.
Don't miss out on this fantastic opportunity!

Doors open at 9 a.m. ⎯ *not until 10*
Free tea and coffee provided.

3 When you describe the problems, you should explain what the advertisement said and then say what actually happened. Match the sentence halves, using the highlighted words to help you.

What the advertisement said
1 The advertisement claimed that prices would start at £2,
2 They promised that there would be huge discounts on everything,
3 They said they would open the doors at nine o'clock,
4 The advertisement stated that all CDs were up-to-date.

What actually happened
a) but we did not get in until ten o'clock.
b) However, the newest one was already six months old.
c) but in fact nothing was less than £5.
d) whereas actually there was only a small discount on some products.

▶ Writing reference p.215

4

1 Choose the best alternatives for the first paragraph of a formal letter.

> Dear Sir or Madam
>
> (1) *I am writing / I'm writing* to complain about (2) *an advertisement which appeared / a horrible ad which was in your newspaper* yesterday. The advertisement was for CDs Incorporated. I thought (3) *there were lots of things wrong with it / it was misleading in several ways.*

2 Which ending is best for this letter?

a) I demand that you remove the advertisement instantly.
b) I would be grateful if you could remove the advertisement from the newspaper as soon as possible.
c) I want you to take it out of the newspaper right now.

5 Now write your own answer to the task.

6 When you have finished, check your letter.

▶ Writing reference pp.206, 207

1 There is a mistake with vocabulary in each of the following sentences. Find the mistakes and correct them.

1 The film *Star Wars* has a combine of two themes.
2 I thought that *Moulin Rouge* had a very sad finishing.
3 The film ends with a close shot of the hero.
4 The actress Gwyneth Paltrow made a very emotion speech when she won her Oscar.
5 I was very irritating by what he said.
6 The Olympic Games have place every four years.
7 He just made a glimpse of the tiger in the long grass.
8 It is impossible to me to buy that car.
9 The reality of the situation was starting to fall in.
10 Eggs are known to be high with cholesterol.
11 Would you rather feed out in a restaurant?
12 The taste of the insect was absolutely revolted.
13 I had to eat the insect living.
14 You must have used a fortune buying that car!
15 The shop has a broad selection of electrical goods.

2 Decide what word is missing in each of the following sentences and write it in the correct place.

1 He known her since he was a child.
2 How many times you phone your sister every day?
3 I had this car since I was eighteen.
4 Have you running? You look hot.
5 My sister is lot better at Maths than I am.
6 This ride isn't exciting as the one we went on in Disneyland.
7 Tom is not taller than I am – only about one centimetre.
8 I'm going to Canary Islands for my summer holiday.
9 My father drives slowly than my brother does.
10 He already finished the work when the teacher returned.
11 I usually just have piece of toast for breakfast.
12 I'm watching very interesting series about dinosaurs on TV.
13 The police told me go away.
14 Brad asked Vicky she wanted a drink or not.
15 They advised me not worry as everything would be all right.

Use of English: multiple-choice cloze (Part 1)

3 For questions 1–15, read the text below and decide which answer (A, B, C or D) best fits each space. There is an example at the beginning (0).

MY FIRST FLIGHT

My heart was (0) ..*B*.... fast as I stood at the edge of the cliff with my hang glider for the first time. I looked (1) .... ahead to where the (2) .... disappeared in front of me, and (3) .... that there was nothing between me and the valley lying (4) .... below. My flying instructor went (5) .... the instructions once more, but I was not listening. The idea of jumping off this cliff suddenly seemed totally (6) .... !

I hesitated for a moment. But I had to do it. I (7) .... a deep breath and began to move forwards. After only five steps I was (8) .... up into the air by the wind. I gasped as I flew over the (9) .... of the cliff. Excitement surged through me, and I (10) .... to laugh. I was excited and afraid at the same time, and I loved it. I (11) .... the control bar tightly as if that was the only thing (12) .... me falling as I hung hundreds of metres above the valley (13) .... out below.

All too soon I was over the landing field, and I had to (14) .... hard on getting down safely. When I finally landed, I was triumphant. I had flown like a bird, and I would never be the (15) .... person again.

0 A running	**B** beating	**C** moving	**D** rushing
1 A straight	**B** true	**C** direct	**D** completely
2 A floor	**B** ground	**C** base	**D** bottom
3 A reviewed	**B** reminded	**C** reconsidered	**D** realised
4 A long	**B** far	**C** further	**D** away
5 A over	**B** out	**C** by	**D** in
6 A indecisive	**B** unrepeatable	**C** unreasonable	**D** insensitive
7 A had	**B** took	**C** caught	**D** got
8 A ascended	**B** moved	**C** made	**D** lifted
9 A bit	**B** section	**C** border	**D** edge
10 A burst out	**B** started	**C** set off	**D** felt
11 A held	**B** carried	**C** touched	**D** reached
12 A closing	**B** keeping	**C** stopping	**D** making
13 A extended	**B** spread	**C** closed	**D** covered
14 A attend	**B** consider	**C** concentrate	**D** apply
15 A equal	**B** same	**C** similar	**D** typical

Use of English: open cloze (Part 2)

4 For questions 16–30, read the text below and think of the word which best fits each space. Use only one word in each space. There is an example at the beginning (0).

TEA BAGS

These days, in millions of homes around the world, people make cups of tea **(0)** ...*with*... tea bags. But **(16)** .... first thought of putting tea leaves **(17)** .... small bags? It was an American, in 1919. At **(18)** .... time, the bags were mainly used by tea companies to allow customers to try the tea before buying it. But the idea of the tea bag took **(19)** .... , and by 1935 most were being bought for use **(20)** .... home.

It wasn't long **(21)** .... tea bags started to become popular in countries outside America. But they were not an immediate success everywhere. In Britain, for **(22)** .... , people held very strong views on **(23)** .... to make a good cup of tea. There was a strict procedure which involved warming the teapot, putting one spoonful of tea for **(24)** .... person into the pot and then filling **(25)** .... with boiling water. The pot was then left **(26)** .... five minutes before the tea was poured into cups, and milk and sugar were added last.

However, **(27)** .... this strong tradition, nowadays things **(28)** .... changed. Modern people lead busy lives, and making the perfect cup of tea properly is **(29)** .... important than making it easily and conveniently. These days, over 75% of the cups of tea drunk in Britain **(30)** .... made with tea bags.

Use of English: key word transformations (Part 3)

5 For questions 31–40, complete the second sentence so that it has a similar meaning to the first sentence, using the word given. Do not change the word given. You must use between two and five words, including the word given. There is an example at the beginning (0).

Example:

0 You must do exactly as I tell you.
carry
You must ...*carry out my*........ instructions exactly.

31 'It was me who broke the window,' said Steven.
admitted
Steven .... the window.

32 There are hardly any copies of the book left in the shop.
very
There are .... of the book left in the shop.

33 He's been her boyfriend for a long time.
out
She's been .... for a long time.

34 I only ate a little at lunch, so I'm hungry now.
to
I didn't .... at lunch, so I'm hungry now.

35 Don swims better than Carlos.
well
Carlos .... as Don.

36 They don't know what caused the problem yet.
discovered
They .... of the problem yet.

37 He said that the accident was my fault.
blamed
He .... the accident.

38 It's three years since we worked together.
not
We .... three years.

39 'I'll come with you tomorrow,' said Jaime.
promised
Jaime .... the next day.

40 I prefer watching football to playing it.
rather
I .... play it.

Use of English: error correction (Part 4)

6 For questions 41–55, read the text below and look carefully at each line. Some of the lines are correct, and some have a word which should not be there. If a line is correct, put a tick (✓) at the end of the line. If a line has a word which should not be there, write the word at the end of the line. There are two examples at the beginning (0 and 00).

WHAT I THINK ABOUT ADVERTISING

0 Today, unlike in the past, we are all surrounded by brand names, ✓
00 and newspapers and television are dominated by such marketing. *such*
41 But my friends and I are familiar with all the different of advertising
42 techniques that can be used to because we see them so much, and
43 we know when a company is just trying to sell us a product although
44 whether we need it or not. I do actually quite enjoy advertisements,
45 especially if they are funny or amusing in some way but I try myself
46 not to be too influenced by them when I go for shopping. I remember
47 a good advertising campaign, for a new energy drink, which was used
48 an unusual technique. The company got thousands of empty cans
49 of the new drink and left them lying everywhere – on more café tables,
50 even though in litter bins. We all saw the cans, and wondered what
51 the new drink was like. But when we tried to buy it the drink in cafés
52 and in shops, we couldn't have. When the drink was finally available
53 we all rushed out to buy it. This was unusual for me because that I
54 do normally try to buy things I really want rather than so what
55 advertisements say I should have. I quite enjoyed the drink, though!

Use of English: word formation (Part 5)

7 For questions 56–65, read the text below. Use the word given in capitals at the end of each line to form a word that fits in the space in the same line. There is an example at the beginning (0).

SPACE – FICTION AND FACT

In science fiction, space is a silent, empty place but in (0) ..*reality*.. , **REAL**
things are very different. The (56) .... in a space station can be **EQUIP**
so (57) .... that astronauts working there cannot communicate **NOISE**
with one another (58) .... The noise may affect their work, and **EASY**
may even mean they are (59) .... to sleep. And noise is not the **ABLE**
only problem. Scientists have (60) .... over 8,000 items of **IDENTITY**
rubbish in orbit around the Earth. These (61) .... the safety of **THREAT**
space (62) .... because even a small piece of metal floating in **EXPLORE**
space could cause a (63) .... disaster if it hit a spacecraft. **CATASTROPHE**
Although astronauts (64) .... try to bring most rubbish home, **GENERAL**
there is even an old (65) .... camera among the litter left behind on **BREAK**
the Moon.

UNIT
6 It's your call

Vocabulary 1: technology

1   Put the following words into the correct category below. Some words may go in more than one category. Can you add any more words?

battery   cable   CD   cursor   email
engaged tone   file   film   focus   handset
hard drive   keyboard   keypad   line   monitor
mouse   negative   plug   ring tone   screen
scanner   text message   zoom lens

Computer	Camera	Telephone
	battery	*battery*

2

1 Complete the sentences using words from Exercise 1. You will need to make some words plural.

1 Do you keep the *negatives* of your photographs so you can get copies made if you want to?
2 How often do you have to recharge the .... in your mobile phone?
3 How many fingers do you use when you type on a computer ....?
4 Does your camera have a .... which allows you to take close-ups?
5 Is the .... on a computer screen a flashing line or an arrow?
6 Do you use a .... to save photographs and other documents onto your computer?
7 What kind of .... have you got on your mobile phone?
8 Have you ever had a problem when you sent a .... to be developed (e.g. the shop lost it)?
9 Do you get a headache if you look at a computer .... for a long time?
10 Which finger do you use when you press the numbers on a telehone .... ?

2 Now discuss the answers to the questions with a partner.

Example: *I don't need to keep the negatives any more because I have a digital camera.*

3 Discuss.

What benefits have the camera, the phone and the computer brought to everyday life?

Listening 1: multiple matching
(Part 3)

1 Look at the photos.

1 What is happening in each one?
2 How do you think the people are feeling?

2   You will hear five people talking about photography and the media.

1   Choose from the list A–F which opinion each speaker expresses. Use the letters only once. There is one extra letter which you do not need to use.

A   Modern developments in photography may affect the privacy of ordinary people.

B   Photographs don't always reflect the truth.

C   Modern technology means ordinary people can compete with professional journalists.

D   Media attention is justifiable in certain situations.

E   Technology helps me to take more natural photographs.

F   I was upset when pictures were taken of me without my agreement.

Speaker 1	**1**
Speaker 2	**2**
Speaker 3	**3**
Speaker 4	**4**
Speaker 5	**5**

2   Listen again to confirm your ideas.

3   Match the highlighted phrases to their meanings below. You heard all these phrases in the recording.

1   they'd kill or be killed   **f)**
2   filming on location
3   the whole face of news reporting
4   a breaking news story
5   the celebrity promotion machine
6   they'll do the rounds of
7   they've all been touched up

a) altered and made to look better
b) organised publicity for famous people
c) information that is just beginning to arrive
d) go to several different places in succession
e) out of the studio
f) risk danger and cause danger to others
g) the way something appears to people

4   Do you agree with the following statements? Why?/Why not?

• The camera never lies.
• Celebrities shouldn't expect to have privacy.

Use of English 1: word formation
(Part 5)

1   Read the title and the text below. Does the writer want to be famous or not?

2   Use the word given in capitals below the text to form a word that fits in the space in each line. There is an example at the beginning (0).

> **TIP!** Remember to check if nouns need a negative prefix and/or a plural ending.

WOULD YOU LIKE TO BE FAMOUS?

Most people find the idea of fame **(0)** .*attractive*. But would you **(1)** .... want to be famous? Many people do, but they don't always realise how many **(2)** .... there are for those who live in the public eye. They just see the **(3)** .... things about being a star, or the **(4)** .... benefits, and ignore the problems that go along with it – things like having **(5)** .... around you wherever you go, and **(6)** .... writing things about you in the newspapers that may be **(7)** .... untrue. With this kind of pressure, it's not easy to keep up **(8)** .... with friends, and some people do regret making the **(9)** .... to seek fame. Once you've become well-known you can't go back. So is it actually worth it? It's a **(10)** .... choice but I would hate it!

0	ATTRACT
1	ACTUAL
2	ADVANTAGE
3	ENJOY
4	FINANCE
5	PHOTOGRAPH
6	JOURNAL
7	COMPLETE
8	RELATE
9	DECIDE
10	PERSON

3   Would you like to be famous, even just for a short time? Discuss what might be good and bad about it.

Grammar 1: certainty and possibility

Present

1   Underline the modal verbs in the following sentences, and match them with the descriptions below.

1 Look at this photo I took – I think I might be able to sell it to the newspapers.
2 She must be very pleased with the wedding photos – they've come out really well.
3 The President may be giving a press conference later today.
4 I suppose the reports could be true, but I doubt it.
5 That can't be Nicole Kidman, can it? She looks completely different.

a) It's certainly true. ....
b) It's certainly not true. ....
c) It's quite likely to be true. ....
d) It's possible that it's true. ....

▶ **Grammar reference p.200 (14.2–3)**

2   Complete the sentences with *must, may, might, could* or *can't* and a suitable verb from the box in the correct form. Use each main verb only once.

come   be   explain   stay   feel   find
remember   ~~tell~~   be able to

Example: She *could be telling* the truth – it's hard to say.
1 Simone says she .... to the party, but she's not sure.
2 I'm afraid I can't help, but maybe my brother .... the answer to you.
3 My grandparents .... with us next week – they'll let us know by Friday.
4 You .... Carrie, surely? She used to be in our class.
5 You .... serious – you're not really going to leave, are you?
6 I .... finish the report by Friday – I'll do my best.

7 She .... nervous, having to give a presentation to so many people.
8 You .... this book useful for your essay.

3

1 Match each of the following statements with the best response below.

1 I've won first prize!   *e)*
2 Is it just me, or is it hot in here?
3 I wonder if I can get a cheap flight to New York.
4 I find heavy metal music quite relaxing.
5 I think a lot of telephone calls are unnecessary.
6 I feel like going to the cinema.
7 I can't use my new computer because they didn't install the software.
8 I don't know much about computers.

a) You could try looking on the Internet.
b) You must be in a minority these days.
c) You may have a point there.
d) You might be coming down with something.
e) Well done! You must be thrilled.
f) You may be able to do it on your own, you know.
g) You must be joking! Really?
h) There may be something good on at the Odeon.

2 Listen and check your answers.

3 With a partner, practise the mini-dialogues using appropriate intonation.

Past

4   Choose the best alternatives in the following sentences.

1 The photographer *must / can't* have touched up that photo – she looks a lot older than that really.
2 He *might / can't* have meant to upset you when he said that – he's a very kind man.
3 To take that photo, the reporter *couldn't / must* have been hiding in the garden – or maybe he was even inside the house.
4 I don't think I *could / might* have done what Mother Teresa did – she was a very brave person.
5 He *could / must* have been mad to climb the tower without safety equipment.
6 'I wonder where they are?' 'They *may / can't* have got lost.'

▶ **Grammar reference p.200 (14.2–3)**

5 Correct the mistakes in the following sentences.

1 Bruce can't has been chosen for the job – he doesn't have the right experience.

2 This photograph is very dark – it couldn't have being taken outside.

3 Be careful what you say to him – he can't to be trusted to keep a secret.

4 The police might have watching the house.

5 He can't see that she was there, or he'd have spoken to her.

6 She may have want to come to the film – why don't you ask her?

7 It wasn't a good idea to phone at midnight. I might be asleep.

8 They may been intending to leave the country.

9 You can't still doing your homework!

6 Read this extract from Dave's CV. Dave does not say what he was doing from 2002–2004. How do you think he became Editor of *Hi! Magazine?*

Example: *He might have met someone famous.*

CURRICULUM VITAE

1996 – 1999	Bingly College: Diploma course in Journalism and Photography
1999 – 2002	Reporter/photographer on Crawley Evening News (salary £12,000)
2004 – present	Editor of Hi! Magazine (salary £100,000)

Listening 2: song

1 You are going to hear a song called *We are the Champions.* As you listen, think about this question:

What sort of champion do you imagine the singer might be?

2 Look at the words of the song and complete the collocations using words from the box.

calls   crime   cruise   done   fortune
made   race   share   taken   time

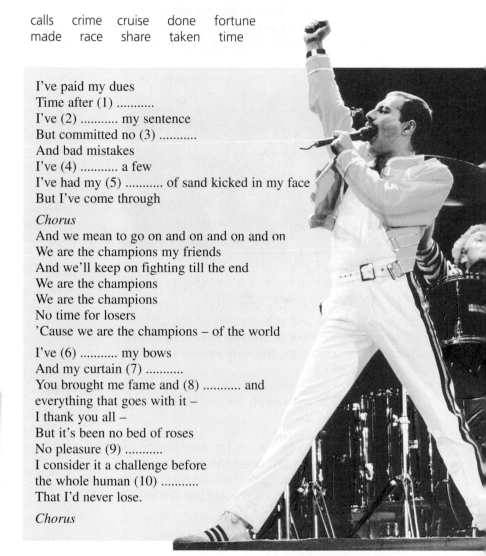

I've paid my dues
Time after (1) ....
I've (2) .... my sentence
But committed no (3) ....
And bad mistakes
I've (4) .... a few
I've had my (5) .... of sand kicked in my face
But I've come through

Chorus
And we mean to go on and on and on and on
We are the champions my friends
And we'll keep on fighting till the end
We are the champions
We are the champions
No time for losers
'Cause we are the champions – of the world

I've (6) .... my bows
And my curtain (7) ....
You brought me fame and (8) .... and
everything that goes with it –
I thank you all –
But it's been no bed of roses
No pleasure (9) ....
I consider it a challenge before
the whole human (10) ....
That I'd never lose.

Chorus

3 Discuss the following questions about the song.

1 What phrases from the song tell us that the singer had a difficult time in the past?

2 The singer says 'I've made mistakes'. What sort of mistakes might he have made?

3 Who do you think the singer means by *you* in the third verse?
a) friends and family   b) the public   c) the media

4 How does the singer feel about the people who have brought him fame?

Reading: multiple matching (Part 1)

1   Discuss the following questions.

1   Do you have a mobile phone? If so, how long have you had it? How important is it to you?
2   Do you send and receive text messages? How often? What are they usually about?
3   What do these messages mean?
a) C U L8R   b) r u OK?   c) Thx 4 yr msg
Check your answers below.
4   What abbreviations do you use in your own language?

2   You are going to read a newspaper article about mobile phones and email.

1   Read the title and subheading of the article. How do you think email and text messaging might be 'changing the way people relate to each other'?

2   Read the first paragraph and compare your ideas.

3   The following questions focus on the main idea of each paragraph. Read the text paragraph by paragraph and highlight the words or phrases that answer each question. Paragraph 0 has been done for you.

Paragraph 0:   What is surprising about the way computer use has developed?
Paragraph 1:   What's one advantage for Alice of text messaging?
Paragraph 2:   Why does Alice prefer to send a text message to someone she doesn't know well, rather than speak to them directly?
Paragraph 3:   What other group of people does Alice use modern technology to keep in touch with?

Paragraph 4:   Professor Briggs gives three reasons for the popularity of text messaging and email. What are they?
Paragraph 5:   What does Annabelle Rose use email for?
Paragraph 6:   What does she dislike about the text messages she receives?

4   Using your answers in Exercise 3 to help you, choose the most suitable heading from the list A–H for each part (1–6) of the article. There is one extra heading which you do not need to use. There is an example at the beginning (0).

A	The only problem
B	Making it personal
C	Future possibilities
D	No need to think ahead
E	Maintaining friendships over the years
F	A more serious purpose
G	Confidence to make the first move
H	An unexpected benefit

5   Discuss these questions.

1   The article mentions several advantages of mobile phones and emails. Can you think of any more?
2   Do you agree with Annabelle that text messaging is encouraging bad habits of spelling and grammar? What other problems are there?

6

1   Match the numbered words and phrases in the text to the following meanings.

a) stay in contact
b) a group of people or things that are connected in some way
c) someone you know indirectly
d) between only two people
e) looking directly at someone

2   Underline three more phrases in the text (e.g. phrasal verbs and collocations) that you would like to remember and use.

c) Thanks for your message.
b) Are you OK?
a) See you later.

Now we're getting the message

Text messaging and email are changing the way people relate to each other. Sara Gaines reports

0   **H**

When computers first started to be used on a wide scale, some people predicted that we would spend so long staring at computer screens that we would end up forgetting how to talk to one another. But in fact, the rapid expansion of electronic communication in the 21st century has had the opposite effect. Rather than retreating into themselves, people are using new technology, in particular email and text messaging, to find more and more ways to expand their [1]*network* of friends.

1

Alice Thompson, 23, is known as the Text Queen to her friends because she sends so many messages. 'My friends and I take our phones out with us and send messages to other friends saying, "We're in this club and it's really good. Come and meet us,"' she said. 'It means we don't have to spend ages planning a night out. You can just send the same message to everyone.'

2

Alice has found that text messaging has other advantages too. 'If there is a guy I like, I find it easier to send text messages initially rather than phone him up,' she said. 'Because we're not [2]*face to face*, I don't feel nervous. There is one guy, [3]*a friend of a friend*, who I don't know that well, but we've started to text message each other and that's how we communicate. I would never have phoned him up but this way it feels OK.'

3

Text messaging and email also help Alice [4]*keep in touch* with old schoolmates she would probably have lost contact with otherwise. She finds it's much easier to send a message saying 'Hi, thinking of you,' rather than having to write a long letter.

4

It seems these forms of communication have filled a gap, offering something that [2]*face-to-face* conversation does not. Professor Pam Briggs, a psychologist at the University of Northumbria, believes they have become popular because they offer people a chance to present themselves in the way that they want to. 'People seem to really enjoy sending text messages and emails,' she says. 'They can take their time planning their message, and they can be a bit more playful, adding jokes and little bits of video clips and so on. They prefer it to the [5]*one-to-one* communication of speaking on the phone to each other – maybe also because this way they can choose when they want to respond to someone.'

5

The fact that text messages are so quick and easy is a big part of the attraction. Many people also find text messaging more informal than making a phone call or writing a letter, and therefore simpler to use. Annabelle Rose, who teaches at a London sixth form college, uses email and text messaging to keep in touch with her students. They often email or text her with questions about their work. 'They don't find it so difficult to keep in touch that way, whereas they might feel that a phone call is more of an interruption,' she said. 'I have always given my number out to students and told them to call me if they have any problems. But no one ever did before text messaging really started taking off.'

6

So is it all good? Annabelle has identified one negative result of text messaging. 'The popularity of this way of writing among my students can cause a few difficulties as they have started using these abbreviations in their normal writing, like writing 'tomoro' for tomorrow,' she said. 'But they are never rude. If I text them back answering their queries, they always send another message saying 'Thx', even though it's not really necessary.'

Adapted from THE GUARDIAN

Grammar 2: passives (1)

1

1 When did the events below happen? Write the correct year in each gap.

1992   1876   1971   1844   1975   1895

1 The first telegram was delivered in ....; today, telegrams have been replaced by email.

2 The first phone call was made in ...., and phone calls are still being made every day across the world – but today the majority are made by mobile phone.

3 The first words transmitted by wireless could be heard in .... – and who knows – maybe transmissions will be received from other planets in the future!

4 The first personal computer was launched in .... and once they had been developed, they changed the way we work.

5 Millions of email messages are now sent and received every day, but the first one was sent in ....

6 Millions of text messages have also been sent since the first one in ....

2 Underline the passive verbs in the sentences above.

2 Choose the correct alternative in each of the following sentences.

1 Students *are / are being* allowed to use the computers in the library as often as they want.

2 Employers regularly monitor the emails that *are / have been* sent by their employees.

3 I hope that the new building *is being / will be* finished next year.

4 How long did it take for the film *The Matrix* to *be / being* made?

5 As we walked down the road, we realised we *have been / were being* followed.

6 That homework *should have been / should be* finished by the end of last week.

7 They say mobile phone bills *are going to be / have been* cut by 5% very soon.

8 We didn't realise he'd *given / been given* a promotion.

▶ Grammar reference p. 202 (17)

3

1 Read the following advert. What is special about the iCEBOX?

KITCHEN COOL

Slaving in the kitchen will never be the same again, thanks to the iCEBOX, an Internet-enabled entertainment centre that fits under your kitchen cupboard.

Flip open its colour LCD monitor and you'll be able to send emails to your friends or surf the web using the touch-sensitive screen. You can also use the iCEBOX to watch TV and DVDs and listen to CDs and the radio. iCEBOX comes with a wireless keyboard, which is washable to deal with those inevitable kitchen spills.

iCEBOX has opened up huge possibilities – you'll find it hard to catch up if you don't have one!

2 The following report gives the same information as the advert above, but the language is more formal. Complete the text using passive forms of the verbs in brackets.

Makers of the iCEBOX claim that working in the kitchen will be much more enjoyable once this new device (1) .... (*install*) there.

The iCEBOX is an Internet-enabled entertainment centre that (2) .... (*may/fit*) under a kitchen cupboard. The device (3) .... (*conceal*) at first but when the colour LCD monitor (4) .... (*flip open*), it reveals a touch-sensitive screen, allowing the user to send emails or surf the web. The iCEBOX (5) .... (*could/also/use*) to watch TV and DVDs or listen to CDs and the radio. The iCEBOX (6) .... (*accompany*) by a wireless keyboard, which is washable so that any kitchen spills (7) .... (*can/deal with*) easily.

The makers claim that anyone who does not have an iCEBOX (8) .... (*will/leave behind*).

4

1 Complete the responses using the verbs in brackets in the correct form. Then listen to check.

1 A: I want to learn French.
 B: Why? Spanish .... (*speak*) by a lot more people.

2 A: What's Ken planning to do when he finishes his course?
 B: Well, I think he .... (*offer*) a job with a telesales company.

3 A: I've got backache. I think I need to see a specialist.
 B: Can't it .... (*treat*) by your ordinary doctor?

4 A: I think that Marlowe wrote *Hamlet*.
 B: Oh no – I'm sure it .... (*write*) by Shakespeare.

5 A: That building looks really dangerous.
 B: Yes – it'll .... (*have to/pull down*) soon.

6 A: I think that bad weather causes a lot of accidents.
 B: Well, I think more .... (*cause*) by dangerous driving.

7 A: Did you go to the party on Saturday?
 B: No, I .... (*invite*).

2 Answer these questions using a passive form.

1 Why is it useful to learn English?
2 Was it Renée Zellweger who played the part of Rose in *Titanic*?
3 What do you think causes accidents on the roads?
4 What's your favourite book and who wrote it?

Use of English 2: open cloze
(Part 2)

1 Look at the title of the text and the photo.

1 What do you think happened to Dave Mill?
2 What part do you think the mobile phone might have played in the story?

2 Read the text to see if you were right.

3 Read the text again and think of the word which best fits each space. Use only one word in each space. There is an example at the beginning (0).

All thanks to the mobile phone

Dave Mill owes his life **(0)** ...*to*.... his mobile phone. He was trying to make history by walking to the North Pole alone, without any help or support. But after 50 days of extremely bad weather, during **(1)** .... the temperature dropped **(2)** .... low as minus 30°C, Dave **(3)** .... forced to abandon his attempt.

He had completed 185 miles of the 375-mile journey and had suffered several mishaps. He had broken his sunglasses, **(4)** .... followed by polar bears and fallen into freezing water twice. Then, after **(5)** .... the decision to give up, he had some more bad luck and found **(6)** .... stranded on a floating piece of ice that was slowly melting.

The weather was too bad for any rescue attempt to **(7)** .... made. Dave waited **(8)** .... three days, hoping that conditions **(9)** .... improve. But the rescue planes could not land because dense fog prevented **(10)** .... from seeing the surface of the ice. It was a race **(11)** .... time.

Then he remembered his mobile phone. He marked out a runway on the ice and **(12)** .... a photograph with his digital camera. Then he used his phone to email **(13)** .... to the waiting air rescue team. Using **(14)** .... photograph to guide him, the pilot was able to land in **(15)** .... of the weather, and Dave was lifted off the ice to safety.

4 Discuss these questions.

1 Do you think that people should try to undertake this kind of expedition? Why?/Why not?
2 Can you give any other examples of people whose lives have been saved by technology?

Vocabulary 2: communicating with others

1

1 Complete the sets of sentences using a verb from the box in the correct form. Which verb fits all the sentences in each set?

say   speak   talk   tell

1 a) I've never .... a lie in my life.
  b) I don't believe in .... tales.
  c) You should always .... the truth, no matter how much it hurts.
  d) I'm good at .... jokes.

2 a) I don't .... a word of German, but I'd like to learn.
  b) My teacher sometimes .... so quickly that I can't understand a word he says.
  c) If I get bad service in a shop, I always ask to .... to the manager.
  d) I like people who aren't afraid to .... their mind.

3 a) I .... to my friend on the phone every day.
  b) I enjoy .... politics with my friends.
  c) My boy/girlfriend and I have .... about getting married.

4 a) I'm always .... things I shouldn't.
  b) Everyone .... I would be a good manager.
  c) I can't .... I enjoy learning English.

2 Read the sentences again, and say which are true for you. Explain your answers.

2   Complete the following dialogues with an appropriate preposition.

1 A: I'm so sorry you're leaving.
  B: Me too – but we'll keep .... touch.
2 A: I'm calling to check on my pizza order – it hasn't been delivered yet.
  B: I'm sorry – did you order .... phone or .... person?
3 A: Can I contact you .... email?
  B: Yes, of course – I'll give you my email address.
4 A: Steven's missed a lot of classes lately.
  B: Has he? Maybe we should have a word .... him.

5 A: How did you two get to know one another?
  B: Actually, we met .... a friend.
6 A: Have you known each other long?
  B: Yes, we've been going out .... one another for a year.

3   Work with a partner. Look at the highlighted phrases in the following sentences, and decide what they mean. Then write four short dialogues, ending with the sentence given.

1 OK, I'll send them by post.
2 Could you put that in writing, please?
3 No, I found out about it by word of mouth.
4 You can get more details on their website.
5 It's in the post.

Example:
  A: *I'll email you the details, shall I?*
  B: *I'm not on email.*
  A: *OK, I'll send them by post.*

4   Complete the second sentence so that it has a similar meaning to the first sentence, using the word given. Do not change the word given. You must use between two and five words, including the word given.

1 I asked if I could talk to Sophie.
  word
  I asked if I could .... Sophie.
2 I've got to present the project to the Board of Directors tomorrow.
  presentation
  I've got to .... about the project to the Board of Directors tomorrow.
3 We were able to find a solution to the problem that we could both accept.
  compromise
  We were able .... over the problem.
4 I wasn't ready for the test because I hadn't done enough work.
  preparation
  I hadn't .... for the test.
5 I really enjoy meeting friends and talking to them over coffee.
  chat
  I really enjoy meeting friends and .... them over coffee.
6 I think we should talk about this with the boss.
  discussion
  I think we should .... this with the boss.

Exam focus
Paper 5 Speaking: long turn (Part 2)

About the exam: In Part 2 of the Speaking test, you speak on your own for about a minute. The examiner gives you two photographs on the same topic. He tells you the topic and what to talk about. The task has two parts: you have to compare and contrast the photos **and** give a personal reaction to them.

The other candidate is then asked a question related to the topic and has to give a short answer (about 20 seconds).

Then you change roles.

Procedure
1 Listen carefully to the instructions, especially the second part. Ask the examiner to repeat the instructions if you are not sure what to do.
2 First, describe the main thing the two photos have in common and the main difference, and then describe more similarities and differences (about 40 seconds).
3 Leave yourself enough time for the second part of the task (about 20 seconds).
4 If you have some time left, relate the photos to your own experience.
5 While the other candidate is speaking, look at their photos and listen carefully, but don't say anything. When he/she has finished, be ready to answer the examiner's question.

1   Look at photos A and B. What is the main thing they have in common?

2   You will hear two candidates doing a Part 2 Listening task.

🎧 **1** First, listen to the examiner's instructions. What does he tell Candidate A to do?

🎧 **2** Now listen to the two candidates doing the task.

1 Does the first candidate follow the examiner's instructions?
2 Does she do both parts of the task?
3 Does the second candidate answer the question correctly?

3   Work in groups of three. You are going to role-play Part 2 of the exam.

Student A: You are the examiner. Look at the instructions on page 182 and tell the two candidates what to do.
Students B and C: You are the candidates.
Student B look at photos C and D on page 184.
Student C look at photos E and F on page 186.

4   When you have finished, discuss the task together.

Student A
1 Did the candidates do both parts of the task?
2 Did they manage to keep talking for one minute?
3 What were the good points about their talk?
Students B and C
1 What do you think you did well?
2 What did you find more difficult?

Writing: report (Part 2)

About the exam: In Part 2 of Paper 2, you may be asked to write a report. When writing a report:

- you should use formal English
- you should give your report a title
- you should have an introduction giving the background to your report
- you can use headings and numbered points
- you may include recommendations at the end.

DON'T begin and end like a letter.

1

1 Read the following report, which was written by a teacher for the Head of a Language School. Does the teacher think that mobile phones are a good thing or a bad thing?

USE OF MOBILE PHONES IN CLASS

INTRODUCTION
This report describes problems caused by the use of mobile phones by students, and makes recommendations concerning their use in the school. The information comes from interviews with class teachers and administrative staff.

PROBLEMS
1 There is a rule that students should turn off their phones during lesson time. However, many students either forget or disobey this rule. Their phones often ring during class time and this interrupts the class and disturbs other students.
2 Some younger students use their phones to send text messages or play games during class.
3 We have had many complaints from parents and students that mobile phones have been lost or stolen in the school.

RECOMMENDATIONS
Because of these problems, we recommend that no student should be allowed to bring a mobile phone to school. There are several public phones in the school, which students can use if necessary. These should be regularly checked to ensure they are in good working order.

---

2 Answer these questions about the report.

1 In the introduction, the writer summarises what the report is about. What else does it mention?
2 What recommendations does the writer make at the end? What modal verbs are used?

2

1 Think of some reasons why students might want or need to bring their mobile phones to school. Make a list.

Example:
Students might need to phone home if they have transport problems.

2 Think of some ways in which the problems described in the teacher's report could be solved. Make a list.

Example:
Students should check that phones are switched off before classes start.

3

1 Read this task and underline key words.

You are a student at a language school. Teachers have complained about the use of mobile phones by students in class. As a result, the Director of the school wants to ban them completely.

Write a report for the Director, explaining why mobile phones are necessary for students and recommending ways in which their use could be controlled.

Write your **report** in **120–180** words.

---

2 This report should have three sections. Plan the main points you will make in the second and third sections.

4   Now write your report. The introduction has been started for you. Then check your work.

Introduction
This report explains why mobile phones are important for students, and makes recommendations about their use in the school. The information comes from ...

Writing reference pp. 206, 210

1

1 Complete the following sentences, using the correct form of the word in capitals.

1 Peter thinks that a lot of .... about the future may be wrong. **PREDICT**

2 Janet says that text messages have made .... between friends easier. **COMMUNICATE**

3 Maria feels that people have too many telephone .... on personal matters in public. **CONVERSE**

4 Ron told me that one of the .... of text messaging is its cheapness. **ATTRACT**

5 Sarah explains that text messages use .... to save time and space. **ABBREVIATE**

6 Jose complains that a phone call can be an .... if you are working. **INTERRUPT**

2 Which of the people above do you think want to a) save money? b) work hard? c) make more friends?

2 **What do you think these text messages mean? Say them aloud, then write them as complete sentences.**

1 **I WAN 2 CU 2DAY!**

2 **TALK 2U L8R**

3 **LUV U**

4 **CAN U W8 4 ME?**

5 **TXT ME B4 U GO**

3 **Complete the second sentence so that it has a similar meaning to the first sentence, using no more than five words, including the word given.**

1 They advertised the mobile phone so intensively that it was an immediate success.
was
Because it ...., the mobile phone was an immediate success.

2 The technician solved the computer problem quickly.
dealt
The computer problem .... the technician.

3 Someone must have seen him there!
been
He .... there by someone!

4 Their normal business was continued after a short break.
on
After a short break, they .... their normal business.

5 She may contact him by phone this afternoon.
that
It .... she will contact him by phone this afternoon.

6 There's no chance that Peter was in the house at the time.
have
Peter .... in the house at the time.

4 **Respond to the following statements, using** *may, might, can't, must (have) + verb.*

Examples: I can hear the front door bell ringing.
It might be the postman.
Your friend must have come to see you.

1 Lucy hasn't written to me for ages – I'm quite worried about her.

2 I've got a splitting headache and I keep going hot and cold.

3 I've just heard that Peter failed his entrance exam. He was top of the class!

4 Have you seen my keys? I can't find them anywhere.

5 My mobile phone has stopped working.

5 **Choose the correct alternative in each of these sentences.**

1 I made the order *with / by* phone.
2 *In / On* his letter, he told me he missed me.
3 Can I contact you *by / on* email?
4 He's constantly *at / on* the move.
5 All *by / in* all, it was an enjoyable experience.
6 Could I have a quick word *to / with* you?
7 If you're worried, we can talk it *over / about* tomorrow.
8 We arrived at the station just *in / with* time.
9 I found it *from / on* the Internet.
10 You have to speak to him *in / on* person – you can't phone.

UNIT
7 Back to the future

Listening 1: multiple-choice questions (Part 4)

1 For a television series, a group of volunteers spent seven weeks living as people did in the Iron Age, around 2,500 years ago. Look at the photos, which were taken during the experiment. Think of as many differences as you can between life in the Iron Age and now.

2 You will hear an interview with two people who took part in the experiment. First, read through the questions to get a general idea of what will be discussed in the interview, and highlight key words in the question.

1 Janet says that the main aim of the Iron Age project was
   A to discover how Iron Age people managed to survive.
   B to see if people of the 21st century could live in Iron Age conditions.
   C to find which person on the project could stay the longest.

2 One thing Janet never got used to on the project was
   A the food.
   B the cold.
   C the dark.

3 Daniel thinks that Iron Age people ate
   A an insufficient amount of food.
   B snacks as well as big meals.
   C only one big meal a day.

4 Janet says that while they were working, the people on the project did not
   A find it easy to follow a routine.
   B have enough time to do everything.
   C worry about what they were wearing.

5 Daniel says that in the evenings, the participants
   A sometimes missed having TV and radio.
   B talked about the day's problems.
   C made their own entertainment.

6 How did Janet feel about colour while she was taking part in the project?
   A She appreciated small differences in colour.
   B She missed having bright colours around her.
   C She liked seeing how colours changed during the day.

7 What did Janet realise when she took a hot bath at the end of the project?
   A that the project was really over
   B that she preferred living in the modern world
   C that the project had been a wonderful experience

3
1 Listen and choose the best answer, A, B or C. Then compare your answers with a partner.
2 Listen again to check.

4 Discuss the following questions.

1 If you took part in a project like this, what would be the hardest part of the experience for you?
2 What would you probably do first when you returned to modern life?

5 Complete the second sentence so that it has a similar meaning to the first sentence, using the word given. You heard the second sentence in the recording.

1 Five people left before the end of the project. **dropped**
   Five people .... before the end of the project.
2 Nobody cared about their appearance. **matter**
   It .... you looked like.
3 Nobody else could do it for us. **had**
   We .... all for ourselves.
4 I'll always remember how it was. **never**
   I'll .... it was like.

Vocabulary 1: general nouns

1   Match the following sentence halves.

1 If I lived in the past, I'd miss luxuries   *d)*
2 In the past people didn't have any modern facilities
3 Cold and hunger
4 They used weapons
5 The only types of materials used for clothing
6 Hunting, farming and cooking
7 Of course, there were no televisions or computers
8 But life in those days had many advantages too,

a) were often big problems for them.
b) were skills needed by everyone to survive.
c) or any other types of electrical equipment.
d) like cakes and chocolate.
e) such as lack of pollution and closeness to nature.
f) like central heating or hot showers.
g) were wool and leather.
h) such as swords and spears.

2   Each sentence in Exercise 1 contains a noun with a general meaning, and two or more examples. Find them and make a list.

Example:

1 luxuries – cakes, chocolate

3

1 Match the general nouns from Exercise 2 to one of the following stress patterns.

one syllable	two syllables	three syllables	three syllables	four syllables
o	O o	O o o	o O o	o O o o
		luxuries		

🎧 2 Listen and check your answers. Practise saying the words.

4   Complete the statements using words from the box.

creatures   disasters   equipment
~~facilities~~   inventions   vehicles
subjects   cosmetics

1 Our school has excellent *facilities*, including a library and cafeteria.
2 They shouldn't keep .... such as lions and monkeys in zoos.
3 I think modern .... like television have done more harm than good.
4 Natural .... like earthquakes cannot always be predicted or controlled.
5 .... such as face creams and lipstick should not be tested on animals.
6 Do you think .... like politics and religion should be discussed in schools?
7 It is essential to reduce the number of .... in our cities, especially private cars.
8 Hospitals need up-to-date .... such as scanners and ultrasound.

5   Choose three of these words, and make a mind map for each one.

luxuries   vehicles   leisure facilities
inventions   consumer goods
fabrics   insects

Example:

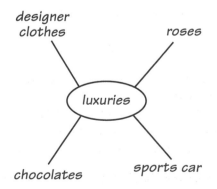

Grammar 1: relative clauses

1

1 Complete the following sentences, using a relative pronoun (*who, which, that,* etc.).

1 Janet and Daniel are ordinary people .... took part in a history project for television.
2 They said it was an experience .... they would never forget.
3 I'd like to go back to a time in history .... there was no pollution.
4 A lot of tourists visit the local museum, ... there are displays of prehistoric pottery and tools.
5 I've visited the site of Machu Picchu in Peru, ... was an amazing experience.
6 Leonardo da Vinci was a scientist .... inventions prepared the way for modern science.
7 .... should we give the award to? (*neutral style*)
8 To .... should we give the award? (*formal style*)

2 Answer these questions.

1 Which of the sentences above can have two different relative pronouns?
2 In which sentence can the relative pronoun be omitted?
3 In which sentence does a relative pronoun refer to a whole phrase rather than to the preceding noun?

— Watch Out! *which, that* ◄

Which sentence is NOT possible? Why not?

1 The car, which he owns, is a red Fiat.
2 The car, that he owns, is a red Fiat.
3 The car which he owns is a red Fiat.
4 The car that he owns is a red Fiat.

► Grammar reference p. 202 (18)

2 Each of the following sentences has a mistake in the relative clause. Find the mistakes and correct them. Don't change the punctuation of the sentences.

1 The thing which I value it the most is my grandmother's necklace.
2 He explained all what his father had told him to do.
3 That's the house where I used to live in.
4 Whose does this book belong to?

5 I can do everything what you can.
6 I want to go to Wales, where my grandfather was born there.
7 Students which want to go on the trip should sign up now.
8 Anyone who he wants to return by bus must pay £5.00.
9 Alison is someone whom I think would do the job well.
10 The girl, that I'd seen before in the restaurant, was dressed in black.

3 The following text is jumbled. Number the sentences in the correct order. Then join them together to make a logical paragraph including four relative clauses.

The history of the parachute

☐1☐ A parachute is a piece of equipment.
☐ Berry jumped from a US Army plane in 1912.
☐ The parachutes were made from strong cotton cloth.
☐ Lenormand jumped from a very tall tree carrying two umbrellas in 1763.
☐ The first person to jump from a flying airplane (and survive the fall) was Captain Albert Berry.
☐ A few years later, some adventurous people jumped from hot-air balloons using primitive parachutes.
☐ The idea was first demonstrated by a Frenchman called Lenormand.
☐2☐ It is used to slow your fall when jumping from a great height.

Example:

A parachute is a piece of equipment which is used to slow your fall when jumping from a great height.

4   Guess the word.

Student A look at page 187.
Student B look at page 188.

You each have a list of words. Take turns to explain the meaning of each word without using the word itself. Your partner must guess what the item is. Begin with phrases like this:

This is a thing/an object/a device which/that …
This is a person who …
This is a place where …

Example:

> A: *This is a thing that a teacher uses for writing on the board.*
> B: *A board marker?*
> A: *Yes.*

Exam focus

Paper 3 Use of English: open cloze (Part 2)

About the exam: In Paper 3, Part 2, you read a text with 15 gaps. You have to complete each gap with one word. The words you need are grammar words (pronouns, articles, prepositions, auxiliary verbs, etc.).

Procedure

1   Read the title and then read through the whole text to find out what it's about. Don't fill in any gaps yet.
2   Read the text again sentence by sentence and write in the missing words in pencil. Look at the whole sentence and especially at the words before and after the gap. Think about what part of speech the missing word is.
3   When you have finished, read through the text again to check your answers make sense.
4   In the exam, you transfer your answers to the answer sheet. Be careful to write each one next to the correct number.

> **DO** make sure you spell the words correctly.
> **DON'T** write more than one word in each gap.

For questions 1–15, read the text below and think of the word which best fits each space. Use only one word in each space. There is an example at the beginning (0).

Example: | **0** | *was* |

THE OLDEST POSTCARD IN THE WORLD

The world's oldest picture postcard **(0)** ..*was*.. sold yesterday to a European businessman. The card, which sold for more **(1)** .... £31,000, was dated 1840. It was addressed to a man called Theodore Hooke, **(2)** .... lived in Fulham, London. Theodore Hooke was a novelist and playwright and was well known **(3)** .... the time for his sense **(4)** .... humour. The picture on the card is a cartoon showing a group of post office workers with pens in **(5)** .... hands sitting round an enormous inkwell. It was printed in black and white, but had **(6)** .... coloured in **(7)** .... hand. Experts think that Hooke may have posted the card to himself for **(8)** .... own amusement.

The card was discovered last year by Edward Proud, a historian who specialises in the history of the postal service. Up to **(9)** .... , it had been thought that **(10)** .... postcard was either an Austrian, German **(11)** .... American invention and that the first one was sent during the 1860s. However, the discovery of Hooke's card has proved that postcards were **(12)** .... fact invented at least twenty years earlier than **(13)** .... 'We know that Hook claimed to **(14)** .... invented the picture postcard, said Mr Proud, 'and this discovery suggests that his claim could well **(15)** .... true.'

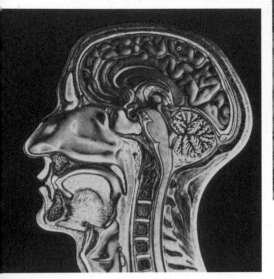

Reading: multiple matching
(Part 4)

1   You are going to read an article about what some highly respected scientists think could happen in the future. First, discuss what you think is the best way to approach this task type. If necessary, look back at the suggested procedure in Unit 2, page 24.

2   Look at the title of the article, and the headings.

1 Have you heard of any of these people?
2 What sort of work do you think each job involves?
3 Can you predict any of the developments they might mention?

3   Look at the example (0), and at the underlined sentence in text B that it refers to.

1 Which phrase in the sentence relates to *modern scientific equipment?*
2 Which word means *very small?*

4   For questions 1–15, choose from the people A–E. The people may be chosen more than once. When more than one answer is required, these may be given in any order. There is an example at the beginning (0).

> **TIP!** If you can't find an answer, leave it and come back to it later. You may spot the parallel phrase while you're reading for a different question.

Which person mentions that

modern scientific equipment can help us understand very small things?	**0 | B**
the distribution of wealth among the world's population is unfair?	**1**
scientists need to get experience of different ways of living?	**2**
the mass media can help people to learn about science?	**3** **4**
some living creatures experience very exciting events?	**5**
the increase in the world's population could be a problem?	**6** **7**
future research will involve combining different areas of science?	**8**
people may be unsure of the value of some scientific advances?	**9**
investment in scientific research should be regarded as a priority?	**10**
children need to be taught science in an interesting way?	**11**
scientists need to find better ways of treating illness? **12**	**13**
research could affect people's view of what the future holds?	**14**
progress may not need advanced technology?	**15**

5   Compare your answers. What parallel phrases in the article helped you find them?

Where is science going?

We asked five well-known scientists to give us their views on some of the
most exciting scientific developments we could see in the next few years

A Susan Greenfield, brain scientist

We're going to see a way of linking information technology with brain research. Already scientists have managed to place an electrode in the brain of a paralysed man who was unable to move any part of his body. This allowed him to use the electrical activity of his brain to move the cursor on a computer screen. This sort of research could have enormous value for people with brain damage and it's important that we continue to look for ways to help patients with conditions like this. However, one thing that worries me is that scientists don't use their imaginations enough. So I'm involved in a project in which young scientists are sent out into the developing world to help people in rural areas. I hope they'll come back more aware of other cultures, and more imaginative and creative about the way they do science.

B Sir David Attenborough, wildlife broadcaster

Natural history film-making has always been very much affected by technology. <u>With the latest technical advances we can take a close-up film of something as minute as the eye of a fly.</u> This means we'll be able to make incredible films about insects like spiders and scorpions which actually have very dramatic lives. And I think these documentaries will change people's opinions of nature programmes and show them that they're not just dry, educational stuff. If you can get people to watch cartoon programmes like *The Simpsons* on TV, you ought to be able to get them to watch films about scorpions too. As far as the future in general is concerned, I think the biggest change on the way is that there will be too many people around. There will be less and less of the emptiness, the wilderness, left in the world.

C Sir Patrick Moore, astronomer

The most important thing in the field of space research will be to find out whether there is life on Mars. If we knew that we were not the only intelligent beings, then it would have enormous implications for our future and how we look at it – our whole philosophy in fact. Personally, I think that there is life on other planets. Why should we be unique? But whether or not we'll find this out all depends on money, and if we go on wasting our money on wars instead of using it for this type of research then of course we won't get anywhere. I also think that in the future we should spend far more than we do now on medical research, especially when the number of people in the world is rising at such a rapid rate. After all, one of the worst dangers we face is disease and we need to understand how to cure it.

D Lord Robert Winston, fertility doctor

I'm excited by the idea of extending women's reproductive life. I don't want to see women of 60 having babies. But women are now healthier, fitter and more able to have babies at 45 or 50 than they've ever been. However, there is a lot of public suspicion of developments like this, and many people question whether we should be doing this sort of work. I think a lot of the problem is ignorance, and what we should be doing is making science in schools relevant so that students don't think of it as a boring subject. And I think there should be recognition that things like television programmes where you have 5 million viewers – I've never had less than 5 million viewers for any programme – are very influential as well.

E Trevor Baylis, inventor of the wind-up radio

I believe that we'll have to go back to go forwards. We have to stop depending on electricity for everything and look instead at other sources of power. For example, the wind-up radio I invented just works by clockwork, without needing batteries or anything, and we now have torches and lights powered like this as well. In general, I think greed is one of the biggest problems that we have to face up to. It's wrong that some people make billions and billions of pounds when there are other people in the world who can't even afford to buy a packet of cornflakes. We have to do something about it.

---

6 Discuss these questions.

1 Which scientist in the text do you think is involved in the most useful or important work?
2 Do you think any of the work described is not useful – or could even be dangerous?

7

1 Complete the following sentences with the correct preposition and highlight the whole phrase in each case.

1 What's your opinion .... nature programmes on TV? Are they dry and educational or exciting?
2 It's important to make people more aware .... environmental problems .... general.
3 Big changes are .... the way. For example, women may be able to have babies when they are over 50.
4 The greatest discovery in the field .... space research could be finding there is life .... Mars.
5 Recent developments in our understanding of the brain could have enormous implications .... our future.
6 We are too dependent .... electricity nowadays.
7 We are wasting our money .... wars when we should be using it .... medical research.
8 It's a good idea to get young people involved .... projects in other countries.

2 Discuss the ideas above. What's your opinion?

"If you put your ear to them you can hear the land."

Grammar 2: conditionals (1)

1

1 Complete sentence b) in each pair so that it has a similar meaning to sentence a).

1 a) It's likely there is life on other planets. If so, we are not alone.
   b) If there .... life on other planets, we .... not alone.

2 a) The world's population will probably continue to increase. If so, we will need more food.
   b) If the world's population .... to increase, we .... more food.

3 a) Other intelligent beings might inhabit the universe. If so, they would be very different from us.
   b) If other intelligent beings .... the universe, they .... very different from us.

4 a) There aren't many TV programmes about science, so people don't know much about it.
   b) If there .... more TV programmes about science, people .... more about it.

5 a) We shouldn't have spent so much money on space research. Instead, we could have solved many other serious problems.
   b) If we .... less on space research, we .... many other serious problems.

2 Complete the following information about conditional sentences.

1 General truth: *if* + present + ...
2 a) Possible/likely in the present or future:
      if + present + ...
   b) Unlikely or contrary to present fact:
      if + past simple + ...
3 Contrary to fact in the past:
   if + past perfect + ...

► Grammar reference p.194 (5)

2 There is a mistake with the verb in the second part of each sentence. Correct the mistakes so the second part follows on correctly from the first part.

1 He will pass his driving test if he will practise.
2 You can borrow the car tonight if you would take good care of it.
3 I wouldn't have made so much food if I knew they weren't coming.
4 If you buy two, you got a third one free.
5 I would have done better if I worked harder.
6 If I had the right tools, I can fix the flat tyre myself.
7 If you'd told me Susan was going to be there, I would never go to the party.
8 If I lived in that house, I will get smoke alarms put in straightaway.

3 Here is a list of developments that could happen in the next few years. Say what you think will or might happen as a result.

1 All phones will have a video component.
2 Colonies will be established on Mars.
3 Protein and vitamin pills will replace the food we eat today.
4 Everyone will speak the same language.

Example:

If all phones have a video component, we will be able to see the person we are talking to. That may not always be a good idea because ...

4 Think of five things you take for granted in your everyday life. Say how and why you use them. How would your life be different without them?

Example:

I drive to work by car every day. If I didn't have a car, I would have to go by bus.

5 Complete the text below using the correct form of a verb from the box. Use each verb once only.

go   have   not have   take   not want

Medicine then and now

Nowadays, if you (1) .... a headache, you can (2) .... a painkiller like aspirin and it goes away. If you were suffering from something more serious and needed an operation, you could (3) .... to hospital and have it done under anaesthetic. But if you'd been born five hundred years ago, you (4) .... any of the medicines we take for granted today, and you certainly (5) .... to have any sort of surgery as there were no anaesthetics.

6 Think of five ways your life would have been different if you had lived 100 years ago.

Example:

If I'd lived 100 years ago, I probably would not have been able to go to university.

Speaking: ranking; discussion
(Parts 3 and 4)

1 Look at the pictures, which show some ways we use electricity. Think about:

1 what each thing is used for
2 how important each thing is.

2

1 Now listen to two students discussing which of the uses of electricity they think are the most important. Complete the conversation.

A: OK, where (1) ....?
B: Well, I think lifts are very important, (2) ....?
A: Yes, if we didn't have them, we wouldn't be able to build tall buildings. So I think that (3) .... And street lights are important too – I hate walking around in the dark!
B: Yes, (4) .... But we (5) .... without street lights, couldn't we? I mean, cars have their own headlights.
A: Yes, I think (6) .... And (7) .... microwave cookers? (8) .... they're not very important?
B: I (9) .... not. Even if we didn't have them, we could still cook our food in the stove. Some stoves use electricity, though.
A: (10) .... What do you think is the least important thing?

2 Practise the conversation with a partner. Try to use similar intonation to the recording.

3 Work with another partner. Imagine you have been asked to suggest ways in which people can save electricity. Put the things in the pictures in order of importance so as to save electricity. Try to keep talking for about three minutes.

4 Discuss some of the following questions, which are related to the topic you discussed in Exercise 3.
Try to keep talking for about four minutes.

1 What would you miss most if there was no electricity?
2 In what ways do people waste electricity?
3 In what ways do you think life today is easier than it was in the past?
4 If you could travel back in time, which period in your country's history would you like to see? Why?
5 Do you think that in the future the world will be a better place than it is today?

Exam focus

Paper 4 Listening: extracts (Part 1)

About the exam: In Paper 4, Part 1, you hear eight short unrelated extracts with people talking in different situations. You answer one question about each extract by choosing from three options. Each extract is repeated immediately.

Procedure

1 Read the questions and the options before you listen. Underline any key words e.g. *who, what, why, how* and any topic words (e.g. *museums* in Question 1 below).

2 The first time you listen, you will hear the question and then the extract. Mark the answer you think is best.

3 The second time, listen to check your answer. Always put something – you don't lose marks for a wrong answer.

4 In the exam, you transfer your answers to the answer sheet at the end of the test.

🎧 **You will hear people talking in eight different situations. For questions 1–8, choose the best answer, A, B or C. You will hear each extract twice.**

1 You hear a woman talking about museums in New Zealand. Why did she like looking at the textbooks?
   A because there was someone to explain about them
   B because they had a personal appeal
   C because she learned about education in the past

2 You hear the presenter of a radio programme. What sort of programme is it?
   A a science programme
   B a history programme
   C a discussion programme

3 In an art gallery, you overhear this conversation. What does the man want to do?
   A come back the next day
   B have a guided tour
   C go to another part of the gallery

4 You hear a woman talking on the radio about her career ambitions. What does she want to be?
   A a writer
   B an archaeologist
   C an artist

5 You overhear two people talking about a football match. How does the woman feel?
   A uninterested
   B disappointed
   C angry

6 You overhear a man talking to a friend about his new job. What good thing about the job does he mention?
   A the pay
   B the travelling
   C the amount of work

7 You hear the weather forecast on the radio. What will the weather be like tonight?
   A cold
   B windy
   C cloudy

8 You switch on the radio and hear part of a radio play. Where does the conversation take place?
   A in an airport
   B in a bus station
   C in a train station

Vocabulary 2: collocations

The Longman *Active Study* Dictionary shows you common phrases and collocations.

im·pres·sion /ɪmˈpreʃən/ *n* [C] **1** your impression of someone or something is the way that they seem to you: **+ of** *What was your first impression of Richard? ...* | **make a good/bad impression** *She made a good impression at her interview.*

spare¹ /speə‖sper/ *adj* **1 spare key/tyre etc** a key, tyre etc that you have in addition to the one you normally use so that it is available if it is needed

1 Complete the following sentences using either *make* or *do* in the correct form.

1 Have you .... the travel arrangements yet?
2 What do you .... for a living?
3 We .... a lot of business with Japan.
4 It's not easy to .... a living from writing.
5 'Please .... sure you're on time.' 'I'll .... my best.'
6 My brother is always .... fun of my clothes.
7 I am writing to .... a complaint.
8 Recently Stefan .... a big effort to improve his English.
9 I don't enjoy .... the housework.
10 At present we're .... research into a vaccine for AIDS.

1 In the following sentences, cross out the adjective which does NOT collocate with the noun.

Example:

Being on the project was a *valuable* / *wonderful* / ~~*pretty*~~ experience for me.

1 I can't afford *spare* / *unnecessary* / *expensive* luxuries.
2 The website advertises a range of *musical* / *scientific* / *cookery* instruments.
3 In the last 100 years we have seen many *historical* / *technical* / *scientific* advances.
4 Some *recent* / *latest* / *modern* developments have had both good and bad effects.
5 Conditions on the roads are *good* / *sunny* / *excellent* today.
6 The nurse said the patient was making *good* / *satisfactory* / *swift* progress.

2 Match the adjectives you crossed out with these sets of nouns.

a) book / classes / lessons
b) day / weather / personality
c) reply / runner
d) pair of shoes / set of keys / room / tyre
e) novel / film / research
f) news / CD / gossip

3 Work with a partner. Ask and answer the following questions.

1 Who does most of the housework in your family? What do you do?
2 Have you ever made a complaint? What about? What happened?
3 Which is your favourite musical instrument? Why?
4 What expensive luxury would you buy if you had lots of money?
5 Do you enjoy listening to gossip?

Use of English 2: multiple-choice cloze (Part 1)

1 Read the text below quickly. Don't try to fill in the gaps yet. What is special about this library?

2 Now read the text carefully and decide which answer (A, B, C or D) best fits each space. There is an example at the beginning (0).

A FAMOUS LIBRARY

The most famous library of all time was **(0)** ...*B*... by Alexander the Great over 2,300 years ago, in Alexandria. It was **(1)** .... at the crossroads of Europe, Africa and Asia, and was the perfect location for a centre of learning. The library was **(2)** .... to have around 700,000 books, and at the time people thought it contained 'all the knowledge in the world'. Copies of these books were **(3)** .... there, and these were then **(4)** .... around countries in the ancient world. But then the library was **(5)** .... by fire. Thousands of works of philosophy, science and literature were lost, and it took centuries to **(6)** .... them.

Now a new, modern library has been built in Alexandria, at a **(7)** .... of £120m. It has a vast reading area seating 2,000 people, and **(8)** .... in the library for eight million books. The **(9)** .... of the building is spectacular, with amazing use of light and space. There is a huge circular roof which **(10)** .... at a special angle. This means that it can **(11)** .... light from the sun into the museum. **(12)** .... of sunlight shine through green and blue glass onto the desks and bookshelves below, and letters from every known alphabet are carved on the walls. People in Alexandria **(13)** .... that the library will once again be a **(14)** .... where scholars from all over the world come to study and **(15)** .... research.

0	**A** originated	**B** founded	**C** instituted	**D** based
1	**A** situated	**B** stationed	**C** installed	**D** inserted
2	**A** stated	**B** told	**C** spoken	**D** said
3	**A** got	**B** made	**C** formed	**D** achieved
4	**A** beamed	**B** sent	**C** transmitted	**D** relayed
5	**A** broken	**B** injured	**C** destroyed	**D** hurt
6	**A** recover	**B** plan	**C** write	**D** reveal
7	**A** price	**B** cost	**C** worth	**D** charge
8	**A** room	**B** place	**C** volume	**D** extent
9	**A** model	**B** creation	**C** invention	**D** design
10	**A** slopes	**B** falls	**C** increases	**D** expands
11	**A** show	**B** mirror	**C** reflect	**D** demonstrate
12	**A** Sections	**B** Pieces	**C** Rays	**D** Slices
13	**A** hope	**B** want	**C** aim	**D** target
14	**A** scene	**B** place	**C** position	**D** part
15	**A** follow	**B** have	**C** accept	**D** do

Writing: composition (Part 2)

About the exam: In the exam, you may have to write a composition in which you present an argument. One way to do this is to present both sides of the argument, and then say which one you agree with.

1 Read the task below. Do you have to write about:

a) whether museums charge too much for entrance?
b) whether museums are important in modern life?

Your class has been discussing what part museums play in life today. Your teacher has now asked you to write a composition giving your opinion on the following statement:

Museums are a waste of money.

Write your **composition** in **120–180** words.

2 Work with a partner.

1 Think of as many ideas as possible either in support of museums or against museums. Use the ideas below to help you.

- cost
- national importance
- interest
- education
- tourism
- research

2 Choose three of your best ideas for each side of the argument and note them down.

Reasons for keeping museums	Reasons against keeping museums

3 When you write a composition like this, you can use four paragraphs.

Paragraph 1: a statement of the topic
Paragraph 2: two or three ideas supporting one side of the argument
Paragraph 3: two or three ideas supporting the other side of the argument
Paragraph 4: a conclusion giving your own opinion

TIP! Before you begin writing, decide on your own opinion. Put the ideas you agree with in paragraph 3, so they support your conclusion.

1 Look at the four paragraph openings below, which come from one student's composition on this topic. Match them to each paragraph above.

A ......

To sum up, it seems to me that ...

B ......

Some people claim that museums use up money which would be better spent on other things.

C ......

However, other people believe that if we understand how things happened in the past ...

D ......

How important are museums to people living in the 21st century?

2 Is this student writing for or against museums?

4 In a composition, it is important to link your ideas.

1 Which of the highlighted linking expressions in Exercise 3

a) introduces a contrasting idea?
b) introduces a conclusion?

2 Choose the correct alternatives in these sentences.

1 Most people think museums are boring and *because of / in spite of* this they seldom go.
2 Museums tell us about our history and *in addition / therefore* people should be encouraged to visit them.
3 *Despite the fact that / Because* museums attract tourists, they should be maintained, *even though / on the other hand* this costs a lot of money.

5 Now write your composition, using your ideas in Exercise 2. You can use the paragraph openings above to help you if you want to.

6 When you have finished, check your work.

Writing reference pp.206, 213, 215

1 Complete the following text using relative pronouns.

Who invented toothpaste?

Toothpaste is an invention (1) .... doesn't seem to have a definite inventor or date. Something like it was known in ancient Egypt, (2) .... people used a paste made of a mixture of ash and powered egg shell, (3) .... they rubbed on their teeth with their fingers.

In 1873 the Colgate Company – the same one (4) .... makes toothpaste today – introduced Colgate Dental cream, (5) .... smelled and tasted much nicer than anything else used until then.
Soon after this, people began to use toothbrushes instead of sticks or fingers, (6) .... made cleaning teeth much easier.

However, most Americans didn't brush their teeth regularly until the 1940s, (7) .... American soldiers (8) .... had spent several years in Europe and learned the habit there, went home after the Second World War.

2 Complete these sentences, giving true information.

1 If I could go anywhere in the world, …
2 In ten years' time, if all goes well, I …
3 I … if I'd lived two thousand years ago.
4 If I was showing a visitor from abroad round my town, I …
5 I … if I have music playing while I'm studying.
6 If I had more free time, I …
7 If I had been able to choose what time to be born in, I …
8 If I was offered the chance to live for 500 years, I …

3 Complete the following sentences with an appropriate linking word.

1 I believe that space exploration is a waste of money .... I don't think it should be banned completely.
2 Life in the past may have been simpler. .... , it was probably more dangerous in many ways.
3 The number of people who read books regularly is declining. .... this, I believe we will always need libraries.

4 The most exciting scientific discoveries may come about .... research into the brain.
5 Many experiments on animals seem unnecessary to me and I .... think they should be banned.
6 There may be life on Mars. If there is, ... , it might be hard to recognise.

4 Use the words given in capitals below the text to form a word that fits in the space in each line. There is an example at the beginning (0).

THE ORIGIN OF THE POTATO CRISP

The potato crisp was the (0) .....*invention*..... of George Crum, in 1853. He worked as a chef at a popular resort in the USA. One day a (1) .... decided that he didn't like the (2) .... of his fried potatoes, and sent them back to the kitchen. Crum made some more, but the man (3) .... these as well, making the same (4) .... Crum got angry and, hoping to annoy the man, he made a third batch which were much (5) .... and could not be eaten with a fork. To his (6) .... , the man loved them – and so potato crisps were invented. Since then, their (7) .... has increased (8) .... , and they are eaten all over the world. But George Crum was (9) .... at the time that his invention would cause great (10) .... in the future between the Americans (who call them *chips*) and the British (who call them *crisps*).

0 INVENT
1 CUSTOM
2 THICK
3 TURN
4 COMPLAIN
5 THIN
6 AMAZE
7 POPULAR
8 DRAMA
9 AWARE
10 CONFUSE

UNIT
8 We are family

Reading: multiple matching (Part 1)

1 Look at the photos. What do you think the relationship between the people could be?

2 You are going to read an article written by an Englishwoman who went to Mongolia to test a theory. First, look at the title and subheading and read the text quickly. Choose the best alternatives in the following sentences.

1 Lucy wanted to prove a theory of *her own / someone else's.*
2 The theory was to do with *how easily people can become friends / how closely connected we all are.*
3 Lucy went to Mongolia to meet *a friend / a stranger.*
4 She feels her journey was *successful / unsuccessful.*

3 Now read the article again and choose the most suitable heading from the list A–I for each part (1–7) of the article. There is one extra heading which you do not need to use. There is an example at the beginning (0).

A A difficult journey
B Coping with a setback
C Laying down the rules
D Two worlds finally connected
E What it all means
F A more ambitious experiment
G A stroke of luck
H Solving a postal problem
I Linking up in the 21st century

TIP! There may seem to be more than one possibility for each heading. To find the correct one, find information in the paragraph that is an exact match for your heading.

Steppe by step

According to a theory, Lucy Leveugle is linked by just six acquaintances to this Mongolian herdsman. So she travelled round the world to put the theory to the test.

| **0** | **I** |

What if everyone around the world was somehow connected to everyone else? In many ways nowadays we are, with the Internet, email, air travel and so on. But I mean more than that. There's a theory called six degrees of separation that says you can make contact with anyone in the world by following a chain of acquaintances. Someone you know knows someone, who knows someone else, and so on – and in six of these steps, you can reach anyone.

| **1** | |

This idea is based on an experiment carried out in 1967 by a social psychologist called Stanley Milgram. He sent parcels to 100 people in different states of the USA. Each person had instructions to try to get their parcel to someone else in another state on the other side of the country. However, the address of the person for whom the parcel was destined was not given – only their name, occupation and a few personal details. Milgram found that, on average, each parcel was passed on from one person to another just six times before reaching its final destination. Although the experiment has never been repeated on a large scientific scale, his idea has **1** *taken off*. There's a play, a film and even an Internet game based on it.

| **2** | |

I decided to **2** *test out* Milgram's theory, this time on a world stage; to **3** *find out* how many steps it would really take to reach someone chosen completely at random on the other side of the planet. And I wanted to make a television documentary about it. I got the backing of a TV company, and **4** *went ahead*. I decided on Outer Mongolia for my target, because I had never met anyone from there. I advertised in Mongolian newspapers, asking for volunteers to be filmed in a documentary, and from the replies I chose Purev-Ochir Gungaa, a nomadic herdsman in the middle of the Mongolian Steppes. I felt that if I could **5** *get to* him, then I could get to anyone.

3 _____

So my journey to reach him began. I set myself guidelines based on the original 1960s experiment. I could only contact someone who I already knew on a first-name basis. That person had to pass me on to someone they knew personally, and so on. I wasn't allowed to use the Internet or any other public resource.

4 _____

I hesitated over whom to choose as my first step as they would be vital in starting the chain that would hopefully lead me to my herdsman. Finally I chose my school friend Francis in Dublin, as I knew he had travelled in Russia. Francis **6***passed* me *on* to his sister Emily, a magazine editor, who sent me to her environmentalist friend Rolf in Geneva. And then, unbelievably, Rolf was able to send me straight to someone he knew in Mongolia. I had reached Mongolia in four steps – so perhaps I really would make it to my herdsman in six.

5 _____

I met my fourth link, Urtnasan, a high-ranking government official, in Ulan Bator, the Mongolian capital. Then language difficulties got in the way, and I realised that I wasn't going to make it in six steps – if at all. But I **7***went on* trying, and was passed on to two more officials, then a businessman who lived several hundred miles away from Ulan Bator. I was getting close. My eighth step was Oyuntuya, who was a teacher in a tiny village – but more importantly, she was my herdsman's mother.

6 _____

When I finally found Purev-Ochir I was amazed that it had not taken me much longer. The 24-year-old lived in a traditional tent in the middle of the desolate, empty and frozen Mongolian Steppes. He lived with relatives and more than 600 horses, cows, sheep and goats. I was the first foreigner that he had met.

7 _____

Our lives were totally different, yet amazingly a chain of only eight different people connected Purev-Ochir and me. Although it had taken me nine steps to reach him, that doesn't prove that the six-degrees theory is wrong – it is quite possible that the average is actually six. What it does prove is that we can take shortcuts through large social networks and that it really is a small world after all.

Adapted from THE GUARDIAN

4   Compare your answers. What parts of each paragraph gave you the answer?

5   Rewrite the following phrases in italics using one of the phrasal verbs (1–7) in the text in the correct form. There is one phrasal verb you do not need to use.

1   In England, the idea of 'six degrees of separation' has *become popular among young people.*

2   Lucy Leveugle *has continued* investigating the theory in a television series.

3   This series, called *Secret Admirer,* aims to *discover* how people can meet someone they admire.

4   Maybe you could volunteer *to see whether* the theory *really works* in your country.

5   Do you think you could *reach* your favourite film star in just six steps?

6   Maybe you have a friend or relative who could *direct* you to someone closer to your idol?

6   *What if?*

1   Look at the following questions and discuss possible consequences, or actions you might take.

• What if you received a letter from a secret admirer asking you for a date?

• What if a friend invited you to a party and your favourite film star was there?

• What if you discovered a long-lost relative in New Zealand?

2   Think of some more *What if?* questions and ask a partner.

Speaking 1: quiz

1   What type of relationship is each person talking about?

acquaintance   best friend   colleague
relative   stranger

1 We work together.
2 I've met her once or twice.
3 I've no idea who he is.
4 I see her at family get-togethers.
5 I can tell him everything.

2   Do the quiz with a partner.

3   Check your results on page 189. Do you agree with the descriptions given?

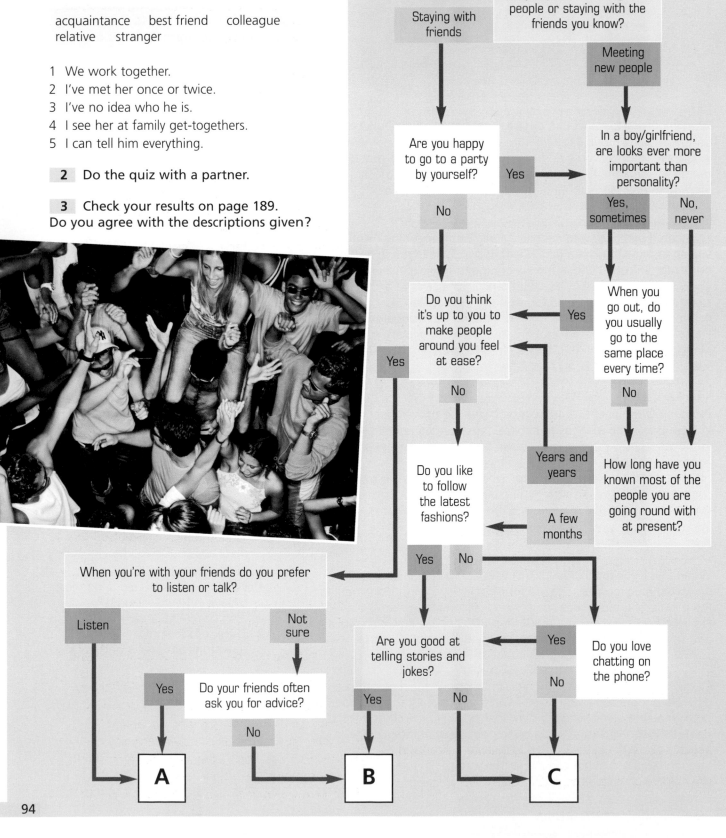

What kind of friend are you?

Start ➤ Do you prefer meeting new people or staying with the friends you know?

Staying with friends

Meeting new people

Are you happy to go to a party by yourself?   Yes

No

In a boy/girlfriend, are looks ever more important than personality?

Yes, sometimes   No, never

Do you think it's up to you to make people around you feel at ease?   Yes

Yes   When you go out, do you usually go to the same place every time?

Yes

No

No

Years and years   How long have you known most of the people you are going round with at present?

Do you like to follow the latest fashions?

A few months

Yes   No

When you're with your friends do you prefer to listen or talk?

Listen   Not sure

Yes   Do you your friends often ask you for advice?

Are you good at telling stories and jokes?

Yes   Do you love chatting on the phone?

No

Yes   No

No

No

A

B

C

Grammar 1: gerunds and infinitives

1   Work in pairs or groups.

Group A complete the letter on page 189 using the verbs in brackets in the correct form.

Group B complete the following letter using the verbs in brackets in the correct form.

Dear Aggie

When I first met Marc we got on really well – and he seemed
(1) .... (enjoy) my company. We liked
(2) .... (do) the same things and we were both keen
on (3) .... (go) to football together. He was my
best friend at that time, and I dropped my other friends
(4) .... (spend) more time with him. He hasn't
changed, but I have. Now I can't bear (5) .... (hear)
the same jokes every time we go out, and I hate having
(6) .... (watch) football on TV all weekend.
        I know he'll be upset – but nothing can (7) ....
(make) me (8) .... (change) my mind – I miss
(9) .... (see) my other friends and I'd rather not
just (10) .... (stay) with him all the time. I've tried
(11) .... (tell) him, but I can't – I'm afraid of
(12) .... (hurt) him. What can I do?

Stephanie

▶ Grammar reference p.196 (8)

2   Work in new pairs, one from Group A and one from Group B.

1   Tell your partner what is in your letter.

2   Decide what advice to give the writer of each letter.

Watch Out! *make/let/allow* ◀

1   What happens when you use *make* in the passive?
a) The teacher made us do the exercise again.
b) We were made to do the exercise again.

2   Which sentence is NOT possible? Correct it.
a) My parents don't let me stay out late.
b) I am not let to stay out late.

▶ Grammar reference p.197 (8.7)

3   Match the sentence halves and explain the difference in meaning.

1   I'd like to meet her
    I like meeting her
    a) on Saturday mornings, because we go shopping together.
    b) at 9.30 tomorrow morning.
2   I stopped to talk to Rose
    I stopped talking to Rose
    a) because I realised I couldn't trust her.
    b) when I bumped into her on the street.
3   I remembered to phone Jack
    I remembered phoning Jack
    a) and he was very pleased.
    b) although I didn't make a note of the exact time.
4   He tried to write his essay in half an hour
    He tried writing his essay in half an hour
    a) but he couldn't do it.
    b) and he got a bad mark for it.
5   I regret to tell you that
    I really regret
    a) encouraging my brother to apply for the job.
    b) your application has been unsuccessful.

4   Rewrite the following sentences using the verbs in brackets in the correct form. Add a preposition where necessary.

Example: We've thought about whether we should move house. (*consider*)
We've considered moving house.

1   She interrupts me all the time – it's really annoying. (*keep*)
2   She wants to invite all the family to the party. (*insist*)
3   The man claimed he was a government official. (*pretend*)
4   She hoped that he would explain everything to her. (*want*)
5   I think it's great when I don't have to get up early on holiday! (*enjoy/not*)
6   I shouldn't have written the letter. (*regret*)
7   Even though I was late, the examiner allowed me to take the exam. (*let*)
8   I hate being dependent on other people. (*rely*)

5   Ask and answer the following questions.

1   What are you thinking of doing this weekend?
2   Have you ever considered working abroad?
3   Is there anything you can't stand doing?
4   Have you ever done something you regretted or regretted not doing something?
5   Have you ever tried surfing? Would you like to?

Vocabulary 1: adjective suffixes

1

1 Match each group of words to the correct adjective suffix. The suffix must fit all three words in the group. What spelling changes do you have to make when you add the suffix?

1	depend, love, wash	a)	-ly
2	truth, hope, harm	b)	-ive
3	act, create, support	c)	-ful
4	nerve, fury, fame	d)	-al
5	nature, nation, culture	e)	-y
6	friend, coward, heaven	f)	-able
7	fun, wealth, health	g)	-ous

2 Which adjectives can you make negative using *un-*, *in-* or *-less*?

Example: lovable – *unlovable*

2 Complete the following sentences using the correct form of the words given. Be careful! You will need make some of the adjectives negative.

Example:
At first I thought Tracey was ...*unfriendly* but then I realised she was just shy. **FRIEND**

1 Mario's friendship is really .... to me – I'd miss him a lot if he left. **VALUE**
2 Couples often break up if one of them becomes very .... **FAME**
3 The whole situation seemed .... until you came along to help. **HOPE**
4 My parents are very .... of me, and encourage me to try new things. **SUPPORT**
5 It's very .... to go without breakfast. **HEALTH**
6 Tom is such an .... person – he's always running around doing something. **ACT**

3 Think about the people you know. Who:

• is always supportive of you, whatever you do?
• would you talk to if you felt nervous or worried about something?
• is friendly to everyone?
• might be famous one day?
• is very active in sports and games?

Write the names in a circle and show your partner. Can your partner match the names to the descriptions?

Example:

Carlotta
Pietro
my grandmother
Kim
my sister

A: *I think your grandmother is always supportive of you.*
B: *Right!*

Use of English 1: word formation (Part 5)

1 Read the title and the text below quickly. Which two of the following topics does it discuss?

a) making friends
b) why friends quarrel
c) what keeps friends together

2 Use the word given in capitals below the text to form a word that fits in the space in each line. There is an example at the beginning (0).

FRIENDS

Everyone wants to have friends, but building up new **(0)** *relationships* is not always easy. A few people are born with outgoing **(1)** ....; they have a **(2)** .... ability to make new friends wherever they go. But not many people are **(3)** .... at ease in a room full of strangers. Most of us feel **(4)** .... when we meet new people, and this can occasionally make us appear **(5)** ...., when in fact we are just shy. In any case, the **(6)** .... of new friendships is a gradual process – it doesn't just happen overnight. Long-standing friendships **(7)** .... have several things in common. The friends enjoy the same sorts of **(8)** ...., and share similar beliefs and values, they are **(9)** .... to one another, and they are also **(10)** .... of one another when they have problems.

0	**RELATION**		
1	**PERSON**	6	**DEVELOP**
2	**NATURE**	7	**GENERAL**
3	**COMPLETE**	8	**ACTIVE**
4	**NERVE**	9	**TRUTH**
5	**FRIEND**	10	**SUPPORT**

3 The text mentions four qualities of a successful friendship. What are they? Which one do you think is most important?

Vocabulary 2: relationships

1

1 Some of the following definitions are incorrect. Find them and correct them.

Example:
Your **mother-in-law** is the mother of your friend. *Wrong – she's the mother of your husband or wife.*

1 Your **nephew** could be either your brother's son or your sister's daughter.
2 Your **great-grandmother** is your mother's mother's mother.
3 Your **aunt** could be your mother's sister or your father's brother.
4 Your **cousins** can be either male or female.
5 Your **stepbrother** shares one parent with you, but not both.
6 Your **great-uncle** is the father of one of your grandparents.
7 Your **niece** is your brother's or sister's daughter.
8 Your **brother-in-law** is the husband of your brother.
9 Your **grandson** could be the son of your son or daughter.

2 Say how many of the relatives above you have.

Example: *I don't have a mother-in-law because I'm not married. But I have three cousins.*

2

1 Match the adjectives in the box to the following descriptions.

stubborn	modest	~~optimistic~~	reliable
sensible	sympathetic	sociable	thoughtful
talkative	generous	ambitious	

Example:
My brother always looks on the bright side of life. *He's optimistic.*

1 My cousin Maria will never let you down.
2 My younger sister is the kind of person who makes a party go with a swing!
3 Mark is determined to be a success in life.
4 John always leaves a big tip for the waiter.
5 When Pietro starts on his favourite topic, I just can't shut him up.
6 Carla never boasts about her achievements.
7 My aunt is the right person to go to if you feel depressed.

8 My nephew doesn't let his heart rule his head.
9 My older sister is always thinking of things she can do to make other people feel good.
10 Arek is so sure he's right, it's hard to get him to change his mind about something.

2 Work with a partner and think of the opposite of each adjective above. Use your dictionary if necessary.

3 Describe the different members of your family to your partner. Give examples of their behaviour. Compare yourself with them.

3

1 Complete the following text using words or phrases from the box. There are two extra words or phrases you won't need.

bridegroom	ceremony	honeymoon
got married	bride	got engaged	wedding
bridesmaids	reception	

Jenny met Rob at work and they soon started going out. After a few months they (1) .... , and the following year they (2) .... They had a lovely big (3) .... and invited all their friends and family. Jenny's nieces were the (4) .... The (5) .... was held in their local church, followed by a (6) .... at a hotel with dinner and a band. Afterwards they set off on a romantic (7) .... in Italy.

2 Discuss these questions.

1 Is the relationship described above typical for your country or not?
2 How popular is marriage in your country?
3 Do you think that marriage is outdated nowadays?
4 What do you think is the best age to get married?

Exam focus

Paper 4 Listening: note completion (Part 2)

About the exam: In Paper 4, Part 1, you hear one or more speakers. You have to complete notes or sentences with a word or words from the recording. The information on the page is in the same order as what you hear. You hear the recording twice.

Procedure

1 Read the notes or sentences before you listen. Underline key words and think about what sort of information is missing. Remember that the words in the notes may not be exactly the same as those used in the recording (e.g. *choose* in question 1).

2 The first time you listen, fill in as many gaps as you can, using approximately 1–3 words. You don't need to change these words in any way.

3 If you can't fill a gap, look ahead to the next one.

4 The second time you listen, check and complete your answers. Always put something – you don't lose marks for a wrong answer.

5 In the exam, you are given time to transfer your answers to the answer sheet at the end of the test. Be careful not to make mistakes when you do this (e.g. with singular/plural).

🎧 **1** You will hear part of a radio talk about how to organise a wedding. For questions 1–10, complete the notes.

Wedding advice

One year ahead:
* choose (1) .... for wedding
* choose best man and bridesmaids
* decide on locations for the (2) .... and reception, and make bookings
* make a (3) ....

Six months ahead:
* choose bride's and bridesmaids' dresses
* choose (4) .... (according to what will be in season)
* choose (5) .... for reception (according to budget)
* reserve (6) .... for guests
* finalise arrangements for the (7) ....

Three months ahead:
* check (8) .... is valid
* organise (9) ....
* think about the (10) .... (e.g. by bridegroom and possibly by bride)

Most important thing – enjoy the wedding!

2 Discuss these questions.

1 How much of the advice in the notes above would apply to weddings in your country?
2 Is it better to spend a lot on a big wedding ceremony or save the money for the future?
3 Why do some people want to have a big expensive ceremony?
4 Tell a partner about the last wedding you went to. Who was there? What was it like?
5 What other celebrations are important for families? Describe the last one your family had.

Grammar 2: expressing hypothetical meanings

1   Read Cris's story. Then match each sentence 1–8 to one of his wishes a)–h) below.

1   I think I'm in love with Eleanor.   *g)*
2   She's going out with Carlo.
3   He's the captain of the basketball team.
4   He's very rich and he drives a silver BMW.
5   Eleanor's eyes light up when she sees him driving it.
6   I heard there was a big party yesterday for the basketball team and Eleanor was there.
7   They say Carlo drove another girl home from the party and Eleanor was crying.
8   But I know she'll never leave Carlo, even though he'll never make her happy.

a)   I wish she would look at **me** like that.
b)   I wish I'd been invited.
c)   I wish I'd had a clean tissue to dry her tears.
d)   I wish I had lots of money and a big car.
e)   I wish she was going out with me instead.
f)   I wish I could get picked for the team too.
g)   I wish she'd never met him. I could make her much happier.
h)   I wish I wasn't – I don't have a chance with her.

2   Underline the verb forms after *I wish* in a)–h). Which ones refer to:

• the present or future?
• the past?

Watch Out!   *wish and would*

Decide which sentence in each pair is NOT possible. Then match the correct sentences to the explanations below.

1   a) I wish I would have a big car.
    b) I wish I had a big car.
2   a) I wish she would go out with me.
    b) I wish she went out with me.

A   We use *wish* + past simple when we want our own situation to be different.
B   We only use *wish* + *would* when we are referring to another person.

▶   Grammar reference p.198 (11.1–2)

2   Choose the correct alternative in each of the following sentences.

1   I wish I *hadn't lost / didn't lose* my favourite scarf.
2   I really wish my sister *would stop / stopped* smoking so much.
3   I wish I *would / could* dance as well as my friend.
4   If only I *didn't have / don't have* to take exams next month!
5   I wish I *can / could* get a job abroad.
6   I wish I *wasn't / wouldn't be* so bad at sport!
7   If only a millionaire *will / would* fall in love with me.
8   I wished the concert *would be / was* over – it was awful.

3

1   Complete the following wishes for yourself.

1   I wish I could …
2   I wish I'd never …
3   If only my parents would … , but they won't.
4   If only I had …
5   I wish I was …

2   Now explain your wishes to a partner.

Examples:

I wish I could sing well. If I had a good voice, I could become an opera singer.

I wish I'd never gone out with Sam. If I'd gone out with Peter instead, I would have enjoyed myself much more.

4   The following expressions are also followed by past tense forms to show hypothetical meaning.

1 Choose the best meaning for each expression from the alternatives given.

1 It's time we went home.
   a) They have already gone home.
   b) They haven't gone home yet.
2 I'd rather you left.
   a) I am pleased that you left.
   b) I would like you to leave.
3 Suppose I read your email! You'd be in trouble then!
   a) He is thinking about reading the email.
   b) He has read the email.

2 What is the difference in meaning between the sentences in these pairs?

1 a) You talk as if you know all about it.
   b) You talk as if you knew all about it.
2 a) What if we can't find the answer?
   b) What if I couldn't speak English?

▶ Grammar reference p.198 (11.3–6)

5   Complete the following sentences in a logical way.

1 Isn't it time ....? It's already nine o'clock.
2 Suppose .... – wouldn't that be great?
3 I think I'd rather .... than just sit here on my own.
4 You look as if .... Shall we find something to eat?
5 Would you rather we .... or ....?
6 It's high time you .... You can't afford to fail this exam.
7 Suppose I .... – would that help you?

The Backstreet Boys

Listening 2: song

1

1 Match the sentence halves to make the first verse of the song *Drowning*.

1 Don't pretend you're sorry
2 You know you got the power
3 Girl you leave me breathless but it's okay 'cause
4 Now hear me say I can't imagine life
5 Even forever don't seem

a) you are my survival
b) to make me weak inside
c) without your love
d) like long enough
e) I know you're not

2 Now suggest a possible order for the lines of the chorus.

☐ Baby I can't help it, you keep me drowning in your love
☐ Baby I can't help it, you keep me drowning in your love
☐ 'Cause every time I breathe, I take you in and my heart beats again
☐ Every time I try to rise above, I'm swept away by love

🎧 **2**   Listen to the first part of the song to check your answers.

🎧 **3**   Listen to the whole song. What is it about? Choose two answers from the list.

a) The singer feels totally dependent on the girl.
b) The singer wants to escape from the girl's control.
c) The girl gives him a reason to live.
d) The singer wants to leave the girl for someone else.
e) The girl has left the singer and he wants her back.

Speaking 2: how to keep talking/adding ideas (Parts 3 and 4)

1   Work with a partner and do the Part 3 speaking task below. Use the following questions to help you. You should talk for about three minutes.

- What would each activity involve?
- How would it help you to meet people?
- What sort of people would you meet?
- Do you think you'd like these people? Why?/Why not?
- How much do you think you would enjoy the activity?

I'd like you to imagine that a town council wants to create opportunities for local people of different ages to meet one another socially and has asked residents for their views. Here are some ideas they are considering. Talk to each other about how effective each one might be as a way of encouraging people to meet one another. Then say which two you would recommend to the town council.

2   Compare your ideas with the class.

3   In the exam, you must try to keep talking for the full three minutes. Listen to two students. How do they keep the conversation going when they have discussed all the pictures and still have time left?

a) They go back to the first topic again.
b) They think of different activities they could do besides the ones in the pictures.
c) They think of the things that their two favourite activities have in common.

4   In Part 4 of the Speaking test, the examiner asks you to discuss some questions which extend the topic you discussed in Part 3. The examiner may also take part in the conversation.

1   Look at the following question and think of three things that you could discuss in the answer.

- Who do you rely on more – friends or family?

2   Now listen to two students doing the task. Are their ideas the same as yours, or different?

3 Listen again. Tick the phrases the students use to introduce a new idea.

... another thing is that ...
... as well as that ...
... and in addition to that ...
... and also I suppose ...

5   Discuss some of the following questions with a partner. Keep talking for about four minutes.

1   How and where do people in your town meet one another socially?
2   Who do you rely on more – friends or family?
3   Who do you confide in more – friends or family?
4   What sorts of things do you enjoy doing with your family, and what sorts of things do you like doing with your friends?
5   What do you enjoy doing in a large group, and what do you enjoy doing on your own?

Writing: article (Part 2)

1   Read the task below and underline key words.

You see the following notice in an international magazine.

Family celebrations

Families around the world all have their own ways of celebrating special occasions. Write us an article about one family celebration that you have particularly enjoyed recently, explaining the reason for the celebration and describing what made it so enjoyable.

The best articles will be published and the writers will receive £500 each.

Write your **article** in **120–180** words.

2   Read these statements and decide if they are true or false.

1   This article should be based on your own experiences.
2   You should use subheadings and numbered points.
3   You should use a neutral style as it is for an international magazine.
4   You have to describe two different things about the celebration.
5   You need to make recommendations about what should be done.
6   You should include some description.
7   You should begin *Dear Sir or Madam*.
8   You should have an interesting title.

▷   Writing reference p.211

3

1   Decide what celebration you will write about. You could choose one of the following:

• a wedding   • a birthday   • the birth of a baby
• a religious celebration   • a national celebration

2   Now plan the details you will include in your article. Remember your article should have three sections:

• first paragraph which introduces the topic
• main part of the article with supporting detail
• ending.

Example:

Para 1 – woke up – special day – sister's wedding!
   – background information (how the couple met, etc.)
Para 2 – last-minute preparations
   – ceremony
   – party
Para 3 – end of the celebrations – how I felt

4

1   Here are some titles that other students gave their articles for this task. Which two do you think are the best titles? Why? What is wrong with the others?

a)   A family celebration
b)   **A wonderful wedding in New York**
c)   A family celebration that I enjoyed
d)   Family reunion – 21st century style

2   Think of an interesting title for your own article. Don't just repeat the words of the question in your title.

5   Look at three opening paragraphs and answer the questions.

1   What sort of celebration is each person writing about?
2   Why are they all good openings to an article?

A   What's the first thing that comes into my mind when I think of Christmas?

B   Any French child knows that the 14th of July is a very special date for our country. Why?

C   Why was last year special for me and my family? Because that year, we celebrated a new arrival in our family.

6   Write your article, using three or four paragraphs. Remember to read through the task again carefully and include all the information needed.

7   When you have finished, check your work.

▷   Writing reference pp.206, 211

1 Complete the second sentence so that it has a similar meaning to the first sentence, using no more than five words, including the word given.

1 You must remember your camera.
   bring
   Don't .... your camera.

2 The officials allowed us to take photographs in the museum.
   let
   The officials .... photographs in the museum.

3 I'd like to buy a mountain bike.
   interested
   I'm .... a mountain bike.

4 Susie and I are very good friends.
   on
   Susie and I .... with one another.

5 Jack feels bad about not writing to his friend earlier.
   wishes
   Jack .... his friend earlier.

6 I think you should go home now.
   time
   I think .... home.

7 I wish I could speak Spanish.
   being
   I regret .... speak Spanish.

8 I wish I was still in contact with my old school friends.
   touch
   I wish I had .... with my old school friends.

9 You ought to buy some new shoes.
   high
   It is .... some new shoes.

2 Read the text below and decide which answer (A, B, C or D) best fits each space. There is an example at the beginning (0).

FRIENDSREUNITED.CO.UK

Have you ever looked (0) ..*B*.... what happened to your old friends? *Friends Reunited* is a website which puts old school and college friends back in (1) .... with one another. It was (2) .... by a husband and wife (3) .... when the wife, Julie Pankhurst, decided she wanted to track (4) .... some of her own school friends. The website now has over five million (5) .... and is one of the most popular websites in the UK. You pay a small (6) .... to join, and then add your name and email address to a list. This list is (7) .... by school and year, so it is easy to find people.

Thousands of reunions have now (8) .... place across the UK, and the idea has spread to many other countries. So if you join *Friends Reunited*, you can find the person who was your (9) .... friend when you were eight, even if he or she's now living on the other (10) .... of the world. There may even be some surprises (11) .... for you! You might (12) .... that the quiet boy who everyone used to (13) .... in school has now become a professor of Physics, and the tall shy girl has now become a top fashion (14) .... with her picture in *Vogue* magazine. Or, (15) .... , you might find that no one you knew has changed much at all!

0	**A** out of	**B** into	**C** up to	**D** about
1	**A** connection	**B** association	**C** meeting	**D** touch
2	**A** set up	**B** made out	**C** put on	**D** got down
3	**A** team	**B** group	**C** crew	**D** band
4	**A** out	**B** down	**C** for	**D** in
5	**A** players	**B** holders	**C** users	**D** consumers
6	**A** price	**B** fee	**C** fare	**D** expense
7	**A** organised	**B** demonstrated	**C** managed	**D** controlled
8	**A** made	**B** given	**C** taken	**D** done
9	**A** ideal	**B** perfect	**C** superb	**D** best
10	**A** section	**B** side	**C** piece	**D** half
11	**A** in store	**B** on order	**C** in place	**D** en route
12	**A** invent	**B** discover	**C** investigate	**D** identify
13	**A** smile	**B** laugh	**C** joke	**D** tease
14	**A** example	**B** image	**C** model	**D** brand
15	**A** in effect	**B** in particular	**C** on the whole	**D** on the other hand

UNIT
9 A new look

Reading: gapped text (Part 3)

1 Look at the photos. What do you think is the connection between the people?

2 Read the title, the subheading and the main part of the text to check your ideas in Exercise 1.

3 Seven paragraphs have been removed from the article. You have to choose from the paragraphs A–H the one which fits each gap (1–6). There is one extra paragraph which you do not need to use. There is an example at the beginning (0).

1 Read the first paragraph of the article, then the example paragraph H in the box. Decide why H is correct. Key phrases have been highlighted to help you.

2 Look at the rest of the gaps and decide what type of information could fit in each gap.

Example: *Gap 1 could have more information about what is not right with Ken's appearance.*

3 Read through the extracted paragraphs A–G in the box. Decide which one describes:

1 early events after Ken's meeting with Cindy.
2 why Ken thinks looking good is important (two paragraphs).
3 details of what Ken's face looks like now (two paragraphs).
4 Ken's present feelings for Cindy.
5 how Ken looked before surgery.

4 Now do the task, using your answers in Exercise 3 to help you.

Making a new man of himself

Inspired by the doll-like looks of Cindy Jackson, known as the 'Queen of Plastic Surgery' because of the amount of surgery she has had, Miles Kendall has spent £40,000 turning himself into a real-life boy doll.

'Sorry I'm not looking my best. I had a late night – I didn't get to bed until 5.00 a.m.,' laughs Miles Kendall at the beginning of our interview. He needn't apologise because it's impossible to tell whether he's had a late night or not.

0	H

His status as a celebrity is due to the fact that he has had plastic surgery, and lots of it. Thanks to the encouragement of his good friend the plastic surgery queen Cindy Jackson, he has spent £40,000 sculpting and reshaping his face. It's hard to say exactly what he looks like now. At first sight he strikes you as a pleasantly good-looking chap, but at the same time there's something not quite right about his appearance.

1	

Miles' self-transformation began when he saw Cindy talking about her experiences of plastic surgery on television. 'I looked at her and thought, "Why can't my life be like hers: glamorous and full of celebrity parties and things?" So I emailed her and told her, "I want to be a male version of you." '

2	

Together, the three of them planned a new face for Miles that would make him feel more acceptable to society. Miles then underwent a series of operations to make this dream a reality. 'Look at this,' he says, showing me a photograph of his face before the operations. 'See! That's what I looked like before – I looked awful.'

3	

'I don't think I'm incredibly handsome now,' he says, 'but I do think I'm above-average looking. I'm the same person underneath but the way people treat me now is completely different. I went to a business lunch the other day and people turned to look at me, and a couple of women even came up to me and said: "Oh God, you're gorgeous."'

A 'After that we got to know one another a bit. Then when she was sure that I really meant it, and it wasn't just a crazy idea, she took me to meet her plastic surgeon and told him what I wanted,' he explains.

B 'If things had been different, I'd have loved to, of course. But anyway, she's a great friend and really beautiful inside as well as out,' says Miles.

C 'It's true I had originally chosen to live my life like that,' he explains, 'but then I also chose to do something about it. And I couldn't have changed my life or had what I've got now if I hadn't changed my looks.'

D I've been so unused to being attractive that it's a bit strange, but that sort of thing happens all the time now. Society treats good-looking people much better, and I've basically done it to be treated better.'

E Well, actually he didn't. He appeared to be unhappier, certainly, and perhaps slightly more stressed – but he wasn't particularly unattractive.

F Maybe this impression is due to the fact that his new face is curiously immovable. When he smiles his eyes almost disappear and his teeth gleam at you, ruler-like in their straightness. His surgeon has given him Brad Pitt's nose, George Clooney's lips and Russell Crowe's chin, but the overall effect has been to transform him into a rather shark-like ex boy-band member.

G Because of these concerns, Miles has no plans to have surgery on any other part of his body. 'If I want to change my body, I can go to the gym.'

H In fact, it's hard to work out anything at all from his face. For Miles Kendall, who says he will be '35 this July', facial expressions are few and far between.

4

His life, says Miles, has altered immeasurably. Whereas in his former life he used to be a computer programmer, he has now taken on a new venture – he runs a bar called Bar Miles. Cindy Jackson was guest of honour at the opening. 'She's great,' he says enthusiastically. 'I'm really, really happy because running a bar was my life's ambition. And my social life is fantastic because Cindy's introduced me to all these celebrities. Before, I was totally bored the whole time. I never did anything but work. I didn't have any friends and I never went out.'

5

Perhaps surprisingly, Miles and Cindy have never been romantically involved. 'I'm not really her type as she's into older men. We've talked about having a relationship but we've never even kissed.'

6

He flashes me a final, dazzling smile. 'People think we're shallow, but really, we're not,' he says.

Adapted from THE SUNDAY TELEGRAPH

5 Complete the following sentences using the word given in capitals in the correct form.

1 Miles Kendall has spent £40,000 sculpting and .... his face. **SHAPE**

2 The writer of the article thinks Miles is .... good-looking. **PLEASE**

3 However, he finds something slightly odd about Miles' .... **APPEAR**

4 Because of the surgery he has undergone, it's difficult for Miles to show any .... expressions. **FACE**

5 Nevertheless, Miles feels more .... to society as a result of his transformation. **ACCEPT**

6 He has received a lot of help and .... from Cindy Jackson. **ENCOURAGE**

7 He talks about her .... **ENTHUSIASTIC**

8 .... , Miles and Cindy do not have a romantic relationship, however. **SURPRISE**

6 Discuss these questions.

1 Why did Miles decide to have plastic surgery? Do you think it was a good reason?

2 Would you ever think about changing your appearance? Why?/Why not?

Grammar 1: present and past habit

1

1 Choose the correct alternatives in the following sentences. In some sentences, both verb forms are possible.

1 When I was young, I *lived / used to live* in the country.
2 We didn't have a car so we *would walk / used to walk* everywhere.
3 My parents *never used to let / were never letting* us go out on our own in the evening.
4 In those days, children *used to be / would be* brought up more strictly.
5 We all *had / used to have* special jobs to do in the house, like washing-up.
6 Because of this, we *weren't having / didn't have* much free time.
7 We *didn't use to have / wouldn't have* televisions in our bedrooms, like children do today.
8 Nowadays my grandchildren *are taken / will be taken* everywhere by car.
9 These days, children *are always complaining / would always complain* about being bored.
10 But I think they *are having / have* a much easier time than I did as a child.

2 Compare your answers with a partner and discuss these questions.

1 Which three forms can be used to express habit in the past?
2 Which two forms can be used to express habit in the present?
3 Why are *would* and *used to* both possible in sentence 2, but not in sentence 7?

▶ **Grammar reference p.197 (9)**

3 Do you agree with what the writer says in sentences 9 and 10 above?

┌─ **Watch Out!** *used to/be used to/get used to* ◀─
│
│ What's the difference in meaning?
│ 1 I'm *used* to this hairstyle.
│ 2 I'm *getting used to* this hairstyle.
│ 3 I *used to have* a different hairstyle.
└─

2 **Find and correct the mistakes in the following sentences.**
getting up
Example: I'm not used to ~~get up~~ at 6.30 a.m. I usually get up at 8.00.

1 Maths was use to be my favourite subject.
2 Did you used to live in London?
3 I'm sure I will soon be get used to living here.
4 My brother is getting used his new job.
5 He is get the bus to the office at 8 o'clock every morning.
6 My grandfather would to walk 10 kilometres to school every day.
7 I would enjoy playing on the beach when I was young.
8 Alison is always try to look different from her friends.

3 **Choose three different years in your past, for example, when you were 5, 12 and 15 years old. Write sentences to describe the things that were true then, but are not true now.**

Example: *When I was 12, I used to ride my bike to school, but I don't do that now.*

4 **Think back to the day you started at your present school, college or job. Describe the things that you have got used to since then, or that you can't get used to.**

Examples:
I've got used to the long journey.
I can't get used to all the paperwork.

5 **Imagine that you are going to do one of the following. What will you have to get used to? What will you find easy or difficult to get used to?**

• live in another country
• move to a new town
• share a flat with a friend
• stop using your car

Examples: *(living in Australia)*
I'll have to get used to speaking English.
I'll find it difficult to get used to being so far away from my family.

1

2

Vocabulary 1: fashion

1

1 Look at the photos of Stuart. Read through the descriptions below, ignoring the gaps, and match them to the correct photo.

2 Complete each description using words from the boxes.

A

'This is the sort of outfit I expect an employee to wear. The suit is (1) .... grey (2) .... It's a (3) .... cut, so it won't date. The shirt is (4) .... blue (5) .... , and the tie is (6) .... , striped yellow and blue. And black (7) .... (8) .... shoes, of course.'

| classic | cotton | dark | slip-on | leather | pale | silk | wool |

B

'I think Stuart can wear (1) .... colours. I think this green (2) .... sweater really suits him – it (3) .... his eyes. And the jacket's very practical, it's (4) .... , and a nice unusual colour. It (5) .... good with these (6) .... trousers and (7) .... (8) .... shoes.'

| beige | bright | brown | looks | matches | casual | round-neck | waterproof |

3 Discuss these questions.

1 Which look is a) formal and professional? b) smart but casual?
2 How fashionable is each outfit?
3 Who do you think is speaking in each description, A and B?

2 Work with a partner.

1 Plan a new outfit for Stuart. Think about:

• the general look and image (e.g. formal, smart-casual, casual)
• what items of clothing Stuart would look good in
• the colour, material and design.

2 Write a short description of the outfit you think would suit him.

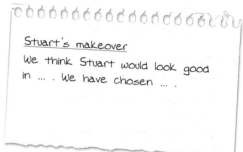

Stuart's makeover
We think Stuart would look good in ... . We have chosen ... .

3 Discuss the following questions.

1 What sort of clothes do you like wearing for school/for work/at home?
2 What is your favourite item of clothing? When and where did you get it? Why do you like it?
3 Have you ever bought an item of clothing that you have never worn? Why did you buy it? Why haven't you worn it?
4 How has fashion changed in the last five years? Do you like to keep up with the latest fashions?
5 Is there any type of modern fashion that you would never wear?

Use of English 1: error correction (Part 4)

1 Look at the title of the text below. What are *vintage clothes*? Why do you think people might want to collect them?

2 Now read the text quickly to see if you were right.

3 Read the text again and look carefully at each line. Some of the lines are correct, and some have a word which should not be there. If a line is correct, put a tick (✓). If a line has a word which should not be there, write the word at the end of the line. There are two examples at the beginning (0 and 00).

TIP! Remember to read the text sentence by sentence, not line by line, so that you understand the meaning and structure of each sentence. Check the first and last word in each line in case either one is the extra word.

COLLECTING VINTAGE CLOTHES

0 If you look up in the fashion magazines nowadays, you may   *up*
00 find that the latest fashion is something copied from the past.   ✓
1 Designers are getting ideas from old styles, and many of followers
2 of fashion are taking this idea further, and actually searching
3 for old clothes. What there is called 'vintage fashion' has become
4 the hottest style around, with famous people such like Julia Roberts
5 wearing vintage clothes in the public. But second-hand is not cheap.
6 As old clothes that become popular, their price rises. The name on
7 the label still matters, but the fashion is to be wear something made
8 by a designer from the past, and it is so a special challenge to find
9 something which made by a designer before he was famous. As
10 well as also this, vintage clothes may be valuable because of their
11 condition and the quality of the material. If a celebrity owned them or
12 was photographed been wearing them, this also adds to their second-
13 hand price. But if you buy such clothes as an investment, take this
14 advice on what you should and shouldn't do it. Don't alter the clothes,
15 store them carefully, and only get them dry cleaned by an expert.

4 What vintage fashions do you like best?

Vocabulary 2: phrasal verbs with *up*

1

1 Match each phrasal verb with the best ending.

1 I wrapped up   *j)*
2 I closed up
3 I finished up
4 I tidied up
5 I zipped up
6 I sewed up
7 I gathered up
8 I washed up
9 I drank up
10 I saved up

a) all the sandwiches but I was still hungry.
b) the shop and went home.
c) my books and left the library.
d) my jacket to keep the wind out.
e) the hole in my jeans.
f) all the dirty dishes.
g) enough money to buy a car.
h) my orange juice.
i) the whole house.
j) Jane's birthday present.

2 What do all the phrasal verbs above have in common?

a) They are all to do with upwards movement.
b) They are all to do with completing something.

2 Think of some phrasal verbs to do with upwards movement.

Example:
pick up – I picked up my suitcase.

Speaking 1

1 In a popular TV series, members of the public were visited by a team of professional designers, who completely transformed a room in their home. The owners were not allowed to see the results until the transformation was complete. They were then taken into the room and their reactions were filmed.

Look at Photos A and B, which show the same room before and after it was transformed. Describe the room in photo A. Then compare it with photo B. How has the room changed?

2 Discuss these questions.

1 Which room do you prefer?
2 How would you feel if this was your room?

Exam focus

Paper 4 Listening: selecting from answers (Part 4)

About the exam: In Paper 4, Part 4, you hear one or more speakers. You have to answer seven questions and select from two or three possible answers, e.g: true/false, yes/no, three-option multiple choice or which speaker said what. You hear the recording twice.

Procedure

1 Read the introduction to the task carefully. This will tell you something about the speakers and the topic, and will also explain the task you have to do.

2 Read the sentences or phrases and underline key words. Think about the sort of information you need to listen for.

3 The first time you hear the recording, listen for words and phrases with a similar meaning to the key words and mark the answers you are sure of.

4 The second time you listen, check and complete your answers.

5 In the exam, you are given time to transfer your answers to the answer sheet at the end of the test.

1 You will hear an interview in which Phil Bradshaw talks about his experiences on a TV programme. For questions 1–7, decide whether the statements are TRUE or FALSE. Write T for TRUE or F for FALSE.

Phil expected to take part in the make-over of his room. **1**

Phil hoped that the designers would replace his curtains. **2**

Phil wanted a complete change of image for his room. **3**

Phil disliked the choice of white as a colour for his room. **4**

When Phil first saw his redecorated room, he hid his true feelings. **5**

Phil was pleased with the storage space in his new room. **6**

Phil says that the producers of the programme want to film people who are looking pleased and happy. **7**

2 Read these extracts from the recording. What does each comment refer to?

1 It wasn't all plain sailing. *The TV company offered to redecorate Phil's flat, but it wasn't a good experience.*
2 They'd definitely seen better days.
3 We had a quick chat.
4 They'd gone for this sort of tent image.
5 I just burst into tears.
6 That's the only good thing that came out of it.

Vocabulary 3: things in the home

1

1 Where might you find the following items of furniture? Put them into the best category in the table below. Some may go in more than one category.

Study-bedroom	Classroom	Office

blinds   bookshelves   a carpet   a coffee table
a sofa   a computer   a cupboard   curtains
easy chairs   a filing cabinet   a wardrobe   pictures
cushions   a photocopier   upholstered chairs
a water cooler   an electric fan   a rug
a hot drinks vending machine   a reading light

2 Can you add more items to the table?

3 Which items do you have in your own room? Which would you like to have?

2

1 Choose words from the box that apply best to your own room. Then describe your room to a partner, explaining why you have chosen the words.

tidy   cluttered   messy   organised   comfortable
cramped   neat   relaxing

Example: *My room is messy because I never put my clothes away.*

2 If you could change one thing in your room, what would it be?

3 Work with a partner. Plan a makeover for your partner's room. You don't have much money to spend, so you have to set priorities. Think about these points:

- What things will you keep? What will you replace?
- What style of decoration will you choose? For example, will you go for a theme like oriental/futuristic/traditional?
- What colours will you choose for the walls, curtains and floor covering?

Exam focus

Paper 3 Use of English: word formation (Part 5)

About the exam: In Paper 3, Part 5, you read a text with ten gaps. At the end of each line, there is a word in capital letters. You have to change the form of this word into the correct part of speech to fill the gap.

Procedure
1 Read the title and the whole text to get an idea of what it is about. This makes it easier to decide the form of the missing word.
2 Read the text again, stopping at each gap. Think about the meaning and grammar of the whole sentence and decide if the word needs to be positive or negative, singular or plural.
3 Fill in the space with the word in the appropriate form.
4 When you have finished, read the text again and make sure your answers make sense.
5 Transfer your answers onto the answer sheet.

DO make sure you spell the words correctly.

1 Do the exam task on page 111.

2 Now discuss these questions.

1 Do you/Have you had to share a room with anyone else? What are/were the advantages and disadvantages of this?
2 Are you easily annoyed by other people's noise?
3 What kind of room do you like to work in?
4 Do you enjoy being alone? When?

For questions 1–10, read the text below. Use the word given in capitals at the end of each line to form a word that fits in the space in the same line. There is an example at the beginning (0).

Example: | 0 | *complaints* |

SHARING SPACE

Many people make **(0)** *complaints* about their working environment. Those   COMPLAIN

in open-plan offices often dislike the noise and especially the lack of **(1)** ....   PRIVATE

Making telephone calls where **(2)** .... information is discussed is   CONFIDENCE

almost **(3)** .... , and it may also be difficult to concentrate when the   POSSIBLE

person sitting next to you is on the phone. However, the **(4)** .... of   DIVIDE

the workspace into smaller offices can lead to a feeling of **(5)** .... An   ISOLATE

(6) .... approach is needed to solve these problems. Why not allow   ALTERNATE

people to choose to work in different places **(7)** .... to what they are   ACCORD

doing – a coffee bar or meeting room for sociable and **(8)** .... activities,   NOISE

or a small room for quiet work? The idea of individual desks would **(9)** ....   APPEAR

in this system and be **(10)** .... by a different approach to using space.   PLACE

Grammar 2: participle clauses

1

1 Read the first part of a description of someone's home. Compare the highlighted phrases with the relative clauses below.

> I used to love visiting my grandfather's house. It had a blue front door, which opened into a large hall. A picture of my grandmother, painted in 1930, hung on the wall and there was a thick blue rug covering the floor.

- ... which was painted in 1930.
- ... which covered the floor.

2 The highlighted phrases are reduced relative clauses. They contain a present or past participle. Which type of participle has an active meaning and which has a passive meaning?

▶ Grammar reference p.202 (16)

2

2 Read the rest of the description and rewrite the highlighted clauses without using a relative pronoun. Make any necessary changes.

> Off the hall, there was a corridor (1) which led into different rooms. In the living room there used to be a huge chandelier (2) which hung from the ceiling. Around the walls there were bookcases full of interesting books (3) which had been collected by my grandfather.
> A flight of wooden stairs led from the hall up to the first floor. Upstairs there were four bedrooms, (4) which were all decorated in different colours. In the main bedroom was a huge painted wooden chest (5) which contained my grandmother's linen. The house also had a wonderful garden (6) which stretched down to a stream at the bottom.

3

3 Work with a partner. Describe your home or the home of a relative and say why you like it.

4 Read the following description of Birmingham, the UK's second city. Then complete the text using the present or past participle forms of the verbs in brackets.

A new face for Birmingham

Once considered to be the last place anyone would want to live, the city of Birmingham is getting a new look. Birmingham, previously (1) .... (*think of*) as dirty and unglamorous, has suddenly become a cool place to be. Architecture is at the heart of the revolution. The city, once (2) .... (*despise*) for its ugly concrete buildings, has undergone a major facelift at a cost of billions of pounds.

Everywhere you look, there are new shopping malls (3) .... (*compete*) to attract shoppers (4) .... (*look for*) high-quality designer goods. The hugely unpopular Bull Ring, a grey shopping centre (5) .... (*build*) in the 1960s, has been knocked down and completely rebuilt. Birmingham's canals, once (6) .... (*hide*) away among decaying factories and (7) .... (*treat*) as rubbish tips, are now surrounded by modern offices, apartments, terrace bars and eateries. Young people come here in their hundreds every evening to see and be seen. In the east of the city, formerly (8) .... (*consider*) one of the poorest areas, an old custard factory has been converted into a lively complex of studios, galleries and café-bars.

For anyone (9) .... (*consider*) a move to a new town, Birmingham is well worth a look.

5 Complete these sentences, giving true information.

1 One of my town's oldest buildings is .... , located ...
2 The liveliest area is .... , offering young people the chance to ...
3 A typical dish of our region is .... , made from .... and served with ...
4 One of the most famous people of my country was .... , born in .... and celebrated because ...

6 Discuss how the place where you live has changed in the last five years. Is it better or worse than it used to be?

Use of English 3: key word transformations (Part 3)

Complete the second sentence so that it has a similar meaning to the first sentence, using the world given. Do not change the word given. You must use between two and five words, including the word given. Here is an example (0).

Example:

0 He said he regretted writing to her. **only**
He said: '*If only I had not* .... written to her!'

1 His last film, starring Julia Roberts, was his best. **which**
His last film, ... Julia Roberts, was his best.

2 When I was a child, I walked to school every day. **used**
When I was a child, ... to school every day.

3 If John was coming, he'd be here by now. **looks**
It .... John isn't coming.

4 Emma found the film extremely boring. **was**
Emma .... the film.

5 It was a more difficult job than they had anticipated. **easy**
The job .... they had anticipated.

6 'Don't touch the wet paint Eddie,' said Kate. **warned**
Kate .... the wet paint.

7 'There's a chance that I left my glasses in the library,' said Chris.
might
Chris said that he .... in the library.

8 The last time I went surfing was ten years ago.
for
I .... ten years.

9 It was unfair that Eva was fired.
deserve
Eva .... fired.

10 Which part of the book interested you most?
the
Which was .... part of the book?

Speaking 2: stressing key information (Part 2)

1 Look at photos A and B and read this task. Then answer the questions below.

❝ Both these photographs show people making changes to a place. I'd like you to compare and contrast the photos, and say why you think the people might want to change these places. ❞

1 What two parts does the task have?
2 In what order will you say the following things?
☐ why people might want to change the places
☐ what is similar
☐ what is different

A

B

2

1 Complete these sentences comparing and contrasting the photos, using words from the box.

> nervous   in good condition   amateurs
> confident   professional   decorating
> private   being rebuilt

1 In the first photo, we can see the outside of a large building, but the other photo shows a room in a .... house.
2 The large building looks as if it's ...., but the house seems to be ....
3 The people working on the large building are .... builders, but the people in the house are probably ....
4 The couple are doing their own ...., but the builders are working for someone else.
5 The man could be rather ...., but the builders are .... about what they are doing.

🎧 **2** Mark the words you think should be stressed. Then listen to see if you were right.

3 Practise saying the sentences and stressing the contrasting information.

3 Work with a partner.

Student A: Do the task in Exercise 1. Try to keep talking for about a minute, and use some of the language in Exercise 2.
Student B: Listen to your partner. When he/she has finished, answer this question (about 20 seconds).

❝ Which place do you think will show the greatest improvement? ❞

4 Now turn to photos C and D on page 185 and change roles.

Student B: Both these photos show people changing the way they look. Compare and contrast the photos and say how you think these people are feeling.
Student A: Listen to your partner. When he/she has finished, answer this question (about 20 seconds).

❝ Do you like dressing up for special occasions? ❞

Writing: report

1

1 Correct the following statements about reports.

1 You should begin *Dear Sir or Madam*.
2 You should use informal language.
3 You should give your own opinion at the beginning.
4 You should not use headings.
5 You should try to use interesting vocabulary.

▶ Writing reference p. 210

2 Look at the task below and underline key words. How many things do you have to do in this report?

The director of the place where you study English wants to set up a new common room for students to use when they are not in class. You have been asked to write a report saying which room in the school should be chosen for the common room, and making suggestions for how it could be made comfortable and attractive.

Write your **report** in **120–180** words.

2 Work with a partner. Brainstorm ideas for the report and complete the notes below.

Example:

New common room
Where?
Furniture?
Decoration
 - walls?
 - floor?
Any extras?

3
Choose four section headings from the ideas below, and decide on the best order for your report. (All the headings are possible – choose the ones you prefer.)

Changes needed

Furniture and decoration

Suggested room

Introduction

Final recommendation

Location of the common room

4

1 Read the following sentences and decide which section of your report they should go in.

It seems to me that the best place for the common room would be … because …

I suggest that there should be … as this would …

There could also be … so that …

In my view, it would be best to make these changes quickly, because then …

This report is to …

2 Complete the sentences above, using your ideas from Exercise 2.

Example:

Introduction
This report is to recommend a room in the school for a student common room.

5
Now write your report, making your suggestions and giving reasons.

> **TIP!** Don't worry if your answer is slightly longer than the word limit, but be careful. If you write a very long answer in the exam, you may not have time to check it properly.

6
When you have finished, check your work.

▶ Writing reference pp.206, 210

1 How many types of clothing can you think of for each of the following descriptions?

1 something that you wear on your feet
2 something that's got sleeves
3 something that you wear for sport
4 something that's usually made of wool
5 something formal
6 something for your head
7 something that's more often worn by women than men
8 something that you never wear

2 There is a mistake with vocabulary in each of the following sentences. Find the mistakes and correct them.

1 I did a really late night – I didn't get to bed until after four o'clock.
2 When I first met Jake, he struck me like a rather shallow person.
3 Then I got knowing him and my opinion changed.
4 My society life has been fantastic since I met Corinna.
5 It's a problem, but I'm sure I can make something about it.
6 I can't work up the answer to this maths problem – can you help?
7 That colour really fits you – it goes with your eyes.
8 I'm not very interested in keeping on with the latest fashions – I just wear what I like.
9 The trouble with my flat is that there isn't much store space.
10 When I saw what the decorators had done to my room, I just burst into crying.

3 Think back to ten years ago and answer the following questions.

1 Where were you living at that time?
2 What did you like most about your home?
3 Which room did you use to spend most time in?
4 Which other members of your family did you use to visit? Which visits did you enjoy the most? Why?
5 Did you ever use to stay with other relatives or friends without your parents? What did you do on these visits?
6 Is it a good thing for children to get used to spending time away from their parents?
7 What was your town centre like ten years ago? Did you use to go there often?
8 Do you still like going there? What do you do there now that you didn't use to do?

4 Write a few sentences about a place you know in your local area, saying what it used to be like and what it's like now. Then read your sentences out to the rest of your class and see if they can guess the place that you are describing.

5 Read the text below and think of the word which best fits each space. Use only one word in each space. There is an example at the beginning (0).

THE MEANING OF COLOUR

We may choose (0) ..*to*.. wear a particular colour just because of personal preference or fashion. However, particular colours (1) .... always had special meanings or uses. Black, for instance, is generally thought (2) .... as suitable for serious occasions and in the West it is traditional for funerals. This is (3) .... the case in China, however, (4) .... white is worn at funerals.

Some colours may be chosen for practical reasons. Road workers, who need to (5) .... easily seen, often wear jackets (6) .... bright yellow or orange stripes (7) .... are clearly visible to drivers. Green is generally regarded (8) .... calming, and so it is often used in places (9) .... doctors' waiting rooms. Blue is many people's favourite colour, and there may be a connection (10) .... this and the popularity of blue jeans. Blue also symbolizes loyalty and for (11) .... reason fashion consultants recommend wearing blue clothes to job interviews.

(12) .... the symbolism of colour (13) .... back hundreds of years, colours can change their significance. For example, pink is now seen as a feminine colour, whereas it (14) .... to be popular with men. So the next time you buy something to wear in your favourite colour, stop and think. (15) .... does it say about you?

Listening: sentence completion (Part 2)

1

1 Do you have a good memory? Which of the following do you find easiest/hardest to remember?

- telephone numbers
- people's names
- shopping lists
- things you have to do
- new English words

2 What do you do to help yourself remember these things? Explain your ideas.

Example: *When I have to remember something, I draw a star on my hand in pen or biro. Then when I see it, I remember I have to do something.*

2 You will hear part of a radio programme about a man called Dominic O'Brien, who has an amazing memory. First, read through the gapped sentences opposite to get a general idea of what the programme is about. Answer these questions.

1 Do you think that Dominic has always had a good memory?
2 How do you think he remembers things?
3 How does he now help others?

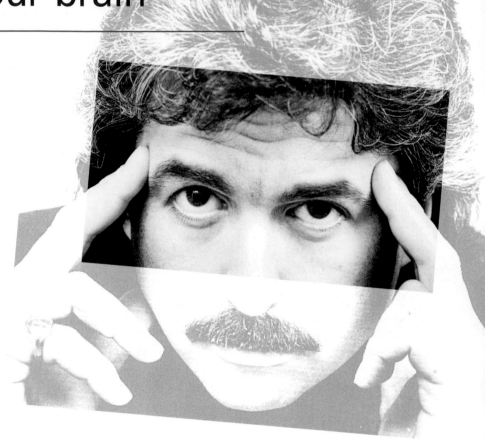

As a schoolboy, Dominic had problems seeing **(1)** .... clearly.

Dominic's teachers thought he was a **(2)** .... student.

Dominic did not manage to complete his education at **(3)** ....

After watching someone on **(4)** ...., Dominic worked out a way of training his memory.

Dominic can now remember a sequence of nearly **(5)** .... cards.

Dominic remembers each card by thinking of it as the **(6)** .... of someone famous.

Dominic makes up a story about a **(7)** .... to help him memorise the order of the cards.

Because of Dominic's skill with cards, he is not allowed to go into **(8)** .... any more.

Dominic now runs courses for people such as **(9)** .... who want to improve their performance.

Dominic thinks his memory will improve as his **(10)** .... increases.

3 Look at sentences 1–5 again and match them to the following extracts from the recording. Use the highlighted words to help you.

a) Then one day by chance he saw ___4___
b) he dropped out before finishing the course
c) He had reading problems – when he tried to look at
d) his teachers regarded him as
e) soon he could memorise all the cards

> **TIP!** The gapped sentences summarise and paraphrase the information you hear in the recording. Listen for the same ideas expressed in a slightly different way.

4 Listen and complete sentences 1–10 with a word or phrase. Remember: don't change the words you hear. Then listen a second time to check and complete your answers.

5 Test your powers of memory.

1 Look at the sequence of playing cards below for 30 seconds. Then close your book and try to remember what the cards were, and what order they were in.

2 Compare what you remember with a partner. Then look at the book again to check.

1 How many cards did you remember?
2 Did you remember them in the right sequence?

> **Did you know?**
> The world record for memorising one pack of playing cards in jumbled order is 34 seconds!

Grammar 1: obligation, necessity and permission

1 Rewrite the following sentences without changing the meaning, using (*don't*) *have to*, *had to*, *can*, *can't* or *could*.

Example:

To remember things, it's necessary to review them several times.
To remember things, ... *you have to* .... review them several times.

1 Is it necessary to pay to go in?
Do you .... pay to go in?

2 They said it wasn't necessary for me to take the exam.
They said .... take the exam.

3 We asked if it was possible for us to take the exam another day.
We asked .... take the exam another day.

4 You're not allowed to use a dictionary in the exam.
You .... use a dictionary in the exam.

5 Staff are not obliged to wear a uniform.
Staff .... wear a uniform.

6 Guests are permitted to use the swimming pool free of charge.
Guests .... use the swimming pool free of charge.

7 I was forced to wait an hour for the bus.
I .... wait an hour for the bus.

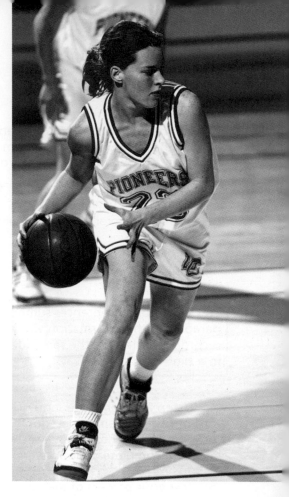

2   Discuss the following questions with a partner.

1   Which sentence is the odd one out? Why?

a) You aren't allowed to wait here.

b) You can't wait here.

c) You don't have to wait here.

2   Which of the sentences below expresses:

a) something the speaker has been told to do?

b) something the speaker recommends?

c) something the speaker wants to do soon?

1   You must see that new film at the Odeon.

2   I have to take my holiday by the end of May.

3   I really must buy some new shoes – these are worn out.

3   Which sentence is the odd one out? Why?

a) You don't need to go yet.

b) You needn't go yet.

c) You don't have to go yet.

d) You mustn't go yet.

4   How can you rewrite these sentences with *should*?

a) You are supposed to speak English in class.

b) You aren't supposed to speak your own language in class.

5   Which sentence is not possible?

a) You shouldn't have done that – it was wrong.

b) You mustn't have done that – it was wrong.

6   Did they actually pay?

a) They didn't need to pay.

b) They needn't have paid.

c) They shouldn't have paid.

▶ **Grammar reference p.201 (14.4–7)**

3   Work with a partner. Choose one of the following and say what is necessary or not necessary to become very good at it. Use appropriate forms of *have to*, *must* or *need*.

- play basketball/chess/ computer games
- speak another language
- ride a bike
- be an actor

4   Complete the second sentence so that it has a similar meaning to the first sentence, using the word given. You must use between two and five words.

1   You can't use a mobile phone in here.
   allowed
   You .... use a mobile phone in here.
2   It wasn't necessary for you to bring all those books.
   need
   You .... brought all those books.
3   You should park on the other side of the road.
   supposed
   You .... on this side of the road.
4   The library was built too far away from the town centre.
   should
   They .... the library nearer the town centre.
5   These exercises should be continued for six weeks.
   must
   You .... on doing these exercises for six weeks.
6   It was wrong of you to give him my address.
   let
   You .... know my address.

5   Complete these sentences giving true information.

1   This week I absolutely must ...
2   At home I'm supposed to ... but I don't always do it.
3   I'm glad I don't need to ... today.
4   My parents say when they were young they had to ... and they couldn't ...
5   I really shouldn't ... but ...
6   I think I should have ...

Use of English: error correction (Part 4)

1   Work with a partner.

1   Look at the title of the text below. Do you know anyone with a bad memory?
2   Now read the text quickly. Can you think of any other ways to deal with this problem?

2   Read the text again and look carefully at each line. Some of the lines are correct, and some have a word which should not be there. If a line is correct, put a tick (✓). If a line has a word which should not be there, write the word at the end of the line. There are two examples at the beginning (0 and 00).

> **TIP!** Remember, the extra word must be actually incorrect. For example, the word *really* in line 0 is not necessary, but it is not incorrect.

MY BAD MEMORY

0	Ever since I was little, I've had a really bad memory, and	*and* ✓
00	which has caused me all sorts of difficulties. I was always	✓
1	getting into the trouble at school because I forgot things	
2	like as my books and my homework. I would forget what	
3	lesson came next and which room I was meant to be in.	
4	One day, when I even forgot that it was a holiday, and	
5	I didn't realise until I had got there all the way to school	
6	and found that the gates were locked. One of my biggest	
7	problems was for remembering things in exams, and	
8	because of that I was never did as well at school as I felt	
9	I could have done it. However, now I'm older I'm slowly	
10	learning myself how to deal with my bad memory. I	
11	always have my diary with me and I make a habit of	
12	writing down everything what I have to do. This helps me	
13	a lot. I did try on an electronic diary, but I decided I	
14	preferred with the traditional version. And I love my job	
15	as an illustrator – my memory isn't making a problem there.	

Vocabulary 1: expressions with *mind*

1   Match the statements or questions 1–8 to the responses a)–h).

1   I just can't decide what to wear.   *g)*
2   Are you going to apply for the job?
3   I'm going to walk to the North Pole.
4   Is something worrying you?
5   Can I have fish?
6   What does *telepathy* mean?
7   I'm really nervous about my interview next week.
8   I'm sure I'm going to fail my exams.

a)   You must be out of your mind!
b)   I thought you wanted chicken – have you changed your mind?
c)   Let's go to a movie – that'll take your mind off things.
d)   Is it to do with reading other people's minds?
e)   Oh, no. The idea never crossed my mind.
f)   You'll pass if you put your mind to it.
g)   Come on – make up your mind!
h)   Yes, I've got a lot on my mind at present.

2   Ask and answer these questions with a partner.

1   Do you find it hard to make up your mind when there's a choice?
2   Have you ever changed your mind about an important decision?
3   What do you do to take your mind off your work or studies?
4   Have you ever done anything that made your friends think you were out of your mind?
5   Would it be a good thing or a bad thing if we could read other people's minds?

Reading 1: multiple-choice questions (Part 2)

1   You are going to read an article about intelligence. First, discuss this question.

Is an intelligent person someone who:
- has a good memory?
- knows a lot of facts?
- is good at passing exams?
- understands new ideas quickly?
- is good at crosswords?
- gets on well with people?
- has a successful career?
- is imaginative and creative?
- knows how to get what they want?

2   Read the title and the first paragraph of the article. According to this article, what has playing computer games to do with intelligence?

3   Now read the whole article. Choose the answer (A, B, C or D) which you think fits best according to the text. Look back at the suggested procedure in Unit 4, page 44 if necessary.

KEEP PLAYING THAT

There used to be a general feeling that computer games were bad for you, and books were good. Now people are not so sure. Researchers have found that computer games,
5 television and the Internet have become key factors in boosting children's IQs up to levels never reached by past generations.
    The idea that intelligence can be measured was first suggested about a century ago, but at that time it was hard to find tests that gave useful results. Over the past two decades, however, tests have become more subtle and complex and researchers have
10 found that IQ scores can give a good indication of what children's future exam results will be. Some experts have even claimed that IQ scores can accurately predict what level of income and status young people will achieve in adult life.
    Why are today's youngsters doing so much better than their
15 grandparents? Of course, better nutrition, higher standards of living and improved education all play their part in raising general levels of intelligence. But there seems to be more to **it**   *line 17* than that. Scientists are attributing the change in intelligence levels to the complexity of modern life.
20   In today's fast-moving world, young people are required to interact constantly with electronic gadgets and equipment. Research has shown that they are constantly exposed to an increasingly complex and visual world – a world far more stimulating than previous generations lived in. This is developing
25 youngsters' brains in ways that older generations never experienced. Computers are one of the major sources of stimulation, and activities such as playing games and using the Internet seem to be particularly important.
    There are still some things that remain unexplained, however.
30 For example, the increase in children's IQ scores varies according to the type of intelligence being tested. It appears that nowadays people are better at abstract thinking than their ancestors were – but their verbal and mathematical abilities have

"Mum, Dad, good news!
My IQ test proved negative."

1   In the first paragraph, the writer says that computer games
    A have got much better recently.
    B are not as good for children as reading.
    C can improve the intelligence of young people.
    D are now used in many different ways by children.

2   According to the article, in the last twenty years IQ tests have become
    A a substitute for examinations.
    B more difficult than they were in the past.
    C a way of increasing young people's income.
    D more reliable than they used to be.

COMPUTER GAME?

35 remained the same as those of previous generations. No one knows why this is the case. Nevertheless, during the last few years there has certainly been a general upward trend, and it has been found that the present generation have IQs about 15 points above their parents.

40 Although this is clearly good news, the surging popularity of computer gaming and other activities has caused concern in some quarters, for two reasons. Firstly, there have been claims that the high levels of violence in the games could encourage children to be aggressive. There have also been fears that children could become 45 addicted to the games, and so be unable to stop playing them. But a recent study found no reliable evidence to prove that computer games contribute to long-term violence or anti-social behaviour.

Indeed, it has been claimed that, in moderation, 50 computer gaming is positively good for youngsters. It requires positive qualities such as perseverance, fast thinking and rapid learning. However, it seems that improvements in IQ may not last very long without continuing stimulation. The brain seems to be like a 55 muscle and requires repeated and vigorous exercise to stay fit and healthy. When it comes to IQ, it's a case of 'Use it or lose it'.

Others argue that computers have only limited value. They fear that young people who spend too much time 60 playing computer games alone will never learn to think independently. They claim that the danger with a computer is that doing repetitive tasks can actually reduce intelligence. In the end, computer games are no substitute for real-life 65 experience and for imagination.

3 'It' in line 17 refers to
  A the use of tests.
  B the effect of education.
  C the increase in intelligence.
  D the improvement in food standards.

4 What does the writer say about young people and electronic equipment nowadays?
  A They sometimes find the equipment confusing.
  B The equipment makes things too easy for them.
  C The equipment is an important part of their daily lives.
  D They depend on the equipment for their entertainment.

5 According to the writer, what remains unexplained about children's intelligence?
  A why levels of some types of intelligence have remained unchanged
  B why there has been such a rapid rise in general intelligence
  C how children can develop their verbal and mathematical skills
  D how the improvement in intelligence levels can be continued

6 Research indicates that violence in computer games
  A can sometimes be addictive for children.
  B may lead to aggressive behaviour in children.
  C can make some children nervous or afraid.
  D may have little effect on children.

7 Some people say that playing computer games encourages youngsters
  A to keep trying at difficult tasks.
  B to be creative in other areas.
  C to develop muscular control.
  D to make decisions on their own

4

1 Complete each sentence using the correct form of the word in capitals.

1 Intelligence tests can .... predict how much money people will earn in the future. **ACCURATE**
2 The .... of modern life can be stressful as well as stimulating. **COMPLEX**
3 The .... of computer games is likely to increase among older people. **POPULAR**
4 Violent computer games can make the people who play them very .... **AGGRESSION**
5 Computer games do not really stimulate people's .... **IMAGINE**
6 Fears that playing computer games can make you less intelligent are .... **GROUND**

2 Now say whether you agree with each statement or not.

5 If you would like to try some IQ puzzles to test your mental agility, turn to page 190.

Grammar 2: *it is, there is*

1

1 There are seven mistakes in the use of *it* and *there* in the following sentences. Find the mistakes and correct them.

Example: ~~It~~ *There* used to be a feeling that computers were bad for you.

1 There's going to be really hot tomorrow.
2 It's no need to hurry.
3 It's a pity that you can't come.
4 It once used to be a river here.
5 There was very crowded in the market.
6 It is said that fish is good for the brain.
7 It's no point in getting upset.
8 It's a long way to the town centre.
9 It is no charge for admission.
10 There's not worth worrying about.

2 Now complete the rules with *it* or *there*.

A We use .... to begin a sentence describing whether or not something exists. This is often followed by an indefinite noun (e.g. *a river*).

B We use .... to begin a sentence giving information about time, weather and distance.

C We use .... as the subject of a sentence to refer forwards to a clause with *that*, an infinitive or an *-ing* form.

▶ Grammar reference p.200

2

1 Complete the descriptions of three different games using *it* or *there*.

2 Then decide what game is being described. Use the jumbled letters in the box to help you.

A

This is a board game for two players. (1) .... is believed to have come from India originally. (2) .... is a board with 64 squares, and each player has 16 pieces, or 'men', to play with. (3) .... is said to be one of the most complicated games in the world. Nowadays (4) .... is possible to play the game against a computer.

B

This is a quick game and (1) .... is easy to play because (2) .... is no special equipment. (3) .... is played with two people, who use their hands to represent objects. (4) .... are three choices of object. The players have to make a movement with their hands simultaneously, and (5) .... is a system to decide who wins each time.

C

(1) .... is one in most daily newspapers, and many people are addicted to this game. (2) .... is a word game, in which you write the answer to questions in a pattern of numbered boxes. Sometimes (3) .... is a prize for the first person to send in the correct answers. (4) .... is claimed that this game keeps your brain active and helps to improve your vocabulary.

- DSROSROCW ZULEZP
- SHESC
- PPARE, SCSISROS, TSNOE

3 Discuss these questions.

1 What kind of board games do you enjoy playing?
2 What word games do you know?
3 Which games are you best at?

4 Write a short description of another game or puzzle, without giving the name. Then give it to another student and ask him/her to guess what the game is.

Vocabulary 2: education

1   Read the following text and choose the correct alternative in each sentence.

I really enjoyed my first experience of school. I went to the local (1) *primary / nursing* school where the (2) *classes / lessons* were small and the (3) *professors / teachers* were kind and friendly. At eleven I went to a secondary school and although I didn't enjoy studying all the (4) *subjects / topics* I did like learning languages and I loved learning to play the guitar. I got especially good (5) *points / marks* in music! My older brother tried to (6) *teach / learn* me everything I didn't understand in Maths, and he spent a lot of time (7) *revising / reviewing* with me before I (8) *took / made* my exams. It was due to his help that I (9) *succeeded / passed* my final exams and I didn't have to (10) *retake / remake* them. Now I'm at university and I'm enjoying the (11) *course / study* very much. I'm (12) *following / studying* Sociology.

2   Think about your own experiences of education, either now or in the past, and discuss these topics:

- similarities with or differences from the description in Exercise 1
- your most/least favourite subjects
- your experiences of examinations
- how much you enjoyed/are enjoying your education

3

1 Read the following extracts from a college handbook. The words in italics are in the wrong place. Decide where they should go.

Archaeology

This is one of the most popular degree
(1) *lectures* at the university. The three-year course is made up of a variety of short (2) *field trips*, covering different subject areas. There are formal (3) *courses* as well as group (4) *examinations*, and the course also includes (5) *modules* for practical research away from the university. There are practical and theoretical (6) *seminars* taken at the end of the final year that students must pass.

Graphic Design

This is a rapidly growing course with a very
(1) *projects* approach. After the first two years of
(2) *placement* taught in the university, students do a year's (3) *coursework* working with a company before returning to the university for the final year. Students will need to have their own computer for this course, as some of the work involves doing special (4) *continuous assessment* which need to be submitted electronically. A system of
(5) *practical* is used and there are no final examinations.

2 Which of the two courses above would you prefer to take? Why?

4

1 Read the following sentences and match the highlighted phrasal verbs to their meanings.

1 I can't work these figures out in my head!   *e)*
2 I was so nervous that I couldn't take in what he was saying.
3 He catches on to new ideas very quickly.
4 He's good at getting complex ideas across.
5 She couldn't get down to her homework.
6 She picks up languages very easily.

a) begin to understand
b) concentrate on something
c) explain something to someone
d) learn something without trying
e) calculate something
f) understand something you listen to or read

2 Work with a partner and ask each other questions using the verbs above.

Example: *Can you work out Maths problems in your head?*

5   What do you think is the main purpose of going to school? Is it:

- to learn facts?
- to pass exams?
- to learn how to get on with other people and develop social skills?
- to learn skills that help with real life?

Reading 2: multiple matching (Part 1)

1   You are going to read an extract from a book about how to learn effectively. First, look at the advice below on how to study and discuss these questions.

1   Which of these pieces of advice do you follow when you study?

2   What other advice would you give?

- Set aside specific times for studying.
- Make sure your work place is tidy before you begin.
- Give yourself regular short breaks as you work.
- Make sure all other business is done before you settle down.
- Have a light snack if you need one to keep your energy up.

2   Read the title of the extract, then read through the text quickly.

1   How much of the advice in Exercise 1 does this student follow? Why does this advice not work for him?

2   In what ways, if any, does this student sound like you?

3   Read the text again and choose the most suitable heading from the list A–H for each part (1–6) of the text. There is one extra heading which you do not need to use. There is an example at the beginning (0).

A   Reasons to be optimistic

B   An interruption resisted

C   Earlier than intended

D   A final attempt

E   A social commitment

F   Well worth reading

G   Bigger and better

H   A tidy workspace

101

0	H

The Six-o'clock-In-The-Evening-Enthusiastic-Determined-And-Well-Intentioned-Studier-Until-Midnight is a person with whom you are probably already familiar. At 6 o'clock he approaches his desk, and carefully organises everything in preparation for the study period to follow. Having everything in place, he carefully adjusts each item again, giving himself time to complete the first excuse: he recalls that in the morning he did not have quite enough time to read all items of interest in the newspaper. He also realises that if he is going to study it is best to have such small items completely out of the way before settling down to the task at hand.

1	

He therefore leaves his desk, browses through the newspaper and notices as he browses that there are more articles of interest than he had originally thought. He also notices, as he leafs through the pages, the entertainment section. At this point it will seem like a good idea to plan for the evening's first break – perhaps an interesting half-hour programme between 8 and 8.30 p.m.

2	

He finds the programme and it inevitably starts at about 7.00 p.m. At this point, he thinks, 'Well, I've had a difficult day and it's not too long before the programme starts, and I need a rest anyway and the relaxation will really help me to get down to studying …' He returns to his desk at 7.45, because the beginning of the next programme was also a bit more interesting than he thought it would be.

3	

At this stage, he still hovers over his desk tapping his book reassuringly as he remembers that phone call to a friend which, like the articles of interest in the newspapers, is best cleared out of the way before the serious studying begins. The phone call, of course, is much more interesting and longer than originally planned, but eventually the intrepid student finds himself back at his desk at about 8.30 p.m.

ways to
avoid studying

4

At this point in the proceedings he actually sits down at the desk, opens the book with a display of physical
40 determination, and starts to read (usually page one) as he experiences the first pangs of hunger and thirst. This is disastrous because he realises that the longer he waits to satisfy the pangs, the worse they will get, and the more interrupted his study concentration will
45 be. The obvious and only solution is a light snack. This, in its preparation, grows as more and more tasty items are piled on the plate. The snack becomes a feast.

5

Having removed this final obstacle the desk is returned to with the certain knowledge that this time there is
50 nothing that could possibly interfere with the following period of study. The first couple of sentences on page one are looked at again … as the student realises that his stomach is feeling decidedly heavy and a general drowsiness seems to have set in. Far better at this
55 juncture to watch that other interesting half-hour programme at 10 o'clock after which the digestion will be mostly completed and the rest will enable him to really get down to the task in hand.

6

At 12 o'clock we find him asleep in front of the TV.
60 Even at this point, when he has been woken up by whoever comes into the room, he will think that things have not gone too badly, for after all he has had a good rest, a good meal, watched some interesting and relaxing programmes, fulfilled his
65 social commitments to his friends, digested the day's information, and got everything completely out of the way so that
70 tomorrow, at 6 o'clock …

*From USE YOUR HEAD
by Tony Buzan*

4   There is a mistake in each highlighted expression in the following sentences. Correct the mistakes. Look back at the text to check your answers.

1 I try to give myself room to finish my work properly rather than rushing through it.
2 I try to plan for an interval about halfway through my period of study.
3 It's easy to leaf among the pages of a textbook quickly without reading it properly.
4 I find that drinking coffee can help me come down to studying.
5 Eating enough before you start can undo an obstacle to studying.
6 Noise in the street outside my room can interfere to my concentration.
7 Sometimes I have to force myself to get down to the task by hand.
8 It's a good idea to digest your social commitments before you start studying.

5   Work with a partner. Make a list of your seven best ways to avoid studying. Then compare with the rest of the class. What are the most popular ways?

6   What do you think are the five most important characteristics that make an ideal student?

125

Exam focus

Paper 5 Speaking: collaborative task/discussion (Parts 3 and 4)

About the exam: In Part 3 of the Speaking test, you and your partner discuss a situation or task outlined by the examiner. You are given some pictures to base your discussion on. In Part 4, you have a conversation with your partner and the examiner which extends the topic of Part 3.

Procedure

1 Listen carefully to the instructions for Part 3. If you don't understand exactly what you have to do, ask the examiner to repeat them.
2 Discuss the visuals with your partner, and finally come to a conclusion together. You have to talk for three minutes, so you need to discuss at least some in detail. You don't have to agree.
3 In Part 4, try to initiate discussion as well as answering the examiner's questions.

DO respond to what your partner says and ask him/her questions.
DON'T try to dominate or interrupt your partner in an abrupt way.

1　You will hear two students doing a Part 3 task.

1 Look at the pictures on page 186 and listen to the examiner's instructions. What two things do the students have to do?

2 Now listen to the students, Agna and Martin, doing part of the task. Which student:

1 interacted well with his/her partner?
2 had the best range of vocabulary and grammar?

2　Work in groups of three.

1 You are going to role-play Parts 3 and 4.

Student A: You are the examiner. Turn to page 184 and tell the candidates what to do.

Students B and C: You are the candidates. Turn to page 186 and follow the examiner's instructions.

2 When you have finished, form new groups and change roles.

3　Now discuss the activity. How well did the candidates follow the suggested procedure?

Writing: article

1　Read this task and underline key words. Then answer the questions below.

Your college magazine is producing a special edition on education. Students have been asked to write articles on the following topic:

How do you learn best? Tell us about your favourite ways of studying, and the things that help you to learn.

Write your **article** in **120–180** words.

1 Who are you writing this article for?
2 What style should you use?
3 How many things do you have to write about?
4 Are you giving general facts or personal information?

2　Plan your article. You can look back at Unit 8 page 102 for help with planning.

3　Look at the sentences that students have written. Find and correct the mistakes.

1 I find that it helps a lot to vary a way that I study because then I no get boring.

2 I prefer to study with other peoples, rather than to studying alone, because it's more motivating.

3 When we are discuss ideas together, they are easier to remember but I always need to write them down.

4 If I am study something difficult, I like to have music playing as it helps me to feel relax.

5 We aren't need to write our compositions on computer, but if I do this I find it easier to see my mistake and correct to them.

4　Now write your article. When you have finished, check your work.

Writing reference pp. 206, 211

1 There is a mistake with vocabulary in each of the following sentences. Find the mistakes and correct them.

1 The battery of my mobile phone needs refilling.
2 The two stars were upset at being snapped by journalism during their honeymoon.
3 I need to do an urgent phone call.
4 She claims she never says lies.
5 You shouldn't speak bad things about people in your family.
6 It doesn't matter how you look like here.
7 Several people dropped out the project before the end.
8 The shop sells microwaves, toasters and other types of kitchen equipments.
9 The school has excellent facility, including a swimming pool and computer centre.
10 The design of the new library is spectacle.
11 Lucy carried an interesting experiment.
12 My grandmother was always very supporting of me, and helped me a lot.
13 I don't feel confidence about making a speech.
14 I can't make my mind what to wear tonight.
15 Scientists can be rather unaccurate in their predictions.

2 In each of the following sentences there is an extra word which should not be there. Cross it out.

1 That must to be a photograph of my grandmother when she was young.
2 You could try with looking on the Internet.
3 Ben might have been gone abroad in 2003.
4 Once personal computers they had been developed, their use spread quickly.
5 It's likely that you will have be offered a job.
6 I've found the book you left it in my house.
7 The village where I used to live in has changed a lot.
8 If I will have a headache, I take an aspirin.
9 If she would have take the car, we would be able to get there more quickly.
10 You won't make me to change my mind.
11 It's high time Benjy has had his dinner.
12 When we were young, we were used to go to bed at seven o'clock.
13 I have two brothers, which both older.
14 Surely you needn't to go just yet?
15 It's necessary for to check his work carefully.

Use of English: multiple choice cloze (Part 1)

3 For questions 1–15, read the text below and decide which answer (A, B, C or D) best fits each space. There is an example at the beginning (0).

A MODERN ROMANCE

I 'met' Christie early one Friday evening in an Internet **(0)** ....*B*...... room. She was American, and I was completely **(1)** .... by her. We began emailing each other immediately. The first few days of our **(2)** .... were wonderful, and although it felt **(3)** .... we already knew each other, there were still lots of things to **(4)** ....

As the days became weeks, I realised I was **(5)** .... in love with her. Soon we found that we were spending a **(6)** .... on phone bills, and so we decided that we had to meet. She was at college and couldn't **(7)** .... to come to England, so I flew out to New York. It was incredibly romantic. As I walked into the arrivals **(8)** .... at Kennedy Airport our eyes **(9)** .... , and even though we had never exchanged photographs we immediately **(10)** .... each other.

We just talked and talked for a week. Our relationship felt perfect, but we both knew that if it was going to **(11)** .... , one of us would need to **(12)** .... the idea of moving to the other **(13)** .... of the world. In the end, we tearfully decided that it was not possible, and we **(14)** .... We still write and talk on the phone from time to time, and I think **(15)** .... Christie as one of my dearest friends.

0	**A** talk	**B** chat	**C** speak	**D** tell
1	**A** secured	**B** caught	**C** held	**D** charmed
2	**A** link	**B** delivery	**C** connection	**D** correspondence
3	**A** as though	**B** in case	**C** if only	**D** such that
4	**A** make out	**B** look in	**C** find out	**D** take on
5	**A** dropping	**B** falling	**C** going	**D** slipping
6	**A** quantity	**B** treasure	**C** fortune	**D** sum
7	**A** afford	**B** spare	**C** spend	**D** account
8	**A** department	**B** room	**C** foyer	**D** lounge
9	**A** met	**B** touched	**C** joined	**D** contacted
10	**A** recollected	**B** recognised	**C** revealed	**D** recalled
11	**A** operate	**B** run	**C** work	**D** perform
12	**A** accept	**B** receive	**C** take	**D** agree
13	**A** surface	**B** section	**C** part	**D** side
14	**A** broke up	**B** cut down	**C** put off	**D** went out
15	**A** on	**B** to	**C** of	**D** for

Use of English: open cloze (Part 2)

4 For questions 16–30, read the text below and think of the word which best fits each space. Use only one word in each space. There is an example at the beginning (0).

SAFE AT HOME

Most people are concerned about (0) ...*what*... their houses look like – but maybe they should be more worried about how safe they are. Every year, over two million people in England injure (16) .... at home.

Injuries are often caused (17) .... falls on the staircase. But every room in the house has (18) .... own special dangers. Accidents may happen in bedrooms if people climb up (19) .... reach a high shelf, or fall (20) .... things on the floor. Shoes, (21) .... particular, seem to cause a lot of injuries. In the bathroom, faulty electrical wiring or a tube of toothpaste left lying on the floor could cause you or (22) .... else in your family to end (23) .... in hospital. Your living room may seem a safe place, but last year more (24) .... 35,000 people needed hospital treatment after accidents involving chairs and sofas. Toys also cause injuries not (25) .... to children but to all age groups. However, (26) .... most dangerous place in the house seems to be the kitchen, (27) .... to the presence there of sharp knives and hot liquids, as (28) .... as electrical equipment.

Even outside the house (29) .... are dangers. In the garden you may be bitten by insects or fall from a ladder. Garden equipment such (30) .... spades can be especially dangerous. But nearly all these accidents can be avoided with just a little care.

Use of English: key word transformations (Part 3)

5 For questions 31–40, complete the second sentence so that it has a similar meaning to the first sentence, using the word given. Do not change the word given. You must use between two and five words, including the word given. There is an example at the beginning (0).

Example:

0 You must do exactly as I tell you.
  carry
  You must ...*carry out my*... instructions exactly.

31 You should make an effort to stop smoking.
  up
  You should try .... smoking.

32 He was very impressed by the biography.
  impression
  The biography .... him.

33 Edward has the ability to succeed in his exams.
  capable
  Edward .... in his exams.

34 I would really like to be able to play the piano.
  wish
  I .... play the piano.

35 The number of people studying information technology has increased sharply.
  rise
  There has .... the number of people studying information technology.

36 She learns new things very quickly.
  catches
  She .... new things very quickly.

37 You answered all the questions so I'm sure you passed the exam.
  must
  You answered all the questions so .... the exam.

38 Writing a letter is not necessary in this case.
  need
  You .... write a letter in this case.

39 I hated my new school at first, though now it's not so bad.
  getting
  I hated my new school at first, though I .... now.

40 It was Julia Roberts who wore that dress.
  by
  That dress .... Julia Roberts.

Use of English: error correction (Part 4)

6   For questions 41–55, read the text below and look carefully at each line. Some of the lines are correct, and some have a word which should not be there. If a line is correct, put a tick (✓) at the end of the line. If a line has a word which should not be there, write the word at the end of the line. There are two examples at the beginning (0 and 00).

THE INTERNET – FRIEND OR ENEMY?

0	There has never been exist anything like the Internet in the	*exist*
00	history of the world, but it is not without its dangers. After	✓
41	all this, when you log on to the Internet you are linking up to	
42	a vast network of computers which is extends all over the	
43	world. The Internet doesn't belong to any single only person,	
44	organisation or government, and controlling it is not easy.	
45	Millions of people use it, and some may use it in the wrong way.	
46	There are three main problems which to watch out for. The first	
47	is people who they pretend to be someone else. The second is	
48	unsuitable material, and the last is by dishonest on-line shops.	
49	But the Internet also offers its users a huge benefits. You can	
50	find out information about anything in the world, in just a few	
51	seconds. You can watch part of an old movie, or enjoy to hearing	
52	a new song by your favourite group. If you are aware of the	
53	possible dangers and use it carefully, the Internet is a one	
54	wonderful opportunity to learn about and be entertained, and to	
55	communicate with such people from other countries and cultures.	

Use of English: word formation (Part 5)

7   For questions 56–65, read the text below. Use the word given in capitals at the end of each line to form a word that fits in the space in the same line. There is an example at the beginning (0).

HOW TO BOOST YOUR BRAIN POWER

Many people would like to know how to improve their (0) *intelligence* .   **INTELLIGENT**
Here are some (56) .... ideas to help you do this without too much   **PRACTICE**
(57) .... First of all, try to eat more fish! You can do this quite   **DIFFICULT**
(58) .... and it is supposed to be very good for the brain. Eating   **EASY**
vegetables is also said to keep brain cells (59) .... Another idea   **HEALTH**
is to take up something (60) .... such as drawing, which uses the   **ART**
(61) .... part of your brain. If you've left school, you can still   **CREATE**
find various (62) .... to stimulate your brain. Why not give some   **ACTIVE**
(63) .... to joining an evening class? And if you decide to learn a   **THINK**
foreign language, try to use new and (64) .... ways of recording   **USUAL**
vocabulary, to help you to (65) .... the new words and expressions   **MEMORY**
you meet in class.

Speaking 1

1 The quiz below aims to help people decide what sort of work might be suitable for them. Do the quiz with a partner.

2

1 Work out your score.

A = 5 marks
B = 10 marks
C = 15 marks

2 Now look at page 190. Do you agree with the results?

3 Decide with your partner which of the jobs below would be best for you. Think about:

• what the job involves
• what qualities are needed for the job.

architect   director
doctor   fire fighter
illustrator   interior designer
nurse   vet   politician
Press Officer   actor
Public Relations (PR)
sales assistant   sports coach
writer   marketing executive
magazine editor   teacher

PERSONALITY QUIZ

☆ Are you a 'people person'? ☆

1 You have just joined a Keep Fit class. Do you:

A stand at the back and avoid everyone's gaze?
B stand in the middle and say hello to the person next to you?
C join the big group at the front and start chatting?

2 You've been invited to a party but your best friend can't go. Do you:

A stay at home? There's no way you're going without them.
B call the person down the street who you've been meaning to make friends with and ask if they want to go with you?
C go to the party on your own – it'll be fun meeting new people!

☆ Are you a leader or a team player? ☆

3 You've been asked to look after your six younger cousins. Do you:

A refuse?
B agree unwillingly and send them to bed immediately so you can watch a video?
C arrive early with a pile of toys and games to play with them?

4 You are working in a coffee bar on Saturdays and the manager is off sick. Do you:

A wait for one of the others to tell you what to do?
B make a list of the jobs to be done and share them out fairly between you?
C tell the others to do the work while you think up new ways to improve business?

☆ How do you feel about change? ☆

5 You and your friends are planning a holiday. What's your idea of fun?

A camping out in a local camping area
B two weeks by the sea with lots of nightlife
C a round-the-world ticket for three months

6 Which of the following phrases best describes you?

A You love just being at home.
B You want to try new things but thinking about it can be a bit scary.
C You're hungry for adventure. You're not afraid to try anything!

☆ What motivates you? ☆

7 Which of these things would you find the most satisfying?

A shopping for designer clothes
B a bike ride on a sunny day
C painting a mural on your bedroom wall

Exam focus

Paper 4 Listening: multiple matching (Part 3)

About the exam: In Paper 4, Part 3, you hear five short related extracts. They may be about the same situation or about the same topic. You have to match five sentences or phrases to the extracts. There is an extra sentence which does not match any of the extracts. You hear all the extracts twice.

Procedure

1 Read the rubric, which tells you the general topic of the extracts. You will also hear the rubric in the recording.
2 Read the sentences or phrases and underline key words.
3 When you hear the extracts the first time, listen for phrases with a similar meaning to the key words. Remember that the actual words in the recording will probably be different.
4 When you listen the second time, check your answers and match any items you didn't get the first time.

> **TIP!** If you change one of your answers the second time you listen, remember that this may affect your other answers as well.

1 You will hear five people talking about what it's like to live and work in a big city.

🎧 **1** Choose from the list A–F what each speaker says about his or her job. Use the letters only once. There is one extra letter which you do not need to use.

A It's easy to travel around the city I live in.
B People in my job can get free entertainment.
C Living in the middle of the city is convenient for me.
D I wish I could meet a bigger variety of people.
E I feel safe in the city at night.
F I don't manage to save any money.

Speaker 1   **1**
Speaker 2   **2**
Speaker 3   **3**
Speaker 4   **4**
Speaker 5   **5**

🎧 **2** Listen again to check.

2 You heard the following statements (1–7) in the recording. With a partner, take turns to read a statement aloud and choose the best response from a)–g) below.

1 My flat's only five minutes' walk from the office.
2 I still get a real buzz out of my job.
3 Another perk is the travel.
4 I have to commute to work every day.
5 I'm under a lot of pressure at work.
6 I meet people from all walks of life.
7 It's a 24-hour-a-day city.

a) I'd love to go to different places as part of my job.
b) You must find it really interesting talking to them.
c) So you don't have to spend anything on transport.
d) Maybe you should look for an easier job.
e) So there's always something to do.
f) So you haven't started to get bored with it?
g) You must be tired out before you even start!

3

1 Choose two of the people from the recording and complete the notes.

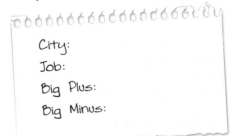

City:
Job:
Big Plus:
Big Minus:

2 Compare your notes. Who do you think has the best and worst job and lifestyle?

4 Discuss these questions.

1 Would you be interested in doing any of the jobs described in the recording?
2 Would you go to another city or country to work? Why?/Why not?

Vocabulary 1: employment

1

1 Read the advice on how to find a job in the UK and put the sentences in the correct order.

HOW TO FIND A JOB

☐ You should enclose an up-to-date Curriculum Vitae (resumé) with your letter.

☐ If you decide you want to apply, write a letter of application or phone for an application form.

[1] Look at jobs advertised in the newspaper, your local Job Centre or on the Internet.

☐ Once you get an interview it's up to you!

☐ Make sure it includes details of your qualifications, any previous work experience and the names of two referees.

☐ Send off your letter or application form and wait to see if you are invited for an interview.

2 Discuss these questions.

1 Do you apply for jobs in the same way in your country? What differences are there?

2 What kind of things can you do to make a good impression at a job interview? What things should you avoid doing?

3 Describe an interview you have attended. Were you successful?

2 What do you look for in a job? Read the list and add more ideas of your own. Then rank the ideas in order of importance for you.

☐ location
☐ opportunities to travel
☐ flexible working hours
☐ long holidays
☐ benefits (e.g. free travel)
☐ good salary
☐ good prospects for promotion

3 Discuss the following questions.

1 What do you think is a good weekly *wage* or annual *salary* in your country?

2 What are the *best paid* jobs in your country? Do you think it's right that they are so highly paid?

3 For what reasons can people *get the sack* or be *made redundant*?

4 What would make you *resign from* a job?

5 What *benefits* can people get from the government if they are *unemployed* in your country?

6 At what age do men and women *retire* in your country? Do they get a *state pension*?

7 Do you think most people look forward to retiring? What are the advantages and disadvantages of being *a pensioner*?

Grammar 1: ability and possibility

1 Look at the first part of an extract from an online magazine. What is the discussion topic?

 You said it!

Opinions about Working Students

People disagree on this topic. What do you think about students working part-time when they are at high school or college? Here's what some readers have said.

I support the idea that students can work, but not that they should work. It should be up to them.
Rudy Chen, Taiwan

There is no denying that working while they are still in school provides students with a chance to learn something that they can't get from formal schooling, like social experience.
Andrew Ie, Taiwan

You can't do two things at the same time – or if you are able to, you won't have a good quality of life.
Fernando Ant. Vega Guillen, Costa Rica

Students have to study hard to enter the college or university that they want to attend. If they work after school, they may not be able to concentrate on their studies.
Daeho-Choi, Korea

For economic reasons, many parents can't support their children at university or college. So by working part-time students can help their parents with their burden. At the same time they can learn to be independent, which will help them in the future.
Ahmad Faiz, Malaysia

2

1 Now read the comments. Who is in favour of students working part-time? Who is against? What reasons do they give? Make notes.

```
FOR
students can learn something
they can't get from school
AGAINST
```

2 Who do you agree with?

3

1 Complete the text below using four of the phrases given.

can   shouldn't be able to   have to be able to
have been able to   should be able to   can't

I honestly think that if teenagers
(1) .... handle working part-time
and attending school, then they
(2) .... make that choice
themselves. Parents (3) ....
provide for their kids all their life, so in order
for teens to feel responsible, they
(4) .... provide for themselves.

2 Write a similar paragraph giving your opinion in 30–50 words.

4   Choose the correct alternatives in these sentences. Both alternatives may be possible.

1 I *don't know how to / can't* type, but it would be useful if I *can / could*.
2 If I don't get a job soon, I *can't / won't be able to* pay the rent.
3 I *could swim / was able to swim* by the time I was three.
4 My sister's *succeeded in getting / managed to get* a job with an international company.
5 Our final assignment was hard, but I *managed to / could* hand it in last week.
6 I'm sorry I *couldn't / wasn't able to* come to your party.
7 I *could become / could have become* a professional football player but I went to college instead.

8 I *couldn't have helped / can't have helped* you even if I'd wanted to.
9 It *is able to / can* rain in August, though it doesn't happen often.
10 My old boss *could / managed to* be very bad-tempered.

▶ Grammar reference p.200 (14.1)

5

1 Look at this list of skills. Say if you can do these things, when you learned how to do them, how well you can do them now and how useful they are. If you can't do them, say if you'd like to be able to, and how they would be useful.

- cook   • touch type
- swim   • speak another language

2 Do you think everyone should learn these skills? Why?/Why not? Are there any other skills you think everyone should learn?

6   Complete the second sentence so that it has a similar meaning to the first sentence, using the word given. Do not change the word given. You must use between two and five words.

1 At school, Jane was the best swimmer in her class. **swim**
   At school, Jane .... anyone else in her class.
2 Do you think you will manage to find the way? **able**
   Do you think .... find the way?
3 You didn't help me, even though you had the chance. **have**
   You .... but you didn't.
4 I wish my spoken English was better. **speak**
   I wish .... English better.
5 I thought I would get the job, but someone else got it instead. **succeed**
   I .... the job.
6 Peter was often quite unpredictable. **be**
   Peter .... quite unpredictable.
7 I knew how to drive by the time I was 17. **to**
   I .... by the time I was 17.
8 Unfortunately, I missed the train. **manage**
   Unfortunately, I did not .... the train.

Reading: multiple matching (Part 1)

1   You are going to read an article about a man called Nick Leeson, who was sent to prison. Look at the title and subheading of the text and the photos.

1   Can you guess what Nick Leeson's job was?
2   What crime do you think he committed?

2   Read through the text quickly and check your answers to Exercise 1.

3   Read the text again and choose the most suitable heading from the list A–H for each part (1–6) of the article. There is one extra heading which you do not need to use. There is an example at the beginning (0).

> **A** An accusation of incompetence
> **B** Running from justice
> **C** A problem doubled
> **D** Hiding a missing fortune
> **E** The end of an institution
> **F** Pushed to achieve more
> **G** Finding out the truth
> **H** Right place, right time

4   Do you think that Nick Leeson deserved his punishment? Why?/Why not?

5   Complete the highlighted phrases in these sentences by adding an appropriate verb. The phrases are all in the text.

1   Nick tried to .... himself out of the mess he'd made, but he couldn't.
2   Sharon believes she can .... a name for herself as a writer.
3   Starting as an office boy, my father managed to .... his way up to the top.
4   The police might .... out a spot check on driving licences at any time.
5   Everything went well for Jake at first, then his luck started to .... out.
6   I have to think of my family – I don't want my marriage to .... down.
7   If unemployment rises, public feeling will .... against the government.
8   The money he owes could .... to more than a million dollars.

The man who brought down a bank

Everything seemed to be going right for Nick Leeson – until he made a gamble that didn't work out.

0	**H**

Nick Leeson came from a poor family in Watford, a small town in southern England. His mother encouraged him to work hard, and was delighted when he managed to get a banking job in London. It was the 1980s, and the world of high finance was doing well. For an ambitious young man like Leeson, the City of London was the place to be. He worked his way up, and quickly made a name for himself as a trader, specialising in buying and selling foreign currency. He was then taken on by Barings Bank, one of the most respected banks in London.

1	

Not long afterwards, Nick went to work for the bank's branch in Singapore, and soon he was Barings' star trader there, making huge profits through his currency deals. By 1993, a year after his arrival in Asia, Leeson had made more than £10 m – about 10% of Barings' total profit for that year. Leeson says the working philosophy at Barings was simple: 'We were all driven to make profits, profits, and more profits.' That year he earned a large bonus of £130,000 in addition to his salary of £50,000. He and his young wife Lisa enjoyed the life of luxury that the money brought. It was a long way from his working-class origins.

2	

Then, in 1994, his luck began to run out. The markets turned against him and he started to lose money. His losses became heavier when a serious earthquake in Japan affected financial markets all over the world. By autumn that year, Leeson had lost £208 m. It was a huge sum of money, but no one realised it was missing. He concealed the losses in a secret account called Error Account 88888, which no one knew about. In an attempt to solve the problem, he asked for and was given extra money to continue his trading activities. As he attempted to get himself out of the financial mess, he made increasingly risky financial deals.

Grammar 2: conditionals (2)

Mixed conditionals

1 Read the following sentences. Which parts of the sentence refer to past time and which to present time?

1 If Nick Leeson hadn't lost £800 m,   *past*
   ... he might still be married to Lisa.   (a)......
   ... Barings Bank could still be in operation. (b)......
   ... he wouldn't have had to go to prison.   (c)......

2 If Nick wasn't such an ambitious person,   (d)......
   ... he wouldn't have taken so many risks.   (e)......
   ... he might not have got into trouble.   (f)......
   ... his life now might be very different.   (g)......

▶ Grammar reference p.195 (5.7)

2

1 Choose the correct ending for each sentence.

1 If she only started the job last year,
2 If I needed money,
3 If they haven't spent all their money,
4 If you don't want to be paid by cheque,
5 If we hadn't spent all that money last year,
6 If she's going to invest in that company,
7 If she hadn't given us all that extra work,

a) they'll be able to get a taxi home.
b) we'd be able to go on holiday now.
c) she probably isn't earning much.
d) you should have told us earlier.
e) we'd have finished by the end of this week.
f) he was always ready to lend me some.
g) she needs to check they're making a profit.

2 Now decide which time (past, present or future) each part of the sentence refers to.

3

1 Complete the following sentences using the correct form of the verbs in brackets.

Example:
   If I .had trained.. (train) as a nurse,
   I .could be working. (work) in a hospital instead of an office now.

3

The end came suddenly. Made suspicious by Leeson's requests for even more money, his bosses carried out a
40 spot check in February 1995. They discovered that Leeson's losses now amounted to more than £800 m, which was more than the value of the bank. How could they have missed such massive losses?

4

Events moved fast once the full scale of the losses
45 was known. When Leeson realised he was going to be discovered, he and his wife went on the run, first to Borneo, then to Frankfurt. Realising the seriousness of his position, he desperately wanted to get back to Britain. However, he was arrested in Germany and
50 sent back to Singapore, where he was charged with fraud. He pleaded guilty, and was sentenced to six and a half years in prison in Singapore. During his imprisonment, his personal problems continued. He became ill and had to have major surgery. His
55 marriage broke down and Lisa remarried.

5

It may have been a personal disaster for Leeson – but it was an even greater disaster for the bank. A few days after Leeson's arrest, Barings, the UK's oldest merchant bank, finally collapsed. It was bought for
60 just £1 by the Dutch bank ING. Dozens of executives who were involved in the failure to control Leeson resigned or were sacked.

6

Leeson himself has claimed that he was not the only one to blame, and after his conviction, he wrote
65 *Rogue Trader*, a book in which he condemned the practices that allowed him to trade with such large amounts of money without any proper checks. His tale remains one of the great disaster stories of the financial world.

1 If I .... (*not/spend*) so much money on clothes last month, I .... (*be able to*) go on holiday.

2 I .... (*be*) much fitter if I .... (*join*) that Keep Fit class Ann told me about.

3 If I .... (*be*) more ambitious, I .... (*rise*) to Managing Director of the company by now.

4 If I .... (*not/be*) so shy, I .... (*ask*) Chris out for a date last weekend.

2 Think of your own life. How would things be different now if the past had been different?

Conjunctions (alternatives to *if*)

4 Choose the correct conjunction in each of the following sentences.

1 You won't get promotion *provided that / unless* you work hard.

2 I'll pay for the meal *as long as / even if* I have enough cash on me.

3 Always keep your money in a money belt *if / in case* it gets stolen

4 I'll lend you the money *on condition that / even if* you pay me back in a month.

5 It's going to be a great day out, *unless / providing* it doesn't rain.

6 I'm pleased I got an interview, *even if / as long as* I don't get the job.

▶Grammar reference p.194 (5.1)

5 Complete the sentences using an appropriate conjunction from Exercise 4 and the correct form of the verbs in brackets. There may be more than one possibility.

1 I told him I wouldn't go with him .... he .... (*pay for*) the tickets.

2 I'll tell you a secret .... you .... (*promise*) not to tell anyone else.

3 I decided I was going to go abroad .... I .... (*have to*) borrow the money.

4 It's a good idea to leave a key with your neighbour .... you .... (*lock*) yourself out.

5 He agreed to take on the extra work, but only .... his salary .... (*raise*)

6 It's a good idea to take some cash with you .... the local shopkeepers .... (*not/accept*) credit cards.

6

1 Can you unjumble these tips?

1 Don't invest in shares unless you get robbed.

2 Never wear jeans to an interview if you are prepared to take risks.

3 Don't carry lots of cash around with you in case you trust them completely.

4 Never let anyone know your cashpoint PIN even if you want the job.

2 Have you got any more useful tips?

Vocabulary 2: numbers and money

1

1 Look at these examples from the text on page 134. Say the numbers aloud.

- *By 1993, Leeson had made more than £10 m – about 10% of Barings' total profit.*
- *That year he earned a large bonus of £130,000.*

2 Match the numbers to the descriptions on the right.

1	10%	a)	a date
2	€15,000	b)	a fraction
3	01783 64 57 38	c)	a time
4	45 kg	d)	a sum of money
5	25° C	e)	a speed
6	34 kph	f)	a weight
7	2¾	g)	an amount of liquid
8	0.75	h)	a telephone number
9	25 m	i)	a temperature
10	23.12.05	j)	a percentage
11	2 L	k)	a decimal
12	6.00 a.m.	l)	a distance

🎧 **3** Say the numbers above. Then listen to check.

🎧 **4** Listen to six extracts and write down only the numbers you hear, together with the correct symbols.

Example: *10 kg*

2

1 Read the following information and complete the text using words and phrases from the box.

current   cash points   cheques   commission
credit card   debit card   deposit   interest
foreign currency   overdraft   savings
statement   travellers cheques

 Our NOW current account offers students a range of special benefits.

■ You will have a (1) .... which you can use to pay bills or to withdraw money from our (2) .... at any time of the day or night.

■ You can also apply for our (3) .... which means you can buy now, and pay up to 56 days later.

■ We'll send you a (4) .... every month telling you how much money you've got in your account – or you can use our Internet banking service to view this online.

■ We know that students are often short of money, so we offer you an (5) .... of up to £1,500 free of charge.

■ Intending to travel abroad? We offer you (6) .... and (7) .... – and you don't even have to pay (8) .... charges.

■ You can use any high street bank or post office to cash your (9) .... and pay money into your (10) .... account.

 Saving up for something special?

With a (11) .... of only £250, you can open a (12) .... account and watch your money grow. (13) .... rates are at present 2–3% but these may vary – enquire at your local branch for details.

2 Discuss these questions.

1 Do you have a bank account? Which of the above facilities does it offer?

2 Are you satisfied with its services?

3 Which is the odd one out? Cross it out.

1 You can pay by *cheque / credit card / receipt*.

2 Waiter, could I have the *check / tip / bill*, please?

3 You can *gain / get / win* a lot of useful experience working abroad.

4 How much money do you expect to *gain / make / earn* in this job?

5 The *worth / price / value* of gold continues to rise.

6 I need to *ask for / take out / withdraw* a bank loan to *pay off / pay for / repay* my debts.

7 You can *change / convert / cash* your foreign currency here.

8 I'm afraid we can't *receive / accept / take* dollars, only local currency.

4 Complete the sentences with the correct preposition.

1 You shouldn't waste your money .... expensive holidays.

2 Banks don't like lending money .... small businesses.

3 You can change your euros .... dollars at any *Bureau de Change*.

4 It's a good idea to invest money .... stocks and shares.

5 Banks charge high interest rates when you borrow money .... them.

6 Why not leave some money .... charity in your will?

5 Read the following statements. Say if you agree/disagree on a scale of 1–5 (5 = strongly agree, 1 = strongly disagree).

1 Money is too important to people nowadays.

2 Everyone should give 5% of their income to charity.

3 You should never borrow or lend money.

4 Money should be saved not spent.

5 Credit cards should be banned.

Listening 2: multiple choice
(Part 4)

1 Think of three things that would make you happier than you are now. Then compare with a partner. Are your ideas similar or different?

2 You will hear a radio interview with a psychologist, Ed Stevens, who is researching what makes people happy.

1 Before you listen, read through the questions below and underline key words.

🎧 **2** Now listen and choose the best answer, A, B or C. Then listen again to check your answers.

1 Ed says that rich people
   A are not as happy as people who have less money.
   B generally want to be richer than they are already.
   C do not become much happier with even more money.

2 Ed claims that, compared to cooler countries, in some hot countries
   A the culture is more interesting.
   B the people are more positive.
   C there are fewer problems to worry about.

3 Ed says that in many cultures, having a good time is less important than
   A getting things you really want.
   B having a satisfying job.
   C having good health.

4 Ed suggests that in certain situations, feeling happy might make it difficult to
   A see danger coming.
   B cope with danger when you meet it.
   C recognise people who may be a danger to you.

5 According to Ed, the word 'happy'
   A has the same meaning in all cultures.
   B does not always have an exact translation.
   C is an easy word in some languages.

6 Ed suggests that one key to lasting happiness is
   A being a parent.
   B having a good marriage.
   C maintaining a positive attitude.

7 What advice does Ed give to listeners at the end of the interview?
   A Accept the level of happiness you have.
   B Try to be happier than you are.
   C Aim to help others to be happy.

3 Look back at the answers. Did anything you hear surprise you? How far do you agree with what Ed Stevens says?

Use of English: open cloze (Part 2)

Read the text below and think of the word which best fits each space. Use only one word in each space. There is an example at the beginning (0).

A PRECIOUS METAL

Throughout history, people have searched for gold. **(0)** ..*But*... this precious metal has not always been associated **(1)** .... happiness. For example, **(2)** .... the 1840s, thousands of people died in the USA looking for gold.

So **(3)** .... is gold so desirable? **(4)** .... from its market value, it has many different uses. Unlike other metals, it won't discolour and it can be shaped easily into beautiful jewellery. It also has some **(5)** .... practical uses than this. Televisions and video players have gold components inside, and **(6)** .... is even used in the instruments **(7)** .... enable astronauts to travel **(8)** .... space. And, of course, it can be used almost anywhere **(9)** .... of money.

For these reasons, gold remains **(10)** .... desirable now as it ever was. Even **(11)** .... gold prices have declined in recent years, the desire to find gold remains strong. But now the focus has changed and **(12)** .... huge leisure industry has developed around it. In the USA, for example, **(13)** .... men fought over gold more than a century **(14)** ...., families can now spend a happy and enjoyable day searching for the precious metal. It seems that for most people, gold still has **(15)** .... power to excite and thrill.

Exam focus

Paper 5 Speaking: a complete test

About the exam: In the exam, the person you will talk to is called an interlocutor. There will also be another examiner, who will just listen to you.

> **DO** speak clearly so that the interlocutor and the examiner can both hear you easily.

1 You are going to do a complete Paper 5 Speaking test. First, look at the areas on which you will be assessed in the exam. Which do you think are your strong points, and which are weak areas?

- grammar and vocabulary
- pronunciation
- how you organise what you say to make your points clear
- how you interact with your partner and react to what he/she says

2 Now listen to two candidates doing the Speaking test. Give them a grade for each category listed in Exercise 1:

poor / satisfactory / good

The photos for Part 2 appear below and the pictures for Part 3 appear on page 183.

3 Now work in groups of four and role-play the test using the same photos and pictures.

Student A: You are the interlocutor. Look at page 180 and tell the candidates what to do.
Student B: You are the examiner. Listen carefully to the two candidates and think about the different categories in Exercise 1. At the end, you can give each candidate feedback on their strong and weak points.
Students C and D: You are both candidates.

4 Now change roles so that Students A and B become the candidates.

Student C: You are the interlocutor. Look at page 185 and tell the candidates what to do.
Student D: You are the examiner. Listen carefully to the two candidates so you can give them feedback at the end.

A

B

C

D

Writing: letter of application

1 Look at the writing task and answer the questions below.

You see the following job advertisement in an international magazine.

International Adventure Course
Do you speak English?
Would you like to meet people from other countries?
We are looking for people of all ages to work on an international adventure course in Canada helping to organise sports and social activities for an international group of young people aged from 9–12.

| You need to be available for at least 4 weeks between July–September. Travel, food and accommodation costs will be covered. | If you are interested in applying, write telling us about yourself and saying why you think you would be a suitable person for the job. |

Write your **letter of application** in **120–180** words.

1 What does the job involve?
2 The task includes two parts. What are they?
3 The following things might all make an applicant a suitable person for the job. Which of them do you think would be **essential**? Tick them. What else would be essential?
 • able to speak English
 • interested in sports
 • experience of being with young people
 • interested in travel
 • enjoys being with people
 • comes from a big family
 • can sing and play the guitar
 • first aid qualification
 • clean driving licence

TIP! In the exam, you don't have to give true information.

2 Read the following letter. Do you think it's a good letter of application for the job advertised? Why?/Why not?

Dear Sir or Madam
I write about your advertisement in the newspaper for the International Adventure Course.
I'm the oldest of a family of five children and I've got lots of young cousins.
I'd really enjoy the chance to use my English in Canada and to work in the international environment.
I'm available between July 13 and September 20. I'm eighteen years old and live in Spain.
I just finished my secondary education and in October I'll be starting a university course in Business Administration. I've already studied English for six years.
I hope you'll write soon.
Yours faithfully

Antonia   (98 words)

3 Read the letter again and anwer these questions.

1 Does the letter begin and end appropriately? ✓
2 Does it include all the necessary information? ✗
3 Is the information organised into logical paragraphs?
4 Is the style appropriate?
5 Are there appropriate fixed phrases for a letter of application?
6 Is the spelling and punctuation accurate?
7 Is the grammar accurate?
8 Does it have the correct number of words?
9 Would the reader want to give Antonia an interview?

4 Work with a partner. Compare and explain your answers.

Example:
1 The letter begins 'Dear Sir or Madam' and ends 'Yours faithfully'. That's correct because we don't know who we're writing to.

▶ Writing reference p.212

5 Plan your own letter of application.

1 How many paragraphs will you write?
2 What information will go in each paragraph?

6 Write your letter in an appropriate formal style.

7 When you have finished, check your letter, using the points in Exercise 3.

1 There is a grammar mistake in each of the following sentences. Find the mistakes and correct them.

1 They could buy the computer if they'd had enough money.
2 I can't speak Spanish, but it would be useful if I managed to.
3 I was late for the train, but fortunately I could just catch it.
4 The weather is able to be bad in July and August.
5 If I hadn't bought that expensive hi-fi system, I will have enough money to go on holiday now.
6 You won't be promoted if you can convince the boss you deserve it.
7 It's going to be a good holiday, providing that it rains.
8 Even although he didn't like the present, he shouldn't have been so rude.
9 I am fitter if I didn't eat so much chocolate.
10 Bring some comfortable shoes provided that we have to do a lot of walking.

2 Complete these sentences giving true information. Then compare your answers with a partner.

1 I'll probably ... this weekend, providing ...
2 I always ... on Saturdays, unless ...
3 When I was younger, I felt frightened if ...
4 I never minded ... even if ...
5 I think it would be useful if I could ...
6 I would love to work in ... as long as ...

3 Choose the best alternative to complete the following sentences.

1 It's time those children were .... to bed.
   A made   **B** had   **C** gone   **D** sent
2 The old man's money was shared .... between his six children.
   A away   **B** out   **C** up   **D** on
3 The theft was discovered when the authorities .... out a spot check.
   A carried   **B** found   **C** counted   **D** worked
4 You needn't include .... of your primary education on a job application form.
   A facts   **B** details   **C** points   **D** items
5 I'm hoping to apply .... a job with an international company.
   A on   **B** to   **C** with   **D** for

6 The job offers a number of .... such as free travel and medical care.
   A prospects   **B** qualifications   **C** benefits   **D** experiences
7 The total bill for the repairs to the house .... to more than €10,000.
   A added   **B** amounted   **C** became   **D** totalled
8 It's believed that he owes the bank a considerable .... of money.
   A sum   **B** number   **C** lot   **D** value

4 Use the words given in capitals below the text to form a word that fits in the space in each line. There is an example at the beginning (0).

THE WORST JOB I'VE EVER DONE

When I was a **(0)** _student_. I once got a job in a factory that made car batteries. I hated it from the first moment! The smell inside the factory was **(1)** .... and the machinery made so much noise that it was **(2)** .... , so workers had to wear ear-plugs all the time to comply with safety **(3)** .... They were very **(4)** .... and I couldn't listen to music. On top of that, my job was terribly **(5)** .... I had to check that all the batteries had the company logo **(6)** .... stamped on them. I stared at the batteries so hard that after a while I couldn't see any **(7)** .... between them – they all looked the same, and my **(8)** .... started creating images of logos that weren't there. After four hours, I made a **(9)** .... I stood up, removed my ear-plugs and walked out, never to return. It was an absolutely **(10)** .... place to work in, and I never regretted giving up the job.

0 STUDY
1 DISGUST
2 DANGER
3 REGULATE
4 COMFORT
5 BORE
6 CLEAR
7 DIFFER
8 IMAGINE
9 DECIDE
10 POSSIBLE

UNIT
12 Strange but true

Reading 1

1 You are going to read an extract from the novel *Rebecca*. Look at the still from the film of the novel. Discuss where the people are and what they are doing.

2 Now read the extract to check your ideas. Then answer these questions.

1 Who is Maxim?
2 Who is the story told by?
3 Who is Rebecca?
4 What is the inquest trying to establish?

3 Read the text again and answer the following questions.

1 How does the narrator feel before she goes to the inquest? How do you know?
2 What has happened just before Maxim's wife goes into the courtroom?
3 How does the Coroner first suggest that Rebecca died?
4 What new evidence does James Tabb then give about the boat?
5 Who does the Coroner think might have been involved in Rebecca's death? How do you know?
6 How does Maxim's wife feel at the end? Why do you think she feels like this?

4 Discuss these questions

1 Do you think that Maxim murdered his wife?
2 What do you think might happen at the end of the book? (Turn to page 188 to check your ideas.)

1 ▶ The inquest was on the Tuesday afternoon at two o'clock. The weather had not broken yet. It was still hot, oppressive. The air was full of thunder, and there was rain behind the white, dull sky but it did not fall.

2 ▶ Lunch was a hurried, nervous meal. I did not want anything to eat. I could not swallow. None of us talked very much. It was a relief when the meal was over and I heard Maxim go out onto the drive and start the car. He seemed quite calm, but my hands were very cold, my heart beating in a funny, jerky way. When we arrived at the court, Frank and Maxim left me in the car and went in.

3 ▶ After a while I got out and started to pace up and down, and found myself outside the building where the inquest was being held. A policeman appeared.

'Excuse me, Madam,' he said, 'aren't you Mrs de Winter? Mr de Winter has just given his evidence. There's only one more to speak, Mr Tabb the boatman.'

'Then it's nearly over,' I said.

'I expect so, Madam,' he replied. Then he said on a sudden thought, 'Would you like to hear the remaining evidence? There is a seat there, just inside the door. If you slip in now, no one will notice you.'

'Yes,' I said. 'Yes, I think I will.'

4 ▶ The policeman opened a door at the end of the passage. I crept in and sat down. The room was smaller than I had imagined, rather hot and stuffy.

5 ▶ James Tabb was standing up, answering the Coroner's questions.

'Was the boat sea-worthy?'

'It was when I fixed it up in April last year.'

'Has the boat ever been known to capsize before?'

'No, sir, never.'

'I suppose great care was needed to handle the boat?'

'Well, sir, everyone has to be careful, sailing a boat. But this one was strong and well-built and Mrs de Winter had sailed her in worse weather than that night. I couldn't understand it sinking on a calm night like that.'

'We would not suggest that you were to blame. It seems that Mrs Rebecca de Winter was careless for a moment, the boat capsized, and she lost her life.'

6 ▶ 'Excuse me, sir, but there's more to it than that. I'd like to make a further statement. After the accident last year, some people said I had let Mrs de Winter use a damaged boat. It was very unfair, but the boat had sunk and there was nothing I could say to defend myself. Well, I went to examine it yesterday to satisfy myself that the work I had done was perfectly good. And it was.'

Tabb paused. 'But what I want to know is this. Who made the holes in the boat?'

I did not look at him. I looked at the floor. It was much too hot. Why didn't they open a window? We should all be suffocated if we sat here with the air like this. Why did the silence last so long?

'What do you mean? What holes?' The coroner's voice sounded very far away.

'There were three of them. Made with something sharp. Open to the sea. With those holes, it wouldn't take more than ten minutes for a small boat to sink. It's my opinion that the boat was sunk on purpose.'

I had to get out. There was no air in the place, and the person next to me was pressing close, close ... Maxim was standing up now but I must not look at him. The heat was coming up from the floor, rising in slow waves.

'Mr de Winter, you heard the statement from James Tabb. Do you know anything of these holes?'

'Nothing whatsoever.'

'It's the first time you've heard them mentioned?'

'Yes.'

'The boat was kept at the private harbour and any stranger trying to damage it would be seen?'

'Yes.'

'James Tabb has told us that a boat with those holes hammered in it probably could not float for more than ten minutes. So it could not have been damaged before Mrs de Winter took it out, or it would have sunk in the harbour before reaching the open sea.'

Maxim nodded.

'Therefore whoever took the boat out that night made the holes. You told us before that when the boat was found, the door and windows were fixed shut and your wife's body was slumped on the floor. Now we are given the information that there were holes in the boat made deliberately – does this not strike you as strange?'

Maxim nodded again.

'I must ask you a very personal question. Were you and your first wife happy?'

It was so hot, no open window, the door was further away than I had thought, and suddenly everything went dark.

Adapted from REBECCA by Daphne Du Maurier
inquest: *official inquiry into the causes of someone's death*
coroner: *someone whose job is to find out the causes of sudden or accidental deaths*

Writing 1: making your writing more interesting

1 In the text describing the inquest into Rebecca's death, the writer has used words and phrases connected with heat and difficulty in breathing to make us aware of how nervous Mrs de Winter is. Find these words in the text:

1 two adjectives describing the weather (section 1)
2 two adjectives describing the sky (1)
3 two adjectives describing the atmosphere in the courtroom (4)
4 a verb meaning *die through lack of air* (7)

2 The writer also uses other words and expressions to make the story more exciting and dramatic.

1 Find verbs in the text that mean:

1 walk nervously in one direction then back again (3)
2 entered the room quietly without being seen (4)
3 stopped for a moment (6)
4 made using a lot of force (8)
5 bent forwards (9)
6 make you suddenly realise something (9)

2 What do these phrases describe in the text?

1 *hurried and nervous*   ....
2 *beating in a funny, jerky way*   ....
3 *strong and well-built*   ....
4 *made with something sharp*   ....
5 *fixed shut*   ....

3

1 The verbs in the box have a general meaning. Match each one to a group of verbs below.

breathe   eat   hit   think   ~~walk~~   look

1 creep/pace/stroll   *walk*..
2 swallow/bite/chew   ....
3 imagine/wonder/believe   ....
4 hammer/knock/bang   ....
5 suffocate/pant/gasp   ....
6 peer/glance/stare   ....

2 How are the meanings of the verbs in each group different? When could you use them? Use your dictionary to help you.

4 Look at the next part of the story. Discuss more interesting and dramatic ways of expressing the ideas. Then rewrite the extract.

Maxim asked Frank to take me back home. Frank drove quickly. For the first time since I had known him, he didn't say anything. That meant that he was anxious. Usually he was a careful driver, stopping at every crossroads, blowing his horn at every corner. When we got to the house, he left me at the front door and drove away, saying that Maxim might need him. I went upstairs and lay down. I thought about what people might say. 'Why should he get off? He killed his wife. He will have to hang for it.'

Example:

Maxim begged Frank to take me back home immediately.

Vocabulary 1: crime and punishment

1

1 Work in three groups, A, B and C. In your groups, put the words below into the correct category.

the accused/defendant   arsonist   (release on) bail
blackmailer   burglar   capital punishment
community service   defence   corporal punishment
find innocent/guilty   fine   forger   hijacker
inquiry   judge   jury   kidnapper   lawyer
mugger   murderer   pickpocket   prison sentence
(put on) probation   prosecution   shoplifter
smuggler   suspended sentence   thief   trial
verdict   witness

Criminals

Law courts

Sentences and punishments

2 Each group should choose one category and check that they know the meaning and pronunciation of the words, using a dictionary where necessary.

2 Now get into new groups of three, with one student from each group A, B and C. Work together to correct the mistakes in these sentences. When you are speaking, put the stress on the corrected information.

Example:

A: *A forger takes people prisoner and asks their family for money to let them go.*

B: *No – a kidnapper takes people prisoner. A forger makes copies of things in order to deceive people.*

1 A mugger steals things from people's pockets in public places.
2 An arsonist goes into people's houses and steals things.
3 A hijacker takes things from shops without paying for them.
4 A blackmailer takes goods into a country without paying tax on them.
5 The judge pleads guilty or not guilty at the beginning of a trial.
6 The lawyer for the defence tries to prove the defendant is guilty.
7 The prosecution lawyer gives evidence about what they have seen.
8 If the defendant is found guilty, the jury passes sentence.
9 If you pay the court a sum of money, you can be given a suspended sentence until your trial.
10 If it is your first offence, you will probably be sentenced to capital punishment.

3 Read the following text and choose the correct alternative in each pair.

Last year my house was broken into and (1) *robbed / stolen.* I immediately informed the police. A police officer came to the house and asked me to make a list of what had been (2) *robbed / stolen.* I told him my neighbours had seen someone suspicious at the time of the (3) *forgery / burglary,* so they had to go to the police station and (4) *make / do* a statement. About a month later the police contacted me to say they had arrested a (5) *defendant / suspect.* When the case came to court, I went to (6) *give / tell* evidence. Of course, the man (7) *admitted / pleaded* not guilty. The (8) *jury / lawyer* decided there was not enough proof to (9) *try / convict* him, and he was (10) *let off / let go.*

Speaking

1 Discuss these questions.

1 What kinds of crimes are the most dangerous?
2 When should a judge send someone to prison?
3 What does the saying *The punishment should fit the crime* mean?

2 Work in groups. Decide what punishment, if any, would be appropriate in the following cases.

1 The children of an English woman, Mrs Amos, regularly played truant from school.
2 David Smith, 34, of New Jersey, created the Melissa computer virus – the first major virus spread by email. The virus caused more than US$80 m in damage.
3 Army Major Charles Ingram went on a TV quiz programme called *Who wants to be a millionaire?* He arranged for his wife and a friend to cough during the quiz to help him get the correct answers. He won a million pounds.
4 Twelve young men were involved in fights and damage to property in the centre of Coventry after a football match.
5 20-year-old Richard Ure, driving on his own, took part in a high-speed car chase with another car containing four teenagers. The teenagers' car crashed, and all four were killed. Richard survived.

3 Now turn to page 188 to find out what the actual punishments were. Were your ideas similar or different?

Listening 1: sentence completion (Part 2)

1 You will hear part of a radio programme about some people who tried to get compensation for injuries. First, read through the gapped sentences below and answer these questions.

1 How many people are mentioned?
2 What do the notes tell you about each person?
3 What sort of information is missing?

Stella Liebeck
An 81-year-old woman called Stella Liebeck bought **(1)** .... from a take-away.
Stella burned her **(2)** .... and claimed this was the fault of the take-away company.
There is now a **(3)** .... based on Stella's case, to find amazing stories about people who claim compensation.

Terrence Dickson
Terrence Dickson was a burglar who got stuck in a **(4)** .... after breaking into a house.
Terrence lived on Pepsi and **(5)** .... for eight days, and claimed compensation for mental suffering.

Kathleen Robinson
Kathleen Robinson claimed compensation when she fell over her **(6)** .... and injured her ankle.

Kara Walton
Kara Walton lost two **(7)** .... when she fell out of a window, and claimed compensation.
Kara was trying to leave a **(8)** .... without paying for her drinks.

Merv Grazinski
Mr Merv Grazinski bought a vehicle called a **(9)** ....
Mr Grazinski got up to make a cup of tea while travelling at **(10)** .... mph and claimed compensation for the resulting accident.

2 Now listen and complete the sentences with a word or short phrase. Then listen again to check and complete your answers.

3 Discuss these questions.

1 Which case do you think is most surprising?
2 Which of the people you have just heard about do you think deserved to be paid compensation?
3 Are there any cases in the news now where ordinary people or celebrities are trying to get compensation for things that have happened to them?

Grammar 1: passives (2)

1

1 Look at the first sentence in each pair and highlight the passive verb forms. Then complete the second sentence, which is active.

Example:

   a) The stolen goods were handed over to the police by the thief.

   b) The thief *handed over* the stolen goods to the police.

1 a) He was given the information he needed.
   b) They .... him the information he needed.
2 a) My little sister likes being read stories.
   b) My little sister likes it when I .... her stories.
3 a) I'm tired of being told what to.
   b) I'm tired of people .... me what to do.
4 a) Johnson was proud to have been promoted.
   b) Johnson was proud that they had .... him.
5 a) I was made to feel like part of the family.
   b) They .... me feel like part of the family.
6 a) The suspect was seen to enter the house.
   b) People .... the suspect enter the house.

2 Look at the passive forms you have highlighted. Find examples of:

• verb + -*ing* form (gerund)   *2,* ....
• verb + perfect infinitive   ....

3 What do you notice about the infinitive form in sentence pairs 5 and 6?

▶ Grammar reference p.202 (17)

2   Change the following sentences from active to passive, using structures from Exercise 1. Omit the agent when it is not necessary.

1 I hope the coach will choose me to play on the team. (present infinitive)
2 I don't like it when the teacher gives us a lot of homework. (-*ing* form)
3 The court awarded $1 m to the defendant.
4 I can't remember my father ever punishing me.
5 Several witnesses heard him shout for help.
6 I hope my parents will let me study abroad.
7 I was not very pleased that they had ordered me to do jury duty.

3   The following sentences tell the story of a man calling himself Count St Germain, who lived in Europe in the 18th century. Match the sentence halves to find out more about him.

1 It is not known where   c)
2 He was said to be
3 It was believed that he knew
4 It was also claimed that
5 At various times he was recorded
6 He is believed to have died
7 His ghost is said to have

a) as having been seen in Europe, Persia, India and West Africa.
b) appeared to Queen Marie Antoinette in 1788, predicting the outbreak of the French Revolution.
c) 'Count' St Germain originally came from.
d) in Germany in 1784 and to have been buried there.
e) the secret of how to turn any metal into gold.
f) enormously wealthy.
g) he had discovered the secret of eternal youth.

▶ Grammar reference p.202 (17.2)

4   Complete the news report using the correct form of the verbs in brackets.

Mystery animal threat to farmers

Several sightings of a large cat-like animal (1) .... (*report*) recently. Several attacks on farm animals in the last few weeks (2) .... (*believe*) to be the work of the mystery creature. It (3) .... (*suggest*) that it could be a panther or a leopard. The animal (4) .... (*think*) to be dangerous, and members of the public (5) .... (*advise*) to inform the authorities immediately if they see anything suspicious.

5   Choose one of the following headlines and write a short newspaper report. Include some of the expressions in the box.

Mystery of burglary still unsolved

Escaped snake terrorises neighbourhood

WITNESSES CLAIM LIGHTS 'COULD HAVE BEEN UFOS'

described being awakened by   thought to have caused
reported to have been seen   said to have escaped
known to be dangerous   members of the public are asked

Listening 2: song

1 How much do you know about the film *Men in Black*?

1 How many of these questions can you answer?

1 Which actors play the two main parts?
2 What is the job of the characters they play?
3 Why do they wear sunglasses?
4 What happens to them at the end of the film?

2 Now turn to page 187 to check.

2 Complete the song lyrics by adding the words from the boxes.

3 Now listen and check your answers.

4 What two things do the Men in Black ask ordinary people to do?

a) try to forget any strange things they see
b) try to find out who the Men in Black are
c) trust the Men in Black to defend them against extra-terrestrial danger

5 Who do you think should be responsible for preventing crime?

- the police
- ordinary citizens
- special task forces

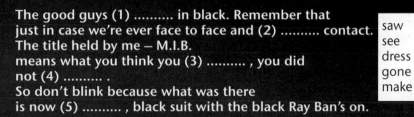

Here come the Men in Black

It's the M.I.B.'s, uhh,
here come the M.I.B.'s.
Here come the Men in Black.
They won't let you remember.

The good guys (1) .... in black. Remember that
just in case we're ever face to face and (2) .... contact.
The title held by me – M.I.B.
means what you think you (3) .... , you did
not (4) ....
So don't blink because what was there
is now (5) .... , black suit with the black Ray Ban's on.

saw
see
dress
gone
make

Walk in (6) .... , move in (7) .... ,
Guard against extra-terrestrial violence.
But yo, we ain't on no government (8) ....
We straight don't exist, no names and no (9) ....
Saw something strange, watch your (10) .... ,
'cause you never quite know where the M.I.B.'s is at.

silence
fingerprints
back
shadow
list

Chorus
Here come the Men in Black
The galaxy defenders
Right on, right on
Here come the Men in Black
They won't let you remember.

From the deepest of the darkest of night,
on the horizon, bright light (11) .... sight tight.
Cameras (12) .... , on the impending doom
But then like BOOM black suits (13) .... the room up
With the quickness (14) .... with the witnesses
Hypnotizer, neuralizer
Vivid memories (15) .... to fantasies.
Ain't no M.I.B.'s, can I please
do what we say that's the way we kick it.
Ya know what I mean? I see my noisy cricket get wicked on ya.

fill
turn
enters
zoom
talk

We're your first, last and (16) .... line of defence
against the (17) .... scum of the universe.
So don't fear us, cheer us.
If you ever get (18) .... us, don't jeer us, we're the
(19) .... M.I.B.'s, freezin up all the flack.
(What's that stand for?) Men in Black.

worst
fearless
near
only

Chorus

Exam focus

Paper 1 Reading: gapped text (Part 3)

About the exam: In Paper 1, Part 3, you read a text from which sentences or paragraphs have been removed and placed in jumbled order after the text. You have to decide where the sentences or paragraphs fit. This part tests your understanding of text structure.

Procedure

1 Look at the title and subheading (if there is one) and think about the topic.
2 Read the base text carefully to make sure you understand what it is about. Read the example (0) as well. This will give you a clearer idea of what the text is about.
3 Try to predict what kind of information is needed in each gap.
4 Look through all the extracts and choose the one that fits each gap best. Look for clues such as topic links and reference words.
5 If you are not sure about an answer, leave it and go back to it later.
6 When you have finished, read through the completed text to check that it makes sense. Make sure you have filled all the gaps and have not used any extract more than once.
7 Transfer your answers to the answer sheet.

1   You are going to read an article about the origins of cities. Eight paragraphs have been removed from the article. Choose from the paragraphs A–I the one which fits each gap (1–7). There is one extra paragraph which you do not need to use. There is an example at the beginning (0). Follow the suggested procedure.

2   According to the last paragraph of the text, *Human civilisation was not born in bloodshed and battle.* Look back through the text and find evidence for this conclusion.

Example: *Instead of weapons they found jewellery …*

3   Discuss these questions.

1 Do you know anything about the origins of the town or city where you live?
2 Are there any ruins or archaeological sites near the place where you live? Are they important? Why?

THE LOST CITY

The origins of city life are a mystery. Did civilisation arise out of violence? Or is there a more peaceful reason why people chose to live in large communities?

Today's modern city is a symbol of human civilisation. But the origins of cities have long been a mystery to scientists. For more than a hundred thousand years, human beings either wandered the world in small family groups, or lived in tiny villages.

0	I

What made people give up the simple life for the city? One theory was that it was something terrifying – warfare. This forced groups of villages to huddle together for their own protection.

1	

But to prove this theory, archaeologists needed to find a 'mother city': the very first big city to appear in the world. After years of searching, they discovered an enormous pyramid in the Casma Valley, in the Peruvian desert. It had the remains of a huge city around it. Excavations revealed simple pottery and crude art, suggesting that the city was very old indeed. When carbon dating showed that it was built in 1500 BC, archaeologists thought they had indeed discovered their 'mother city'.

2	

But that was not the end of the story. An archaeologist called Dr Ruth Shady from the University of San Marcos in Lima heard of some mysterious unexplained mounds in the desert and set off alone to find them. She found the remains of six pyramids, arranged around a central plaza. It was the lost city of Caral.

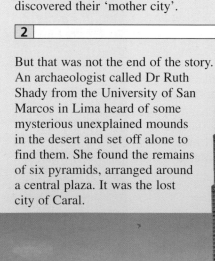

OF CARAL

3

Ruth went back with a team of archaeologists. They looked for pottery, but found none. They looked for metal tools, but the only ones they found were made of stone. Caral seemed to be much older than they'd expected. Eventually, while excavating the pyramids, they found plant remains, which they were able to get carbon dated.

4

But why had the history of civilisation started at Caral? Archaeologists searched for evidence of warfare, but found none. There were no fortifications round the sites, no weapons or carvings of warriors. Instead, Ruth and her team found decorated musical instruments made from the bones of birds, fragments of a fruit used as body paint, and necklaces made from shells.

5

The mystery deepened. They found piles of fish bones from sardines and anchovies which could only have come from the coast. Goods seemed to have been flooding into Caral from all over Peru.

6

They found cotton seeds, lots of them, and discovered a cotton fishing net on the coast dating from the same time. So the people of Caral must have made nets for the fishermen on the coast, who sent fish as payment. More food meant more people could live at Caral and thus it became a booming trading centre. So the driving force that led to the birth of civilisation five thousand years ago was not warfare.

7

Perhaps that is Caral's true legacy. Human civilisation was not born in bloodshed and battle. Great things can come from peace.

A These showed that this was a society where people knew how to have fun. But such things did not occur naturally in that region – so how had they got there?

B Beneath it, they found paint which had not been seen for thousands of years, and a series of staircases. These pyramids would have required craftsmen, architects, a huge workforce and leaders: a whole civilisation.

C And those who organised their citizens to protect and defend themselves in this way emerged as powerful leaders – pharaohs and kings. It seemed that city life was born out of fear.

D Instead, this city of pyramids was built on riches gained through trade. And this peaceful existence continued for almost a thousand years, an achievement unmatched in the modern world.

E 'I was totally overwhelmed by the discovery,' she said. 'This place is somewhere between the seat of the gods and the home of man.'

F Ruth realised the answer to the puzzle lay in the river valleys. Here in the middle of the desert there must have been rivers watering a vast oasis of fruit and vegetable fields.

G And as they continued to excavate, they found carvings of warrior figures with their victims, who had clearly died very violently. It looked as if war really had been the force that gave birth to civilisation.

H The results showed that Caral was built in 2,600 BC. They had found the true 'mother city'.

I And then, suddenly, all this changed. All over the world, in Egypt, Mesopotamia, China, India, Central America and Peru, people started to build cities.

4 Complete the missing words. You have been given the correct number of letters.

Today's modern city is considered to be a s *y m b o l* of human civilisation. Archaeologists have spent years investigating the (1) o _ _ _ _ _ s of city life, believing that it may have been founded on violence. Then Dr Ruth Shady found the (2) r _ _ _ _ s of a huge city in Peru. After detailed investigations, she found no (3) e _ _ _ _ _ _ _ of warfare there. Ruth concluded that the reason for the (4) b _ _ _ _ of civilisation was not warfare, but trade. The (5) p _ _ _ _ of this theory was there in the ruins.

Vocabulary 2: nouns linked by *of*

1

1 Cross out the word which does not belong.

Example: a team of *archaeologists* / ~~computers~~ / *players*
1 a flock of *sheep* / *papers* / *birds*
2 a herd of *cowboys* / *cattle* / *horses*
3 a gang of *thieves* / *dogs* / *boys*
4 a panel of *experts* / *speakers* / *apes*
5 a pack of *cards* / *lies* / *parcels*
6 a bunch of *stones* / *flowers* / *grapes*
7 a collection of *stamps* / *information* / *short stories*

2 Complete the sentences using words from Exercise 1.1.

1 He's got a large .... of .... from all over the world.
2 I don't believe a word she says – it's all a .... of ....
3 A .... of .... attacked the train and got away with $1 m.
4 A .... of .... has been invited to discuss the problem.
5 It's polite to take a .... of .... when you are invited for a meal.

2

1 Choose an item from the box that goes with both nouns.

a bar   ~~a block~~   a fragment   an item   a piece
a pile   a row

Example: *a block* of flats/marble
1 .... of bones/books
2 .... of desks/houses
3 .... of news/paper
4 .... of soap/chocolate
5 .... of pottery/bone
6 .... of clothing/furniture

2 Correct the mistakes.

1 I finished off a whole piece of chocolate by myself.
2 I live in a row of flats.
3 For the examination, students' desks must be arranged in piles.
4 I don't have a single fragment of clothing to wear to the party.
5 A big row of papers lay on my desk.
6 Here's an interesting block of news.

Grammar 2: *have/get something done*

1 **Complete the following sentences using the correct form of a verb from the box.**

check   frame   make   photocopy
paint   take   tell   video

1 I need to get these papers .... in case they get lost.
2 We've just had the house ....
3 I'm going to have my fortune ....
4 She's having her wedding dress .... for her.
5 We're going to have the wedding ceremony ....
6 I think you ought to get your blood pressure ....
7 I want to get this picture .... so I can hang it up.
8 The dentist says I'll have to have the tooth .... out.

2 **Respond to the statements below with advice using *have/get something done* and a suitable verb.**

Example:
A: *I need another house key – I keep leaving mine behind.*
B: *You'd better get another one made.*

1 My hair's too long.
2 Someone's broken the window!
3 I've finished the film in my camera.
4 I've got a mark on my new jacket.
5 My car is making a funny noise.
6 I want a special photograph of my graduation.

3 **Put the words in the questions into the correct order. Then ask a partner. Find out more details about the answer.**

Example: you had ever anything have stolen?
A: *Have you ever had anything stolen?*
B: *Yes, I have.*
A: *What?*
B: *I had my purse stolen a few years ago.*

1 you when last did cut your hair get?
2 taken photograph had recently your you have?
3 you tooth out have had a ever taken?
4 you last your eyes get tested did when?
5 have ever coloured had hair you your?
6 would your ever get pierced you nose?

▶ Grammar reference p.198

Use of English: multiple-choice cloze (Part 1)

1 Read the title and the text quickly. What is the buried treasure referred to in the title?

2 Read the text again and decide which answer (A, B, C or D) best fits each space. There is an example at the beginning (0).

BURIED TREASURE

Artist Kit Williams was always interested in trying new things, so when it was **(0)** ...A.... that he should **(1)** .... a book, he **(2)** .... to write his own story rather than work with someone else's. He hit **(3)** .... a new idea. What better way to attract people's **(4)** .... to his work than to give his readers the **(5)** .... to take part in a treasure hunt? So Kit made a golden pendant in the **(6)** .... of a hare and buried it underground at a secret location. The words and pictures in his book, *Masquerade*, **(7)** .... clues as to where the hare was buried. Almost two million readers from all over the world joined in the rush to **(8)** .... the puzzle. The race was open to all, and no one had any advantage – the treasure was as **(9)** .... to be found by a clever child of ten as it was by a university professor.

After more than two years, the golden hare was found by a businessman who called himself Ken Thomas, although this was actually a **(10)** .... name. It appears that 'Thomas' subsequently sold the hare for a large **(11)** .... of money. Afterwards some people **(12)** .... that the discovery of the hare was not **(13)** .... purely on the information in the book, but was the result of a complex **(14)** .... in which 'Thomas' was helped by a former girlfriend of Kit Williams. However, 'Thomas' has always firmly **(15)** .... these claims.

0 A suggested	**B** told	**C** known	**D** believed
1 A paint	**B** picture	**C** draw	**D** illustrate
2 A selected	**B** preferred	**C** picked	**D** liked
3 A at	**B** in	**C** off	**D** upon
4 A attention	**B** eyes	**C** interest	**D** curiosity
5 A destiny	**B** fortune	**C** chance	**D** luck
6 A pattern	**B** figure	**C** shape	**D** appearance
7 A supported	**B** made	**C** identified	**D** provided
8 A guess	**B** solve	**C** correct	**D** settle
9 A probable	**B** possible	**C** suitable	**D** likely
10 A wrong	**B** dishonest	**C** false	**D** deceptive
11 A sum	**B** figure	**C** rate	**D** profit
12 A charged	**B** threatened	**C** claimed	**D** accused
13 A found	**B** based	**C** established	**D** decided
14 A narrative	**B** tale	**C** story	**D** plot
15 A disapproved	**B** refused	**C** denied	**D** objected

Writing 2: story

1 Look at this task and answer the questions.

1 Who will read your story?
2 Is the main character a man or a woman?

You have been asked to write a story for a student magazine beginning or ending with the words:

Steve turned his back on them and walked slowly into the house.

Write your **story** in **120–180** words.

2 Work with a partner. Think of some ideas for your story. Ask yourself questions like the ones below and note down answers.

- Who was Steve?
- Who were the other people?
- What had happened before this?
- Had he been talking to someone?
- Did they bring good or bad news?
- What was it about?
- Why did he go into the house?
- Why was he walking slowly?

3 Plan your story.

1 Decide if your ideas are mostly about what happened before Steve went into the house, or after. This will help you to decide whether to use the sentence to begin the story, or to end it.

2 Plan how your ideas will fit into paragraphs. Look back at Unit 3 page 40 for the four stages to include in a story. There is an example on the next page.

> **TIP!** Remember that you only have 120–180 words to write your story so your plot should be simple.

Example:

Para. 1 Steve stopped outside his house - had run home

Para. 2 (background info) terrible night - went out with friends - lost his wallet - spent hours looking for it

Para. 3 (later actions) taxi stopped, friends got out. They'd found wallet - it was empty

Para. 4 (ending) - Steve was grateful but evening spoiled. Turned and went into house.

3 Think of a good title for your story.

4 Compare your ideas with other students.

5 Remember that your writing will be more interesting if you use a range of vocabulary.

1 Read the first part of one student's answer to the task and look at the highlighted verbs. Choose the best verb from each group below to replace them.

The wallet

It had been a terrible evening and Steve just wanted to get home. He went down the street as fast as he could, then stopped outside his house. His heart was beating and he felt as if he was unable to breathe. Passers by looked at him, wondering what was wrong. He stood there, breathing quickly, remembering what had happened.

1 a) hurried   b) strolled
2 a) going   b) pounding
3 a) gasping   b) suffocating
4 a) noticed   b) stared at
5 a) crying   b) panting

2 Complete this paragraph with suitable adverbs and adjectives from the box.

frantically   aimlessly   nervous   oppressive   suddenly

He'd arranged to meet his two friends Craig and Tas in town at eight o'clock. The three of them had walked around the streets (1) ...., wondering what to do. The weather was hot and (2) ...., and for some reason Steve felt (3) ...., as if something bad was going to happen. They decided to go to the cinema, but as soon as they got there Steve (4) .... said, 'Where's my wallet?' and started searching all his pockets (5) ....

3 Now finish the story. Use a range of vocabulary.

6 Do this writing task. Follow the procedure below.

You have been asked to write a story for a student magazine beginning or ending with the words:

I had never felt so nervous in my life, but I knew that I had to do it.

Write your **story** in **120–180** words.

- Decide if you want to begin or end your story with the words provided.
- Think of some ideas for your story.
- Make notes and organise them into paragraphs.
- Write your story. Make sure you use tenses correctly and try to include interesting vocabulary. This will make it easier for the reader to imagine the situation.
- When you have finished, check your work.

TIP! Check the information given about your main character in the first sentence. Is it a man or a woman? Or is the story in the first person using *I*? The rest of the story should continue in the same way.

Writing reference pp.206, 208

1

1 Match a word from A with a phrase from B to make collocations.

A		B	
1	commit	a)	a statement
2	plead	b)	someone on bail
3	convict	c)	trial
4	let	d)	someone guilty/innocent
5	release	e)	a suspect
6	give	f)	guilty/not guilty
7	pass	g)	someone of a crime
8	put	h)	a crime
9	arrest	i)	sentence
10	make	j)	someone go free
11	stand	k)	someone on probation
12	find	l)	evidence

2 Decide who does each action.

Example: *A criminal commits a crime.*

2 Complete the phrasal verbs using the correct preposition or particle.

1 Someone who commits a crime should not be allowed to get away .... it.
2 First time offenders may be let .... with a warning by the police.
3 Burglars often break .... houses during the day when the owners are at work.
4 It can take a long time to get .... the shock of being burgled.
5 Statistics show that the majority of young criminals give .... crime in their late twenties.
6 Take care to avoid being taken .... by credit card fraudsters.

3 Complete the second sentence so that it has a similar meaning to the first sentence, using no more than five words, including the word given.

1 They made me feel really welcome
   was
   I .... really welcome.
2 There is a rumour that he committed the crime.
   said
   He .... committed the crime.
3 I need to ask the dentist to take this tooth out.
   have
   I need to .... out.

4 People say that the police will arrest the thief soon.
   expected
   It .... the police will arrest the thief soon.
5 When I was a child, I didn't like it when anyone cut my hair.
   having
   I didn't like .... when I was a child.
6 They didn't let journalists interview the suspect.
   allowed
   Journalists .... interview the suspect.
7 You'll need to take this suit to the cleaners soon.
   get
   You'll have .... soon.
8 After searching for years, they discovered the city.
   occurred
   The .... after years of searching.
9 Trade was the basis of the city's civilisation.
   built
   The city's civilisation .... trade.
10 The artist was able to sell his carvings for a lot of money.
   sums
   The artist was able to charge .... his carvings.

4 Rewrite the postcard using a different adjective to replace each use of *nice*.

We're having a ¹nice time here! We're staying in a ²nice five-star hotel with very ³nice gardens and a swimming pool. All the people who work here are ⁴nice and polite, and the food is really ⁵nice. I'm eating too much! We're lucky because the weather is ⁶nice. I'm spending a lot of time relaxing on the beach reading a ⁷nice book about an unsolved mystery. Everything is great!
See you soon.

Jose

Reading 1: multiple matching (Part 4)

1 Look at the photos. These animals all have something in common. What do you think it is?

2 Read the title and subheading of the text opposite and scan each section quickly to check your answer to Exercise 1.

3 For questions 1–15, choose from the sections A–E. The sections may be chosen more than once. When more than one answer is required, these may be given in any order. There is an example at the beginning (0).

Which section of the article mentions

a person who was often in a different country from their pet?	**0** C
a person who gained a skill at an early age?	**1**
someone who behaved in a way that was not typical of them?	**2**
a person who got a pet by chance?	**3**
a creature that started to behave in a disturbed manner?	**4** **5**
a person who was very upset about leaving their pet?	**6**
a statement which was not believed by another person?	**7**
a creature that was able to predict an event happening at irregular intervals?	**8** **9**
a pet that got angry when its owner went out?	**10**
a situation that could have been more serious than it was?	**11**
someone who recognised a sound made by their pet?	**12**
a pet that appeared to be jealous?	**13**
a creature that predicted a change in a routine?	**14**
a creature that only reacted in a particular way when its owner was involved?	**15**

4 Compare your answers with a partner and explain your choices. What parallel phrases did you find in the paragraphs to help you?

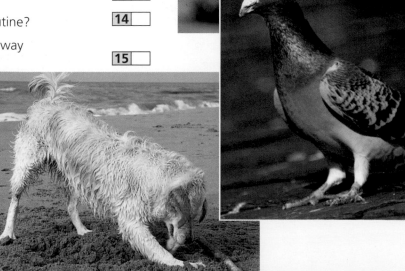

The unexplained powers of animals

Do animals have special powers that people have lost? Rupert Sheldrake looks at the evidence.

A

Some pets seem to have an amazing ability to locate their owners. Twelve-year-old Bobby Chesson came across a racing pigeon in his back yard in West Virginia, USA. He looked after it, calling it pigeon 167 after the identification number on its leg-ring, and it became his pet. Then Bobby was taken to hospital for an operation. One dark, snowy night about a week after his admission, the boy heard a fluttering at the window of his hospital room. He asked his nurse to open the window, telling her that his pigeon was outside. Just to humour him, she did so – and in flew pigeon 167, having flown over 100 miles to find him.

B

Unusual powers are not confined to pet birds but are seen in other animals which have a close bond with their owner. Herminia Denot grew up on a ranch in Argentina, and learned to ride almost before she could walk. She was very attached to her horse Pampero, but the time came when she had to go away to boarding school in the capital, Buenos Aires and, much to her dismay, Pampero could not accompany her. The *gaucho* (cowboy) who looked after the horse said that at the end of each term, as the time of Herminia's return grew near, 'Pampero would go crazy. He used to gallop around the field neighing.' When she was due to arrive, the horse would stand by the gate, looking south towards the train station. But on one occasion, Pampero stood looking in the opposite direction. And this time Herminia arrived by road – from the north.

C

Anticipatory behaviour is common in various creatures. David Waite worked from his home in Oxford, but his job as a public relations consultant also involved lengthy trips abroad. In his absence, David's parents used to stay in the house to deal with telephone calls from his clients and to feed Godzilla, his cat. David used to ring home frequently to check that all was well and get any messages.

'Whenever I called,' says David, 'Godzilla would run and sit beside the telephone as it started to ring. My calls were made at many different times of day – they weren't regular. And she totally ignored all the other calls. The only explanation I can think of is that it was some kind of telepathy.'

D

Sometimes telepathic communication can work from pet to owner. Dolores Katz, from New Mexico, tells the story of a time when her dog, Eric, seemed to communicate with her telepathically. 'One day while I was at work it started to thunder and rain. As I worked, I got more and more agitated. Somehow I knew that Eric needed me. At last I couldn't take it any more. I hardly ever take time off, but this time I dropped everything and rushed home.' Dolores found Eric lying in the back room surrounded by broken glass, with his paws bleeding badly. Frightened by the storm, he had run into a glass door. Fortunately, a possibly tragic situation was avoided as she was able to get Eric to the vet in time to deal with his injuries.

E

Occasionally, a pet's attachment to one particular owner can show itself in strange ways. Celia and David Watson, who live in Sussex, England, used to have a parrot called Oscar. 'I couldn't go near Oscar when David was in the room – he seemed to resent me taking David's attention,' says Celia, 'The bird would just try to attack me without warning. I couldn't give him his food or even touch his cage. And when David left the room, Oscar would fling himself against the side of the cage in fury.' The parrot was quite calm when David was away at work, but started to get excited ten to twenty minutes before David arrived home. 'Oscar used to run around in his cage making little noises and fluttering his wings,' says Celia. 'He always knew when David was going to arrive.'

5 Find words or phrases in the text that mean the same as:

1 keep someone happy by agreeing to their wishes (section A)
2 very fond of (section B)
3 one time (section B)
4 when he was away (section C)
5 everything was OK (section C)
6 took no notice of (section C)
7 couldn't accept the situation (section D)
8 have a break from work (section D)
9 sometimes (section E)

6 Rewrite the following sentences, using a phrasal verb formed with the verbs in brackets. Then check your answers in the text.

1 Bobby *took care* of the pigeon. (*look*)
2 Herminia was *brought up* on a farm. (*grow*)
3 David's parents used to *take care of* his phone calls. (*deal*)
4 Dolores' dog had *hit* a glass door. (*run*)
5 The parrot used to *move about* quickly in its cage. (*run*)

7 Do you know any similar stories about animals that have shown unexplained powers? Can you think of any scientific explanation for any of these stories?

Vocabulary 1: animals

1

1 Complete the mind map below using words from the box. You don't need to use all the words.

bark   beak   bite   cage   claw   feather
flutter   fur   gallop   hoof   jump up   kennel
miaow   neigh   nest   paw   peck   purr
scratch   sing   stable   snarl   tail

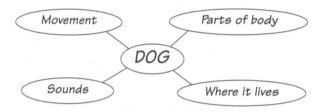

2 Now make mind maps for these animals. Try to add some extra words for each animal.

CAT   HORSE   BIRD

2 Match the sentence halves. Then decide what pet each sentence is describing – a dog, a cat or a bird.

1	It wags	a)	with its claws.
2	It flutters	b)	a cage.
3	It sometimes wears	c)	its tail.
4	It might scratch you	d)	a collar.
5	You can take it for	e)	its wings.
6	It's often kept in	f)	a walk.

3 Try to work out the meaning of the expressions in italics. Use a dictionary if necessary.

1 It's not far away *as the crow flies*, but it's miles by road.
2 Mary *took* the new girl *under her wing* and made sure she felt welcome.
3 The whole thing's *a can of worms* – as soon as we solve one problem, something else pops up.
4 I'd like to get out of *the rat race* and go and raise chickens in the country.
5 Don't worry if he shouts at you. He doesn't mean it – *his bark is worse than his bite*.
6 I didn't want to tell anyone I was leaving, but then my friend *let the cat out of the bag*.

Speaking 1

1 Can you match the celebrities and their pets? Check your answers on page 187.

1

◁ **Robbie Williams, singer**
Likes: talking, football, wearing trainers

2

◁ **Leonardo Di Caprio, actor**
Likes: pasta, rap music, holidays in Germany

3

◁ **George Clooney, actor**
Likes: tennis, Italy, motorbikes

a

◁ **Max, potbellied pig**
Likes: being scratched, rolling in the mud

b

◁ **Missy, Rottweiler**
Likes: chasing her tail, yoghurt

c

◁ **Bearded dragon**
Likes: chopped peaches, live insects

2 Discuss these questions.

1 Why do people keep animals as pets?
2 What are the advantages and disadvantages of owning a pet a) for children? b) for old people?
3 What sort of animals do you think make the best and the worst pets?
4 Have you ever had a pet? Do you have one now? What pet would you choose if you could have any sort of animal?

Exam focus

Paper 3 Use of English: multiple-choice cloze (Part 1)

About the exam: Paper 3, Part 1 tests your knowledge of vocabulary, including words with similar meanings, collocations, fixed phrases, phrasal verbs and prepositions.

Procedure

1 Read the title and then read through the whole text to find out what it's about. Don't try to fill in any of the gaps yet.
2 Read the text again, stopping at each gap. Try to think of the missing word before looking at the options.
3 Choose the best option. If you're not sure, read the whole sentence again and check the words on each side of the gap. Is it a collocation or a fixed phrase?
4 Finally, read through the complete text again to check your choices make sense.
5 Transfer your answers to the answer sheet.

> **DON'T** choose more than one option for any one question.
> **DON'T** leave any answers blank. If you're still not sure when you read the whole text for the last time, then guess.

For questions 1–15, read the text below and decide which answer (A, B, C or D) best fits each space. There is an example at the beginning (0).

Example:

0 A exactly   **B** really   **C** absolutely   **D** totally

0	A	B	C	D
	▬	▭	▭	▭

IT'S A DOG'S LIFE

Will it ever be possible for us to know **(0)** ....A.... what our pets are thinking or feeling? Actually, this day may not be so **(1)** .... away. A Japanese toy-making firm has **(2)** .... up with a gadget that can read a dog's emotions. The company calls their **(3)** .... the 'Bowlingual'. The device is **(4)** .... to a special collar which the dog **(5)** .... around its neck, and can **(6)** .... information about the dog's feelings electronically to a handset kept by the dog's owner.

The company **(7)** .... that the Bowlingual can **(8)** .... six different feelings, including fear, happiness and sadness, by interpreting the different ways in which the dog barks. But how does the Bowlingual actually **(9)** ....? Scientists analysed the barks they recorded from a number of dogs in various different situations and **(10)** .... six general patterns of sound **(11)** .... to different feelings. The Bowlingual is programmed with these patterns and can **(12)** .... them to the sound a dog makes and then translate this into a sentence that can be **(13)** .... understood. Some examples of what dogs apparently say are 'I'm lonely,' and 'Please play with me a bit more!'

The device is also fitted with a diary that **(14)** .... the whole of the dog's day with **(15)** .... such as 'We've done so many good things today. What a happy day!'

1	**A** much	**B** distant	**C** far	**D** long
2	**A** come	**B** put	**C** taken	**D** made
3	**A** construction	**B** development	**C** invention	**D** building
4	**A** carried	**B** attached	**C** communicated	**D** planned
5	**A** fetches	**B** holds	**C** wears	**D** transfers
6	**A** extend	**B** spread	**C** push	**D** send
7	**A** pretends	**B** claims	**C** persuades	**D** tells
8	**A** accept	**B** know	**C** realise	**D** recognise
9	**A** work	**B** play	**C** find	**D** go
10	**A** shared	**B** divided	**C** identified	**D** associated
11	**A** relating	**B** accompanying	**C** concerning	**D** applying
12	**A** suit	**B** match	**C** design	**D** give
13	**A** easily	**B** simply	**C** fluently	**D** surely
14	**A** takes on	**B** gives out	**C** puts away	**D** sums up
15	**A** proverbs	**B** accounts	**C** statements	**D** questions

Listening: sentence completion
(Part 2)

1 Charlotte Uhlenbroek makes wildlife programmes for television.

1 What qualifications and skills do you think you need to do a job like this?
2 What dangers or difficulties might you face?

2 You will hear an interview with Charlotte. First, read through the following sentences and think about the type of information needed for each gap.

Charlotte's mother is English and her father is
(1) ....

Charlotte was brought up in Nepal, where she went to a good **(2)** .... school.

In her first job, Charlotte worked as a
(3) .... with the BBC.

While in Africa, Charlotte studied for her PhD, which was on **(4)** ....

Charlotte says that making a TV programme was like talking to a **(5)** .... about her subject.

Charlotte likes television work because she doesn't have to use **(6)** .... language.

Charlotte's most frightening experience was being chased by **(7)** .... in the jungle.

On one occasion, a young gorilla
(8) .... Charlotte and then a second gorilla sat on her.

From her research, Charlotte has become more aware of the way humans use **(9)** .... in communication.

Charlotte says the future of chimpanzees is threatened because baby chimpanzees are being sold as
(10) ....

3 Now listen and complete the sentences with a word or short phrase. Then listen a second time to check and complete your answers.

4 Would you like to have a job like Charlotte's? Why?/Why not?

5 Work with a partner. You are going to role-play an interview with a famous conservationist called Jane Goodall.

Student A: You are the interviewer. Look at page 187.
Student B: You are Jane Goodall. Look at page 189.

Grammar 1: *so, such, too, enough, very*

1 Complete the following sentences using a word or phrase from the box.

enough (x 2)   so   such   such a   too   very (x 2)

1 Charlotte has travelled .... much that she feels at home in most places.
2 She lived with the chimpanzees for .... long time that they got used to her.
3 I don't think I'm patient .... to be a wildlife photographer.
4 I don't have .... money to go to Africa.
5 .... few people have seen a gorilla in the wild.
6 I was having .... fun at the party that I didn't want to go home.
7 I think I'll have an early night. I'm feeling .... tired.
8 That cat's .... old and fat to catch any birds.

> **┌ Watch Out! *very and too* ◀**
> Which sentence has a negative meaning?
> 1 The gorillas were very friendly.
> 2 The gorillas were too friendly.

▶ Grammar reference p.205 (20.4)

2 Join the following sentences together using *so/such … that* or *too/enough … to*.

Example:
   1 – e) *I was **so** tired **that** I stayed in bed all day.*

1 I was tired.
2 The car is very big.
3 I had a good time on holiday.
4 I don't have much money.
5 The day was hot.
6 I don't have many qualifications.

a) I can't pay the bill.
b) I had to stay indoors in the shade.
c) I won't get the job.
d) I didn't want to go home.
e) I stayed in bed all day.
f) It won't fit in that space.

3 Complete the second sentence so that it has a similar meaning to the first sentence, using the word given. Do not change the word given. Use between two and five words.

1 Paul was too frightened to move. **that**
   Paul was .... not move.
2 The wind was so strong that we could not go outside. **such**
   There was .... that we could not go outside.
3 I couldn't follow the instructions as they were very complicated. **for**
   The instructions .... to follow.
4 It was the most interesting programme I have ever seen. **such**
   I have .... interesting programme.
5 Sarah was too ill to finish the course. **well**
   Sarah .... to finish the course.
6 The tickets cost so much money that we couldn't afford them. **lot**
   The tickets cost .... that we couldn't afford them.

4 Complete the following sentences, giving true information. You can use words from the box.

Example: *I'd like an elephant as a pet because they're so intelligent. But they're not small enough to live in our apartment.*

boring   relaxing   intelligent   pretty
friendly   convenient

1 I'd like/wouldn't like a spider as a pet because …
2 I like/don't like Sundays because they're …
3 I like/don't like [NAME OF AN ACTOR] because …
4 I eat/don't eat a lot of chocolate because …

Speaking 2: quiz

1 How much do you know about the world around you? Work in groups to do this quiz.

1 How would our lives be affected if the Moon suddenly disappeared?

A Changes in the weather would affect birds and animals.
B The cost of lighting would increase everywhere.
C Gravity would disappear from the planet.

2 Where does the word Earth come from?

A the ancient Greeks
B the ancient Romans
C the Germanic peoples

3 Is it true that lightning never strikes twice in the same place?

A Yes. B No.

4 How much do barbecues affect the environment, compared with other ways of cooking?

A A lot, because they release carbon dioxide.
B A bit, because they create pollution and bad smells.
C Not much, because the fuel comes from replaceable resources.

5 When is the world's supply of oil probably going to run out?

A soon
B after a long time
C never

6 What is the most violent natural phenomenon to have occurred on Earth?

A a meteor strike
B a hurricane
C a volcanic eruption

7 What is a *tsunami*?

A an avalanche
B an earthquake
C a giant wave

2 Now listen to see if you were right. Which answer surprised you the most?

159

Exam focus

Paper 1 Reading: multiple matching (Part 1)

About the exam: In Paper 1, Part 1, you read a text which is divided into sections. You have to match a heading or sentence to each section of the text. This requires you to identify the main idea(s) of the section. There is one extra heading or sentence which you do not need to use.

Procedure

1 Read the title and the whole text quickly to get a general idea of what it is about.
2 Read through the headings or sentences.
3 Read each section carefully to identify the main idea, and decide which heading or sentence best matches it. Cross off the headings as you use them.
4 When you have finished, transfer your answers to the answer sheet.

DO be prepared to go back and check your answers.
DON'T just try to match words in the headings and the text. The same word in the text does not guarantee the correct answer.

1 You are going to read an article about a dangerous natural event. Choose from the list A–H the sentence which best summarises each part (1–6) of the article. There is one extra sentence which you do not need to use. There is an example at the beginning (0).

A	There may once have been *tsunamis* far bigger than those of the present day.
B	The appearance of a *tsunami* wave may not reflect its real nature.
C	Predicting *tsunamis* is a difficult but important process.
D	People may misunderstand the signs of an approaching *tsunami*.
E	The dangerous effects of *tsunamis* have been well documented.
F	*Tsunamis* can have effects on places far away from where they began.
G	*Tsunamis* can be deadlier than the event that creates them.
H	A simple experiment can show how a *tsunami* begins.

Tsunami!

0   **H**

A *tsunami* is a giant wave that can do huge amounts of damage when it hits land. To see how one starts, throw a stone into a pond or lake, and watch the ripples spread out on the surface of the water. A *tsunami* starts in a similar way to one of these ripples, except that it is not caused by a stone, but by something much bigger, such as an earthquake occurring under the sea.

1

Once it has started, a *tsunami* can move across the ocean for huge distances. An earthquake off the coast of South America generated a *tsunami* that travelled west for over 15,000 kilometres and caused enormous damage when it hit the coast of Japan 22 hours later.

2

Tsunamis can be caused by volcanic eruptions as well as by earthquakes. The most deadly *tsunami* in recorded history was the one that followed the eruption of Indonesia's Krakatoa volcano in 1883. About 36,000 people died, and what actually killed most of them was the *tsunami* rather than the eruption itself.

3

It is not only events on Earth that cause *tsunamis*. They can also be generated by a comet or meteor hitting the Earth. No one has actually seen this happen, except on screen in Hollywood films such as *Deep Impact*. But the giant *tsunamis* produced by special effects in such films, big enough to cover the skyscrapers of New York, are theoretically possible, and computer simulations show that they have almost certainly happened in the distant past.

4

In the open ocean, a *tsunami* wave is difficult to see, because most of it is below the surface. The part of the wave that is actually visible may be just one or two metres high. But the wave has enormous power, and can travel at the speed of a jet plane – almost 800 kph. As it eventually approaches land, the wave slows down, and this causes a dramatic increase in its height. By the time it actually reaches the land, it can be up to 30 metres high.

5

Tsunami waves can hit the land in different ways. Sometimes the sea seems to pull the water back at first, uncovering a large expanse of shoreline. When the sea withdraws like this, the *tsunami* wave is not far behind, and curious people who have walked out onto this newly exposed

2

1 Work with a partner. Unjumble the questions below, then find the answers in the article.

1 three *tsunami* can start What cause things a to?
2 far How travel can *tsunamis*?
3 Why see are difficult in *tsunamis* to the ocean open?
4 land What happen before a hits just can *tsunami*?
5 common are Where most *tsunamis*?

2 Write a paragraph summarising the information about *tsunamis*.

3 Think of a film you have seen or a book you have read which is about one of the following types of natural disaster. Tell a partner about it.

a meteor strike   an earthquake   a flood
a volcanic eruption   a hurricane   an avalanche

- Did anyone try to prevent the disaster from happening?
- What damage did the disaster cause?
- What happened in the end?

shoreline may find themselves in great danger. In other cases, the wave arrives suddenly and without warning, a dark wall of water which can uproot trees, knock down stone walls, and smash houses into pieces.

6

Tsunamis occur in all the major oceans of the world, although they are most common in the Pacific area around Japan. Here, there is a complex and detailed system for monitoring the waves and providing warning for those who live in the area. This is a vital service because anyone who thinks that *tsunamis* are just big surfing waves should think again – they are impressive, dramatic, destructive and deadly!

Illustration of the tsunami after the Krakatoa explosion in 1883

Grammar 2: emphasis with *what*

1 Read these pairs of sentences. Highlight the emphatic structure in the second sentence of each pair. Then rewrite the second sentence without using *What*.

1 Tsunamis were well known in the Pacific hundreds of years ago. What was the most dangerous thing about them in those days was their unpredictability.
Their unpredictability ...
2 The Tsunami Warning System is an international organisation with 26 member states. What it does is collect information about conditions which could lead to dangerous tsunamis.
It ...
3 Thousands of people go skiing every winter. What many of them forget is that, in certain weather conditions, avalanches may occur.
4 It was once thought that earthquakes occurred when the gods were angry. In fact what causes an earthquake is pressure between rocks on or under the Earth's surface.
5 Hurricanes are strong winds which start over the sea and may move to dry land, causing great damage. What is unusual about them is the way they are named: they are given the name of a man or a woman.

▶ Grammar reference p.196

2 This structure is often used in spoken English.

1 Match the statements and responses below.

1 I've had a really busy day!
2 Do you like skiing?
3 I hate rainy days.
4 My brother keeps complaining he's bored!
5 People keep asking me to do things for them!

a) Oh, I don't mind a bit of rain. What I can't stand is wind.
b) What he should do is take up some sort of sport.
c) What you need is a hot bath!
d) What you have to do is learn to say 'No'!
e) It's OK, but what I really like is snowboarding.

2 Listen and check your answers. Underline the stressed words in the response.

3 Practise reading the dialogues with a partner, using the appropriate stress.

3

1 Complete the responses below.

1 A: Would you like a CD for your birthday?
   B: Well, what I'd really like is ...

2 A: Did you enjoy the film last night?
   B: Yes, but what I enjoyed more was ...

3 A: Do you like reading thrillers?
   B: I don't mind them, but what I really enjoy reading is ...

4 A: Would you like to go shopping on Saturday?
   B: Well, what I'd rather do is ...

5 A: I'm going to the shop – can I get you some milk?
   B: Thanks, I've got milk. What I really need is ...

2 Now practise the dialogues with a partner.

Vocabulary 2: the natural world

1 Put the words into six groups of three.

breeze	climate	cloud	drizzle	fog
shower	frost	gale	hail	lightning
mist	rain	snow	temperature	
thunder	weather	wind	thunderstorm	

2 Choose nouns from Exercise 1 that go with the following sets of adjectives:

1 heavy / light / torrential / pouring ....

2 mild / hot / humid / continental ....

3 thick / dense / patchy ....

4 strong / icy / light / high ....

5 loud / severe / violent ....

6 deep / thick / wet / slushy ....

7 hot / wet / sunny / dry ....

3 Discuss these questions.

1 What kind of climate does your country have?

2 How many seasons do you have?

3 What is the weather like in each season?

4 What different types of weather have you had in the last month?

5 What kind of weather do you like or dislike most?

6 What would be your ideal climate?

4

1 Look at the extracts from radio weather reports. Match the sentence halves and underline all the expressions that refer to severe weather conditions.

1 There will be extremely heavy rain

2 The snow is melting rapidly

3 Driving conditions will be dangerous

4 All ferry services have been cancelled

5 The hot, dry weather will continue

6 Hurricane Katrina is advancing over the Atlantic Ocean

a) towards the coast of Florida with winds of over 130 kph.

b) and avalanches could occur.

c) due to very strong winds of up to 90 kph.

d) with danger of flooding in some areas.

e) and many areas are likely to be affected by drought.

f) due to thick fog and icy roads.

2 Discuss these questions.

1 Does your country experience any of these severe weather conditions? Which ones?

2 Can you remember any recent examples and their effects?

5

1 Complete the idiomatic expressions below with weather words from the exercises above. You have been given the first letter of each word.

1 I haven't got time to go out – I'm s.......... under with work.

2 Don't worry – you'll be as right as r.......... after a good night's sleep!

3 Jenny was in f.......... of tears after breaking up with her boyfriend.

4 She cheers everyone up with her s.......... smile.

5 I'm really happy at the moment – there isn't a c.......... on the horizon.

6 There were s.......... of protest at the plan to build a new road.

2 Highlight the whole of the idiomatic expression in each sentence above. What does it mean?

Speaking 3: individual long turn
(Part 2)

1   Look at the photos, which show people who are affected by the weather. Make sentences beginning like this:

- What's happening in this photo is that …
- What's different about this photo is …
- What they seem to be doing in this photo is …
- What I notice about the person/people in this photo is that …
- What must be most difficult for these people is …
- What I'd find difficult in this situation is …

2   Work with a partner.

Student A: Compare and contrast photos A and B, and say which type of weather is causing the people the most difficulty. You should keep talking for about one minute. Remember to find general areas to compare and contrast between the two pictures. Think about:
- what has happened/what's going to happen
- the weather conditions
- the problems the people are facing
- how they might be feeling.

Student B: Listen to your partner and stop him/her after about one minute. Then answer this question (about 20 seconds):

'*What of type of weather causes most problems in your country?*'

3   Now turn to photos C and D on page 183 and change roles.

Student B: The photos both show people checking the weather. Compare and contrast them, and say why each group of people might be interested in the weather.

Student A: Listen to your partner and time him/her. After about one minute, stop your partner. Then answer the question below, giving a short answer only (about 20 seconds).

'*Do many people in your country watch the weather forecast on TV?*'

Use of English 2:
error correction
(Part 4)

1 Can you answer these questions? Check your ideas on page 188.

1 Do waterfalls freeze?
2 Why is it always windy near skyscrapers?
3 How long will it be before Neil Armstrong's footprints on the moon disappear?
4 Has a tossed coin ever landed on its edge?

2 Read the title and the text below quickly. What do you learn about this topic?

3 Read the text again and look carefully at each line. Some of the lines are correct, and some have a word which should not be there. If a line is correct, put a tick (✓). If a line has a word which should not be there, write the word at the end of the line. There are two examples at the beginning (0 and 00).

THE END OF THE RAINBOW

0	There is an old tradition that there is a pot of the gold	*the*
00	buried at the end of the rainbow, but no one in the	✓
1	world has ever discovered this gold, or even reached to	
2	the end of a rainbow. Why not? In order to see a rainbow	
3	there, you must first have the right weather conditions,	
4	and you must have to be looking at the sky in exactly	
5	the right direction. But then if you move yourself	
6	towards the place where the rainbow seems to end, you	
7	will find that you do not actually get any nearer enough;	
8	the rainbow always stays at the exactly same distance from	
9	you. So you can never get it to the end – the rainbow will	
10	always be ahead of you. In fact, a rainbow doesn't really	
11	have an end at all. It is actually shape a circle, but we don't	
12	see it all because of the Earth gets in the way. In the right	
13	conditions, when the complete circle could possibly be	
14	seen from a plane – if you happened to be in a window	
15	seat! But that still won't help you to find out the gold.	

4 Do you know any traditional stories or beliefs about natural events such as rainbows, thunderstorms, lightning or earthquakes?

Writing: informal letter
(Part 2)

1 Read the task below and underline key words.

An English friend, Pat, has written to ask you for some advice. This is part of the letter you have received.

> I've finally got the chance to come to your country. I hope to stay for about a month, and I can either come in February or in September – I'm not sure which would be better? I'd like to spend most of my time in the countryside and if possible to see some wildlife, especially birds.
>
> Can you give me some advice on the best time to come and which places I should visit, and the best way of getting there?
>
> Best wishes,
>
> *Pat*

Write your **letter** in **120–180** words. Do not write any postal addresses.

2 Which of these features of language are typical of informal writing?

• contractions
• passive forms
• shorter sentences
• colloquial expressions
• phrasal verbs
• connectors such as *therefore, consequently, however*
• connectors such as *and, but*
• exclamation marks (!)

3 Now write your letter. Remember that an informal letter still needs to be well organised and to have clear paragraphs. Check your work when you have finished.

▶ Writing reference p.206, 209

1 Which is the odd one out? Explain why.

1 miaow bark gallop neigh
2 fur bone feathers skin
3 stable cage can kennel
4 beak paw claw hoof
5 flutter fly soar purr
6 fear emotion happiness sadness

2 Which natural disaster is being described in the following sentences?

1 The .... in Alaska in 1964 measured 9 on the Richter scale and caused major damage over a large region.
2 .... leads to lower crop production or crop failure, and may be linked to global warming.
3 What destroyed the ancient city of Pompeii was a ....
4 A .... , or tidal wave, could be caused by a meteor hitting the Earth.
5 Nearly all .... that involve people are triggered by the victims themselves, so skiers and mountaineers should learn how to recognise and avoid danger.
6 .... are the most common and widespread of all natural disasters except fire.

3 Choose the correct alternative to complete each of these sentences.

1 All the evidence suggests that animals can *read* / *understand* your mind.
2 Twins often have a *near* / *close* bond with one another.
3 When the child was *admitted* / *accepted* to hospital, she missed her beloved pet.
4 We were relieved to get a phone call telling us that *all* / *everything* was well.
5 My mother very rarely *takes* / *makes* time off work.
6 The pilot landed the plane safely and a potentially *fatal* / *tragic* situation was avoided.

4 Rewrite the following sentences using phrasal verbs and expressions from the box. Make any changes necessary.

come across	keep on	run out of	make up
take place	put out	take part in	slow down
phone up	go on	end up	pick up

1 I wanted to be a vet, but now I'm working in a bank.

2 We may find that we have no more oil left if we don't try to save energy.
3 *Tsunamis* occur in all the major oceans of the world.
4 The wave starts to go slower when it approaches land.
5 It can take firefighters days to stop a big forest fire.
6 Have you ever been involved in a demonstration?
7 You should continue going to the gym even if you didn't enjoy it – it'll help you to keep fit.
8 I called directory enquiries but the telephone number is ex-directory.
9 I don't know what's happening next door – they're making an awful noise.
10 When I was tidying up my room, I found an old storybook I'd had as a child.
11 Trade Fairs are a good place to get new ideas.
12 If you can't do any of the questions, just invent the answers.

5 Read the text below and think of the word which best fits each space. Use only one word in each space. There is an example at the beginning (0).

LIVING WITH LIONS

Mark and Delia Owens have (0) *been* working to save endangered species for many years. They met (1) .... studying zoology at university and married shortly after (2) .... taken their degrees. They then sold all their possessions (3) .... bought one-way tickets to Botswana, in southern Africa. (4) .... they wanted to do in Botswsana was study lions in a natural setting, but they had (5) .... any money.

They set up camp in a remote valley in the Kalahari desert, (6) .... than eight hours' drive from the nearest town. They had (7) .... little money for petrol that they could only afford to drive to the town once (8) .... few months and the rest of the time they were on (9) .... own. Their life was rewarding but dangerous. One night they were camping out in the desert (10) .... they woke up to find they were surrounded by nine lions. But they knew that (11) .... the lions were hungry, they themselves were probably not in much danger.

After a few years they managed to find (12) .... money to buy a small plane so that they (13) .... track the movements of the lions across the desert. (14) .... seven years, they left Botswana to continue their research elsewhere, but they never forgot (15) .... animals they had come to know and love.

UNIT
14 Getting there

Speaking 1

1 Do the quick quiz below.

> **1 You have won £1,000,000. Would you**
> A *put it in a bank account?*
> B *share it with your family?*
> C *use it to do something you have always wanted to do?*
>
> **2 You can change places with anyone in the world for a week. Would you choose**
> A *a film star because they have such a luxurious lifestyle?*
> B *an explorer because they have such an exciting life?*
> C *a politician because then you could change the world?*
>
> **3 You have the chance to travel anywhere in the world. Would you go**
> A *somewhere completely different from your own country?*
> B *somewhere relaxing?*
> C *somewhere on your own?*

2 Compare your answers with a partner. What do you think your answers say about each of you?

Reading 1: multiple-choice questions (Part 2)

1

1 You are going to read an extract from a novel about a girl called Rowan who dreams of travelling the world. Read the extract quickly and answer the following questions.

1 Where does Rowan grow up?
2 Where does she go to work?
3 Where does she dream of travelling to?

2 What do you know about these places? Would you like to go to any of them?

Rowan was twenty-four years old. She'd been dreaming of travelling the world since she was twelve.

It was Mr Kinear, her geography teacher back home in
5 Scotland, who had first set her dreaming. He cycled to school summer and winter wearing a poncho. He was not a man who kept to the point. Trying to fill young minds with facts – a country's imports, exports, natural resources, populations – did not make him happy. He
10 would gaze across the rows of faces before him, aware of how tired they might be of the process of gathering new knowledge. He would see who was sucking a sweet and who was gazing out of the window and who was passing notes to whom, and he could not bear to think that he was
15 the cause of this boredom.

So instead of teaching, he would tell his pupils about his journeys. He told them about his days of backpacking through Peru and Australia, and about his journey from this little Scottish town where he'd been born down to
20 London, across Europe to India. Not knowing what to think, his pupils continued to suck, gaze and scribble.

Only Rowan in her stiff new school uniform listened. She was spellbound. She wanted to do that, go to places where she was not known, travel the world with just a
25 rucksack and a spare pair of shoes. She wanted to get away from this town, away from her parents and the routine life they led, from strict mealtimes, with breakfast at seven thirty, lunch at a quarter to one, tea at five thirty, and from the family's annual fortnight's trip to the
30 seaside. She wanted to spend years on the move until she found the place where she was meant to be.

In those days, she would get excited just being somewhere where the buses were a different colour. She was convinced there was a place somewhere out there
35 where she would be completely happy. She would find it. One day she would walk into some strange little town, sit down at a table in a small café, look round and say, 'This is it. This is where I am meant to be.'

As soon as she'd finished school, she left the small
40 town where she lived with her parents in Scotland, and got a job as a secretary in London. She did not want to work at moving up the career ladder, but she kept her dreams. She imagined a whole wide gorgeous world waiting for her to tramp across it. Determined to get there,

45 she did not notice the things that were going on around her and so denied herself all sorts of simple pleasures – new clothes, music, nights out – in order to save up for her great adventure.

line 49 The routes she planned to take, following in the footsteps of other travellers, **greater**, she thought, than she would ever be, were
50 carefully marked on the maps that covered the walls of her room. One day, she told herself, she would visit the places on her maps and have her own great adventure. She would stand on lonesome railway platforms waiting for trains to come along with their clattering crowds of people, and travel to wherever the tracks took
55 her. She would go to Africa and watch wide grey lakes turn pink with flamingos. She would visit Patagonia and Peru. She would walk the Great Wall of China. She would trek the Australian outback, guided only by ancient dreaming songs, under southern skies. She would sleep under canvas, whilst beyond her tent a
60 jungle lived and moved. She would wander in the deserts of Sudan. She would do all that and more. She would. She would.

From IT COULD HAPPEN TO YOU by Isla Dewer

2   Now read the text again. For questions 1–7, choose the answer (A, B, C or D), which you think fits best according to the text.

1 The writer suggests that Mr Kinear was
  A unobservant of what was going on in his classroom.
  B successful in involving the students in his subject.
  C sympathetic to his students' feelings.
  D uninterested in his students' problems.

2 Rowan was impressed by Mr Kinear because
  A he described the places he had visited so vividly.
  B he had travelled to places she had always wanted to see.
  C he was an example of someone who had escaped.
  D he understood her frustration with her own situation.

3 During her schooldays, when Rowan thought about travelling, she wanted to
  A see sights that were unusual.
  B experience different cultures.
  C find a place where she fitted in.
  D learn how to adapt to new situations.

4 The writer says that when Rowan went to London,
  A she was frustrated because her pay was too low for her to enjoy life.
  B she was disappointed that her job offered so few opportunities.
  C she was confused by the size and activity of the city.
  D she was unaware of the possibilities the city offered.

5 'Greater' in line 49 refers to
  A Rowan's maps.
  B the routes Rowan planned.
  C other travellers.
  D the journeys of other people.

6 When she was planning her journey, Rowan's aim was to
  A use the cheapest means of transport to get to know the country.
  B get to know local people in the countries she visited.
  C visit areas where no one else had ever been.
  D see as wide a variety of places as she could.

7 What is the main impression the writer gives of Rowan in this extract?
  A She is bored with her unfulfilling job.
  B She is single-minded about fulfilling her dream.
  C She is unrealistic about travel in the modern world.
  D She is prepared to face up to difficult problems.

3   How do you think the story continues? Does Rowan fulfil her dream?

4

1 Divide into three groups. Group A should look at page 187, Group B at page 188 and Group C at page 190. You are each going to read a possible summary of how the story continues.

2 Work with two students from the other groups. Tell each other the summary you have read. Decide:

1 which one you like the best.
2 which you think is the real one.

Vocabulary 1: hopes and ambitions

1

1 Match the sentence halves. Use the words in bold to help you.

1 I can't believe it – he's **scored**
2 If you work hard you should **achieve**
3 The first arrow he shot **hit**
4 Congratulations! You've **met**
5 I hope she will **achieve**
6 He **took**
7 Last night I **had**
8 I hope to **fulfil**

a) **the target** right in the middle.
b) **aim**, and then fired at the target.
c) all your **goals**.
d) **my dream** of travelling round the world.
e) **a dream** about taking an exam.
f) his third **goal** of the match!
g) all her **aims**.
h) all your sales **targets** for this month.

2 What is the difference in meaning between:

1 *score* a goal and *achieve* a goal?
2 *hit* a target and *meet* a target?
3 *take* aim and *achieve* an aim?
4 *have* a dream about something and *fulfil* a dream of something?

3 Discuss with a partner:

1 an aim you'd each like to achieve in the next three months. How could you achieve this?
2 a dream you'd each like to fulfil in the next ten years. What might make it possible?

2

1 Choose the correct phrasal verb in each of the following sentences.

1 In order to *get on / get up* successfully in life you need to have clear goals.
2 You must be prepared to *face up to / face with* problems and difficulties.
3 You mustn't *give out / give up* hope when things don't seem to be going your way.
4 If a problem *comes up / comes across*, you can always ask for help.
5 Often someone else will be able to help you *deal with / deal in* your problems.
6 It's a good idea to *talk round / talk through* your ideas with someone you trust.
7 Working in a team can *bring up / bring round* all sorts of new ideas.
8 You may well *finish off / finish up* achieving more than you expected.

2 Discuss these questions.

1 Do you turn to someone else for help and advice when you have problems, or do you prefer to sort things out on your own?
2 What kind of problems are easiest/hardest to deal with?

Use of English 1: word formation (Part 5)

1 Which of the following makes you want to try harder? Can you add any more ideas?

- your teacher praises you
- your parents praise you
- you win a prize
- someone gives you help with something you find difficult
- you find a new interest

2

1 Look at the title of the text below. How would you answer the question?

2 Read the text quickly to find out if your ideas are mentioned.

3 Use the word given in capitals below the text to form a word that fits in the space in each line. There is an example at the beginning (0).

WHERE DOES MOTIVATION COME FROM?

Most of us are **(0)** _reasonably_ motivated to do well in life. But there's a big difference between those **(1)** .... people who push themselves to be more and more **(2)** .... , and the people who have lower **(3)** .... and who just want to move through life **(4)** .... , step by step. Some experts claim that an adult's level of motivation is fixed in their early **(5)** .... and that highly motivated people have often had to cope with some sort of **(6)** .... experience or with a problem such as an **(7)** .... or a physical disability. They say this inspires people to show that they can overcome even the **(8)** .... difficulties. But psychologists **(9)** .... that this is not the full story and that for both children and adults, **(10)** .... and reward are essential.

0	REASON		
1	AMBITION	6	PLEASE
2	SUCCEED	7	ILL
3	EXPECT	8	GREAT
4	STEADY	9	BELIEF
5	CHILD	10	ENCOURAGE

Listening 1: multiple matching (Part 3)

1 You will hear five people talking about their dreams and ambitions.

1 For questions 1–5, choose from the list A–F what each speaker says. Use the letters only once. There is one extra letter which you do not need to use.

A I don't really expect to fulfil my dream.
B I want to meet people from different countries.
C I'm interested in extreme situations.
D I suddenly found I had a goal for the future.
E The support of my family has been essential to me.
F My choice of career was influenced by a present I received.

Speaker 1		1
Speaker 2		2
Speaker 3		3
Speaker 4		4
Speaker 5		5

2 Listen again to check.

2 Read these quotations from the recording. How does each statement relate to the speaker's ambitions?

1 'It was a real inspiration to me.'
2 'Then hopefully I can make my fortune.'
3 'I really want the best for you.'
4 'I fell out with my coach.'
5 'I'll have to start soon or I'll never make it.'

3 Discuss which speaker's ambition is closest to your own and which is furthest away.

4 Do the following exercise to help you identify what you could or should do with your life.

1 Divide a piece of paper into two columns. In the left-hand column, write down all the things you really enjoy doing. In the right-hand column, write down all the things you are really good at.

What I really enjoy doing	What I'm really good at
seeing different places	

2 Work with a partner. Compare what you have written in each column. Discuss what your partner could do which combines his/her preferences and talents.

"I want to be a role model."

Reading 2: gapped text (Part 3)

1 You are going to read an article about possibilities for tourism in Oman. Look at the title and subheading of the text, and the photos. Discuss these questions.

1 Do you know anything about Oman?
2 Would you like to go there on holiday? What would you expect to do while you were there?

2 Seven paragraphs have been removed from the article. Choose from the paragraphs A–H the one which fits each gap (1–6). There is one extra paragraph which you do not need to use. There is an example at the beginning (0).

3 Complete the following sentences using a word from the box in the correct form. The words are all in the text.

amaze	attract	harm	spectacle
unlike	watch	wealth	

1 Oman is a .... kingdom located on the west of the Arabian peninsula.
2 It contains some of the most .... caves in the world.
3 Louise Hose, a geologist, was invited to carry out the .... task of investigating the caves' potential for tourism.
4 She was .... by the size of the cave called *Majlis al Jinn*.
5 Luckily, she found that this cave does not contain any .... gases.
6 For the local people, the idea of cave tourism may be very .... , as it will lead to increased job opportunities.
7 However, the authorities will need to keep a .... eye on developments, in order to protect the caves and their environment.

4 Discuss these questions.

1 Would you like to visit the cave described in the text? Why?/Why not?
2 Are there any similar places in your country? Are they developed for tourists to visit?
3 What areas of your country do you think should be developed? What do you think tourists would be interested in seeing in your country?
4 What is the most spectacular place you have ever visited? Describe it.
5 What are the advantages and disadvantages of tourism for the local people/the environment?

A NEW DIRECTION

Below the mountains of Oman lies one of the world's most spectacular caves. Gregory Crouch joins Louise Hose, who is investigating whether it could bring adventure seekers to this wealthy Arabian kingdom.

Louise Hose is a geologist who has explored some of the world's deepest caves. Now an unlikely task has brought her to Oman.

0	H

Some day Oman's oil will run out, so planners in the country are looking ahead and searching for ways of generating other sources of wealth, from copper mines to biscuit factories. They hope that the caves can be developed to make them centres for underground tourism. The idea might sound crazy, but Louise plans to test it thoroughly.

1	

I go from the capital, Muscat, to join Louise in her camp high up in the mountains. She is about to explore an underground chamber called *Majlis al Jinn* – the meeting place of the spirits. We both stand shivering around the camp fire with our guide, 18-year-old Salim al Ghadani, and his younger brother Said. Soon their father arrives with a load of water he's brought up by donkey from the river far below. Sixty-year-old Mohammed is a thin man with watchful eyes.

FOR TOURISM?

2 _____

Louise and I put on our rucksacks and walk to the entrance to the cave. Louise has already set up the rope to allow us to descend the 70 metres to the floor of the cave. She goes first. It's ten minutes before I hear her give the signal on the radio to say she's got to the bottom. My turn has come. I begin to edge my way slowly into the hole. The sky becomes a small circle as I gradually lower myself down on the rope.

3 _____

I can just see Louise looking up from the bottom of the cave. She is just a dark shape – I am still 100 metres above her. Several minutes later I finally get there.

4 _____

Directly beneath the skylights there are two high piles of stones and pebbles that have fallen through the holes. Stalactites hang from the ceiling. I am amazed by the sheer size of the chamber – nearly two Great Pyramids would fit inside. I follow Louise around the cave as she investigates it. It is one of the world's largest underground chambers, she tells me.

5 _____

Goat tracks criss-cross the fields below. I ask Louise whether she thinks that development of this cave could provide more opportunities for tourism in Oman.
'It's certainly possible,' she says. 'A road could be built. And a tunnel could be made through the rock to get visitors into the cave.

6 _____

In the meantime, sadly, only a few adventurers are likely to have the chance to explore the underground world beneath the mountains of Oman.

A The giant chamber slowly opens out around me. It feels as if I am hanging under the dome of a colossal cathedral. Sunbeams from the entrance holes cut through the darkness. Glancing down, I can't make out much detail in the dim light.

B Her results might show that the caves are too dangerous, or their ecosystems too fragile, to sustain tourism. On the other hand, it is possible that the caves could be the focus of a new national park, attracting more tourists to Oman.

C 'But the cost would be huge. And even if it succeeds, it will be years before it will be possible for tourists to visit the caves.'

D He shakes his head when I comment on the beauty of the mountains. 'No, no,' he says. 'In winter it is too cold. In summer it is too hot.' He makes a living by herding goats. 'I have many hopes for my sons,' he explains. 'But mostly I hope that they will find good jobs.'

E Eventually I begin the heart-pounding rope climb to the surface. Forty minutes later we're sitting side by side on a rock overlooking the cave entrance, in the open air. We watch a pair of eagles soar across the sky.

F I stop walking and examine a few dead leaves stuck in a crack in the rock. 'That's what will happen to you if the cave floods,' she says. Suddenly the idea of cave tourism seems a little less attractive.

G When we meet up, I realise that despite all her experience of caves around the world, Louise is as amazed as I am. 'This place is huge – and day-lit,' she says.

H She has been asked to examine the country's spectacular cave systems. The authorities want her to investigate ways into the caves, measure how big they are and check for harmful gases.

Vocabulary 2: holidays and travel

1

1 What type of holiday is each speaker describing?

backpacking   a cruise   an expedition
a holiday course   trekking   a package holiday
    a guided coach tour   a city-break

1 'It's really relaxing – and I just love knowing that every day we'll go in to a new port and see a whole new place.'
2 'It's good because it's all done for you – you just look in the brochure and choose what you want.'
3 'I really enjoy them – I've done one on archaeology and one on windsurfing. It's a great way to meet people.'
4 'I really enjoy travelling in a group, with a guide who can explain the history of all the places we drive through.'
5 'I'm going to Nepal – we'll be walking in the mountains for about two weeks. It'll be tough, because the conditions are quite hard, but I'm looking forward to it.'
6 'I've got a round-the-world student ticket and I hope to travel for about four months. I'll be staying in cheap accommodation and living out of a rucksack.'
7 'I'll only be away a short time – I'm going for a weekend to Prague with my friends.'
8 'I love being in the fresh air, and I really enjoy the fact that it's keeping me fit at the same time! The only time I don't like it much is when I have to walk up steep hills!'

2 How many of these types of holiday have you been on? Which ones would you like to try?

2   Work with a partner. The words in the box are all things you could take on holiday with you. Decide which ones you might need for the holidays in Exercise 1. You may need the same things for more than one holiday.

insect repellent   driving licence   boots
digital camera   visa   hat   sunglasses
sleeping bag   smart clothes   guidebook
   phrasebook   map   sea-sickness pills
diary   washing powder   note-pad
towel   security wallet   shopping bag

3   Use words from Exercise 2 to complete the following dialogues. Then listen to check.

1 A: There are a lot of mosquitoes here. I hope I don't get bitten.
  B: Do you want to borrow my .... ?
2 A: I can't understand anything on the menu – have you got the .... ?
  B: Here – there's a good section on food words in four languages.
3 A: The one bad thing about trekking is that you have to carry a .... for when you camp out at night.
  B: Well – at least you can lie in your bed and see the stars!
4 A: I never travel abroad without buying a good .... before I go.
  B: Me too – then I know what the most interesting places to visit are, so I don't waste time when I'm there.
5 A: This .... is really old, but it protects my face from the sun.
  B: I think you should buy a new one as you're going on a cruise. And you'll need .... for the evenings, so you could buy a whole new set of things to wear!
6 A: My sister is a terrible traveller – every time she goes on a boat she feels ill.
  B: Has she asked the doctor for some .... ? They should help.

4   Discuss these questions.

1 Have you ever forgotten to take something important on holiday? What?
2 What is the **one** thing you could **not** manage without on holiday?

Grammar: ways of giving advice

1   Read the information below and find four different phrases used to give advice.

ADVICE TO TRAVELLERS

When travelling in the desert or at high altitudes, you can get sunburned surprisingly quickly. It is advisable to use sun cream, wear a hat and protect your eyes with good quality sunglasses.

You may be tempted to bring back exotic souvenirs, but travellers should remember that buying souvenirs made from animal skins or ivory may threaten endangered species and may also be against the law.

When travelling away from home, it's wise to have a spare pair of glasses or contact lenses plus an adequate supply of any medication that may not be available locally.

The month-long Islamic festival of Ramadan will finish at the end of this month. The celebrations for the end of the festival will last for two or three days and travellers are reminded that most things will be closed during that time.

2   Complete the second sentence so that it has a similar meaning to the first sentence, using the word given. Do not change the word given. You must use between two and five words, including the word given.

1   They advised me to have a course of injections.
advisable
They told .... to have a course of injections.

2   Drinking unboiled water is not advised when travelling off the beaten track. **wise**
It is .... unboiled water when travelling off the beaten track.

3   Trying to climb the mountain on your own is not recommended. **attempt**
You should .... the mountain on your own.

4   'I wouldn't stay out in the sun too long, if I were you,' he said. **advised**
She .... out in the sun too long.

5   Visitors should remember to bring warm clothes.
reminded
Visitors .... will need warm clothes.

6   'You must see the traditional dancers – they're excellent,' he said. **miss**
He told me I should .... the excellent traditional dancers.

7   You shouldn't leave without visiting the cathedral. **ought**
You .... before you leave.

8   It is a good idea for guests to keep their passports in the hotel safe. **recommended**
Guests .... their passports in the hotel safe.

3   Write five pieces of advice for visitors to your country, using the structures in Exercises 1 and 2.

4   Chris had a lot of problems while he was travelling abroad. What should or shouldn't he have done to avoid these problems?

1   'My wallet with my credit card in was stolen from my pocket.'
He should have kept his wallet in a safe place. He shouldn't have kept his credit card in his wallet.

2   'I got terribly sunburned.'

3   'I couldn't understand what anyone was saying.'

4   'I lost my passport.'

5   'My parents got very worried because they didn't know where I was.'

6   'My girlfriend back home started going out with someone else.'

5   Think of a situation in which you did not take advice and something went wrong as a result. Then take turns to tell a partner what happened. Your partner should tell you what you should or shouldn't have done.

Speaking 2: prioritising (Parts 3 and 4)

1 Work with a partner and do the Part 3 task below. You should talk for about three minutes. Remember to consider every item before making your final choice.

'*I'd like you to imagine that you are planning to go on a long camping trip in the mountains with a friend. You have all the necessary equipment like food and clothes. Here are some extra things that you might want to take with you. Talk to each other about how important each item might be for the trip. Then say which **two** you think are the most important to take.*'

2 Compare your ideas with the rest of the class. Did you all choose the same items?

3 Discuss some of the following questions with your partner.

1 What do you like doing on holiday?
2 What's the most exciting holiday you've ever had?
3 Do you think it's better to travel with friends or alone? What are the advantages and disadvantages?
4 Have you, or anyone you know, been on a strange or unusual holiday?

Use of English 2: open cloze (Part 2)

1 Read the title of the text below. Discuss what you know about Mount Everest. Then read the text to see if you were right.

2 Read the text again and think of the word which best fits each space. Use only one word in each space. There is an example at the beginning (0).

MOUNT EVEREST
THE WORLD'S HIGHEST MOUNTAIN

In the past, the Sherpas who lived at (0) *the*.......... foot of Mount Everest never thought of climbing (1) .... Their lives were hard enough. But after Everest (2) .... been identified as the world's highest mountain, its conquest was seen (3) .... the greatest challenge on Earth. The Sherpas, adapted to living at high altitudes, have acted as guides and porters to climbers ever (4) .... Sherpas take great pride in (5) .... work, but it is dangerous. At (6) .... 175 people have died on the mountain since the first attempt (7) .... Everest in 1921.

(8) .... Hillary and Tenzing reached the summit in 1953, it was obvious that others would follow them, (9) .... no one expected there would be so many. (10) .... are now ropes and ladders to help people up the difficult sections. But the danger of the mountain (11) .... still not be underestimated. Not (12) .... ago, eight climbers were killed in one night when a storm blew up suddenly. (13) .... this tragedy, hundreds of climbers visit the mountain (14) .... year, hoping to stand on the roof of the world. Everest has now been climbed by a fifteen-year-old girl – Sherpa Ming Kips – and by a seventy-year-old Japanese man – Yuichiro Miura. So (15) .... it still remain the greatest challenge on Earth?

3 Discuss these questions.

1 What qualities do you think make a good explorer? Discuss why the qualities below might be important, then add two more ideas.
  • curiosity
  • courage
  • determination

2 What do **you** think is the *greatest challenge on Earth*?

Search for the hero

Sometimes the river flows but (1) ....
(2) .... but never leaves.
It's a shame.
Oh life – like love that walks out the door
Of being rich (3) ....
Such a shame.
But it's then, then (4) ....
To make you feel (5) ......
And that's why you should (6) ....
Just seek yourself and (7) ....

Chorus
You've got to search for the hero inside yourself,
Search for the secrets you hide.
Search for the hero inside yourself
Until you find the key to your life.

In this life, long and hard though it may seem,
Live it as (8) ....
Aim (9) ....
Just keep the flame of (10) ....
The missing treasure you must find
Because you and (11) ....
Can build a bridge across the stream.
(12) .... in life's rich tapestry -
Your passport to a feel supreme.

Chorus
Search inside yourself (you've got to search)

Listening 2: song

1 Look at the following extracts from the song above. Do you think the song will be generally positive or negative about life?

a) that faith arrives
b) you will shine
c) you'd live a dream
d) Weave your spell
e) so high.
f) nothing breathes
g) only you alone
h) or being poor
i) truth burning bright
j) keep on aiming high
k) A train arrives
l) at least alive

2 Now decide where the expressions from Exercise 1 fit in the song.

  3 Listen to the song and check your answers.

4 Which of the following sentences summarises the song best? Find some expressions in the song which support your answer.

a) Everyone should try to escape from their problems.
b) Everyone has the ability to succeed.
c) Everyone needs to find someone to love.

Writing: composition (Part 2)

1 Read the following task.

1 Do you agree or disagree with the statement?
2 How will you organise your composition? (Look back at Unit 7 page 90 if necessary.)

After a class discussion on the advantages and disadvantages of travelling to other countries, your teacher has asked you to write a composition giving your opinions on the following statement:

The best holidays are the ones spent in a different country.

Write your **composition** in **120–180** words.

2

1 The following statements are all about holidays abroad. Decide if each one is describing a positive or a negative aspect.

1 You can experience different cultures.
2 The food is different.
3 You can have a break from your normal routine.
4 It gives you a chance to relax.
5 You might not understand the language.
6 It could cost a lot.
7 You can visit famous and unusual places.
8 You can get to know different people.
9 You may find yourself in stressful or dangerous situations.

2 Choose which points above you will include in paragraphs 2 and 3 of your composition. You can also add other ideas of your own. You should have no more than three ideas for each paragraph.

3   In a composition, you should support each main point with a reason, result or example. Complete the following paragraph from the middle part of a student's composition, using appropriate linking expressions from the box.

> so   as well as this   for example   however
> finally   as a result   in addition   and in this way

(1) .... , holidays abroad can also bring problems. (2) .... , you have to do more travelling and (3) .... these holidays are more expensive. (4) .... , if you do not speak the language of the country you are visiting, you can have problems getting around and meeting local people. (5) .... , if you don't know the country you may find yourself in stressful or difficult situations.

4   Now read the following task. Decide:

1 whether you agree or disagree with the statement.
2 what points you could include in your composition.

Your teacher has asked you to write a composition, giving your opinions on the following statement:

Holidays should be times for doing new and challenging things, not just relaxing in familiar places.

Write your composition in 120–180 words.

5   Write a composition in answer to the task in Exercise 1 or 4.

▶   Writing reference pp.206, 213

6   When you have finished, check your work. Which of the techniques below are appropriate:

a) to check written work done for class?
b) to check written work in an exam?

1 Read through your writing once to check the organisation is clear, and that you have a new paragraph for each section. Then read it a second time to check grammar, vocabulary and spelling.
2 Write on alternate lines so that you have space to make corrections.
3 Write a rough version of your essay and then copy it out again.
4 Check words you are not sure of in a dictionary.
5 Be aware of your own problems (e.g. articles, subject–verb agreement) and check for these.

Exam focus
First Certificate in English

How much do you know about the FCE exam? Try the quiz your teacher will give you.

1 There is a mistake with vocabulary in each of the following sentences. Find the mistakes and correct them.

1 When you apply for a job, you may have to give the names of two references.
2 There are good prospects for promoted for the right candidate.
3 At first he made a lot of money but then his luck started to go out.
4 I'm a bit short with cash – can you lend me €50?
5 He invested a lot of money for stocks and shares.
6 A very high percent of payments nowadays are made with credit cards.
7 It wasn't the fault from the restaurant that you ate too much!
8 Far out in the desert were some mystery ruins.
9 Tools such as swords and spears were found.
10 A herd of thieves attacked the security van.
11 Scientists have analysis how animals communicate.
12 Skiers are under great danger if an avalanche occurs.
13 Driving conditions are difficult due to thick foggy.
14 Becky is always in the move – she never stays long in one place.
15 By the age of 30, he had filled all his goals.

2 Decide what word is missing in each of the following sentences and write it in the correct place.

1 Unfortunately, I don't know to type.
2 I believe that people should able to choose the hours they want to work.
3 I didn't succeed passing the exam.
4 Take your phone case you need to contact me.
5 If I stayed at university instead of dropping out, I'd be earning a lot more money now.
6 Even I don't win the prize, I'm glad I entered the competition.
7 I don't like told what to do.
8 They were made wait for over an hour.
9 Alexander the Great believed to have died through drinking unclean water.
10 I have to get eyes tested – I'm sure I need glasses.
11 She's not good at languages to work as an interpreter.
12 I studied for a long time that I'm exhausted now.
13 What you mustn't forget that you will hear the recording twice.
14 I don't like rain much, but I really hate is wind.
15 Passengers are reminded that they not leave their luggage unattended.

Use of English: multiple-choice cloze (Part 1)

3 For questions 1–15, read the text below and decide which answer (A, B, C or D) best fits each space. There is an example at the beginning (0).

THE GREAT STORM

At first, January 14th 1938 was no (0) ...A... from any other winter day in the seaside town of Aberystwyth. The grey sea (1) .... to the horizon, where it met the grey winter sky. But towards evening the wind (2) .... and every wave (3) .... onto the beach with greater force than the last.

As the night (4) .... , the wind increased, howling around the houses which faced the sea. (5) .... agree that the storm (6) .... its height at five o'clock in the morning, when winds were (7) .... to be 150 kilometres an hour. The wind broke windows and smashed front doors, allowing the sea water to (8) .... in.

An even greater drama was (9) .... place in a lonely cottage further down the coast. As the storm grew worse, the three women who lived there decided to abandon their home. No sooner had they (10) .... their coats than an enormous wave burst (11) .... the front door. The next wave brought the roof down, trapping them in the house. Fortunately, the driver of a passing train raised the (12) .... and the women were rescued from the wreckage.

As dawn (13) .... , the terrible effects of the storm became clear. It took many years to repair the (14) .... and reinforce the sea wall in order to (15) .... a repetition of the terrifying events of that night.

	A	B	C	D
0	different	contrasting	separate	altered
1	pulled	stretched	passed	flowed
2	toughened	hardened	lengthened	strengthened
3	crashed	hit	banged	knocked
4	went out	broke down	wore on	grew up
5	Spectators	Viewers	Audiences	Witnesses
6	got	touched	brought	reached
7	estimated	guessed	valued	told
8	spill	pour	drip	rain
9	taking	becoming	having	keeping
10	taken on	put off	picked up	come to
11	through	out	off	up
12	emergency	danger	alarm	crisis
13	broke	went	came	fell
14	hurt	injury	harm	damage
15	check	bar	protect	prevent

Use of English: open cloze (Part 2)

4 For questions 16–30, read the text below and think of the word which best fits each space. Use only one word in each space. There is an example at the beginning (0).

DANNY EAST, UNDERGROUND TRAIN DRIVER

Danny East is (0) ..*a*..... London underground train driver. He has (16) …….. doing the job (17) …….. four years, and has become famous because (18) …….. his announcements to passengers. He produces a light-hearted commentary (19) …….. seems to cheer up regular tube users and tourists alike. He (20) …….. it, he says, because he loves talking, and to help him to concentrate.

As (21) …….. as the train starts, Danny begins his commentary, sounding as (22) …….. he is the captain of a spaceship. 'OK, ladies and gentlemen,' he says. 'For your pleasure and delight,' (one of (23) …….. favourite phrases), 'I am the captain of your journey (24) …….. this underground train. So sit back and enjoy the view.' He produces a stream of information, both funny (25) …….. also more serious, about every (26) …….. of the stations the train stops at, as well as advice such (27) …….. , 'Watch out when you get off because there's a big gap (28) …….. the train and the platform and we don't want to see you falling down it!'

He doesn't know (29) …….. effect he's having on the passengers because he can't see (30) …….. faces. But he gets lots of fan mail from passengers grateful to him for brightening up their daily journey.

Use of English: key word transformations (Part 3)

5 For questions 31–40, complete the second sentence so that it has a similar meaning to the first sentence, using the word given. Do not change the word given. You must use between two and five words, including the word given. There is an example at the beginning (0).

Example:

0 You must do exactly as I tell you.
carry
You must ...*carry out my*..... instructions exactly.

31 Someone should have told her that the coffee was hot.
warned
She .... the hot coffee.

32 My hair is getting too long – it needs cutting soon!
get
I will have .... soon.

33 He eventually stayed in Venice for two weeks.
ended
He .... in Venice for two weeks.

34 She didn't want to pay for the drinks she'd had.
avoid
She tried .... for the drinks she'd had.

35 Gunilla had to take Mrs Carling's children to school.
responsible
Gunilla .... Mrs Carling's children to school.

36 The company has invented a useful piece of equipment.
up
The company has .... a useful piece of equipment.

37 I think it would be a good idea for you to take the job.
were
If I .... the job.

38 I could only just see him in the dim light.
out
I could barely .... in the dim light.

39 Many animal species have become extinct in the last hundred years.
out
Many animal species .... in the last hundred years.

40 Because of the snow I couldn't arrive any earlier.
snowing
If it .... , I would have arrived earlier.

Use of English: error correction (Part 4)

6 For questions 41–55, read the text below and look carefully at each line. Some of the lines are correct, and some have a word which should not be there. If a line is correct, put a tick (✓) at the end of the line. If a line has a word which should not be there, write the word at the end of the line. There are two examples at the beginning (0 and 00).

THE EXCITEMENT OF TRAVEL

0	Travelling can be very exciting, especially when you have been	*been*
00	wanted to visit the place for a long time. I remember the first time	✓
41	I have arrived in Hong Kong and saw the buildings along the	
42	waterfront – the skyline was become familiar because I had seen it	
43	in pictures so many times, but I couldn't believe that I was really there	
44	at last! Many people say so that they have had the same feeling	
45	of disbelief when they are travel. But this partly depends on where	
46	you live. What seems be exciting to people from one part of the	
47	world can seem more ordinary to those who they live in a similar	
48	area. For example, people from New Zealand might be excited	
49	to go to Hong Kong, but less excited than to visit Australia, because	
50	it is nearer and more familiar. Now I've seen Hong Kong, I want	
51	to see more places that up so far I have only seen in pictures.	
52	I would like to visit places that are out of the way, not the usual	
53	tourist destinations, but for that is not so easy nowadays. There	
54	are fewer places that those are unexplored, and tourists now	
55	can get to places that were impossible since twenty years ago.	

Use of English: word formation (Part 5)

7 For questions 56–65, read the text below. Use the word given in capitals at the end of each line to form a word that fits in the space in the same line. There is an example at the beginning (0).

THE UNLUCKY BURGLAR

This is a true story about a rather unfortunate (0) .*criminal*. He was an	**CRIME**
(56) .... persistent burglar, who was busy robbing an empty	**EXTREME**
house when he was suddenly and (57) .... disturbed by the	**EXPECTED**
(58) .... of the two people who lived there. After a short, angry	**ARRIVE**
(59) .... with the couple, he managed to push past them and	**ARGUE**
escape into their back garden. (60) .... for him, he found the	**LUCKY**
garden was (61) .... surrounded by high fences at the sides, and a wall	**COMPLETE**
at the end. Although he had no (62) .... of what was on the other	**KNOW**
side, he decided to get over the wall. Showing great (63) .... ability, he	**ATHLETE**
ran at the wall and was (64) .... in getting over it – but when he landed	**SUCCEED**
on the other side he found to his (65) .... and horror that he was	**AMAZE**
standing in the local prison yard.	

Paper 5 Speaking tasks

Unit 1 Exam focus: introduction (Part 1)
Exercise 3, p.15

Student A, ask Student B the following questions.

1 Where are you from?
2 What do you like about living there?
3 Do you work or are you a student?
4 What kind of jobs do the people in your town do?
5 What do you enjoy most about your work or studies?
6 Do you have any hobbies?
7 What is there to do in the evenings in the place where you live?
8 How do you usually spend your holidays?
9 What do you hope to do in the next few years?

Unit 2 Speaking 2 (Part 2)
Exercise 5, p.27

Student B

Unit 2 Speaking 2 (Part 2)
Exercise 5, p.27

Student A

Unit 11 Exam focus: a complete test
Exercise 3, p.139

Student A (interlocutor)

Part 1 (introduction)

Say: 'Good morning/afternoon. I'm going to ask you some questions about yourselves.'
Ask student C: 'Where do you live?'
Ask student D: 'And you?'
Ask student C: 'What do you enjoy about living here/there?'
Ask student D: 'And what about you?'
Ask student C and D in turn:
'Tell me something about your room.
What do you usually do at the weekends?
What do you usually do in the evenings?
What do you enjoy studying most?
What sort of music do you enjoy?
What kind of transport do you use most?'

Part 2 (long turn)

Say: 'Now I'd like each of you to talk on your own for about a minute. I'm going to give each of you two different photographs.'

Tell Student C: 'Here are your two photographs. (**Point to photos A and B on page 139.**) These photographs show people working hard. Please let your partner see them. I'd like you to compare and contrast the photographs, and say which person you think is working harder.'

Allow Student C to talk for a minute. Then stop him/her. Say 'Thank you'.

Ask Student D this question:

'Do you often work late at night?'

After about 15–20 seconds, say 'Thank you'.

Tell Student D: 'Here are your two photographs. (**Point to photos C and D on page 139.**) These photographs show people who are making money. Please let your partner see them. Compare and contrast the photographs, and say what you think might be good and bad about each way of making money.'

Allow Student D to talk for a minute. Then stop him/her. Say 'Thank you'.

Then ask Student C this question:

'How do you think the person in the second photograph is feeling?'

After about 15–20 seconds, say 'Thank you'.

Part 3 (collaborative task)

Say: 'Now, I'd like you to talk about something together for about three minutes. I'm just going to listen.

Here are some pictures of things we can do to avoid getting stressed. (**Point to the pictures on page 183.**) Talk to each other about how useful each one is and then choose two that you think are the most important for students. It is not necessary to agree with each other. You only have about three minutes for this, so don't worry if I interrupt you.'

After about three minutes, say 'Thank you' and stop Students C and D.

Part 4 (discussion)

Ask students C and D some of these questions, in any order. Stop them after about four minutes. You may not need to use all of the questions.

1 What sorts of things do you do to relax?
2 What industries and jobs are important in your town?
3 What kind of job do you think is most or least stressful?
4 Would you rather work inside or outside?
5 Do you think life is more stressful nowadays than it was in the past?
6 More people are working at home these days. Why do you think this is?

Unit 4 Speaking (Part 3)
Exercise 2, p.51

Imagine that a local gym wants to attract more people. Here are some suggestions for making the centre more popular. First, talk to each other about the advantages and disadvantages of these suggestions. Then decide which one would the most successful in attracting people to the gym.

Unit 6 Exam focus: long turn (Part 2) Exercise 3, p.77

Student A (examiner)

1 Tell Student B:

'Here are your two photographs. (**Point to the photos on page 184.**) They show people keeping in touch. Please let your partner see them. I'd like you to compare and contrast these photographs and say which person seems the happiest. You only have about a minute for this, so don't worry if I interrupt you.'

Allow Student B to talk for a minute. Then stop him/her. Say 'Thank you.' Ask Student C this question:

'Do you often write letters to your friends and relatives?'

After about 15–20 seconds, say 'Thank you'.

2 Tell Student C:

'Here are your two photographs. (**Point to the photos on page 186.**) They show people taking photographs. Please let your partner see them. I'd like you to compare and contrast these photographs and say how you think the people might feel about being photographed. You only have about a minute for this, so don't worry if I interrupt you.'

Allow Student C to talk for a minute. Then stop him/her. Say 'Thank you'. Ask Student B this question:

'Do you like taking photographs?'

After about 15–20 seconds, say 'Thank you'.

Unit 5 Speaking 3 (Part 2) Exercise 5, p.63

Student A

Student B

Unit 13 Speaking 3 (Part 2) Exercise 3, p.163

Student B

Unit 11 Exam focus: a complete test Exercises 2–4, p.139

Part 3 (collaborative task)

Unit 6 Exam focus: long turn (Part 2) Exercise 3, p.77

Student B

Unit 1 Exam focus: introduction (Part 1) Exercise 3, p.15

Student B, ask Student A the following questions.

1   Where were you born?
2   What is the most interesting part of your town or village?
3   Do you have a large family or a small family?
4   How long have you been studying English?
5   Which do you prefer, watching television or going to the cinema?
6   What sort of programmes or films do you like to watch?
7   How do you spend your holidays?
8   Is there anywhere you would particularly like to visit?
9   What kind of job do you hope to be doing in ten years' time?

Unit 10 Exam focus: collaborative task/ discussion (Parts 3 and 4) Exercise 2, p.126

Student A (examiner)

Part 3 (collaborative task)

Say to the other students: 'I'd like you to talk about something together for about three minutes. I'm just going to listen. I'd like you to imagine that a school is producing a leaflet to help students study effectively. Here are some things that can help students to study. (**Point to the pictures on page 186.**) First, talk to each other about how useful each one is. Then choose three that you feel should be included in the leaflet. It is not necessary to agree with each other. You only have about three minutes for this, so don't worry if I interrupt you.'
After about three minutes, say 'Thank you' and stop them.

Part 4 (discussion)

Ask the other students some of these questions, in any order. Stop them after about four minutes. You may not need to use all of the questions.

1   What sort of things help you to study?
2   How important do you think it is to have a good memory?
3   Which part of your education have you enjoyed most so far?
4   What would you like to learn about in the future?
5   How do you think your education has been different from that of your parents or grandparents?
6   What do you think education will be like in the future?

Unit 9 Speaking 2 (Part 2) Exercise 3, p.113

Student B

Unit 11 Exam focus: a complete test Exercise 4, p.139

Student C (interlocutor)

Part 1 (introduction)

Say: 'Good morning/afternoon. I'm going to ask you some questions about yourselves.'
Ask student A: 'Where do you live?'
Ask student B: 'And you?'
Ask student A: 'What do you enjoy about living here/there?'
Ask student B: 'And what about you?'
Ask student A and B in turn:
'What do you usually do at the weekends?
What did you do on your last birthday?
What's the next special occasion you're going to celebrate?
How much exercise do you do?
How easy do you think it is to keep fit and healthy? Why?
What do you hope to do in the next ten years?'

Part 2 (long turn)

Say: 'Now I'd like each of you to talk on your own for about a minute. I'm going to give each of you two different photographs.'
Tell Student A: 'Here are your two photographs. (**Point to photos A and B on page 139.**) These photographs show people working hard. Please let your partner see them. I'd like you to compare and contrast the photographs, and say how you would feel in these situations.'
Allow Student A to talk for a minute. Then stop him/her. Say 'Thank you.'
Ask Student B this question:
'Which person do you think is working harder?'
After about 15–20 seconds, say 'Thank you'.
Tell Student B: 'Here are your two photographs. (**Point to photos C and D on page 139.**) These photographs show people who are making money. Please let your partner see them. Compare and contrast the photographs, and say which person or people have the easiest job.'
Allow Student B to talk for a minute. Then stop him/her. Say 'Thank you'. Then ask Student A this question:
'How do you think the person in the first picture is feeling?'
After about 15–20 seconds, say 'Thank you'.

Part 3 (collaborative task)

Say: 'Now, I'd like you to talk about something together for about three minutes. I'm just going to listen. Here are some pictures of things we can do to avoid getting stressed.
(**Point to the pictures on page 183.**) Talk to each other about how useful each one is and then choose two that you think are the most important for students. It is not necessary to agree with each other. You only have about three minutes for this, so don't worry if I interrupt you.'
After about three minutes, say 'Thank you' and stop Students A and B.

Part 4 (discussion)

Ask students A and B some of these questions, in any order. Stop them after about four minutes. You may not need to use all of the questions.

1 Would you like to work in an office?
2 Do you think some jobs are too highly paid? Which ones?
3 Which is most important, a high salary or job satisfaction?
4 If you had enough money to live on without working, would you still want to work?
5 What sort of jobs used to be important in your country in the past?
6 What do you think life would be like if people didn't have to work?

Unit 10 Exam focus: collaborative task (Part 3)

Exercise 2, p.126

Students B and C (candidates)

Unit 6 Exam focus: long turn (Part 2)
Exercise 3, p.77

Student C

Communication activities

Unit 1, Grammar 2 Exercise 4, p.12

Student A

You've just come back from abroad. You've been …

- doing a holiday job (Say what and where.)
- working quite long hours (Say how many hours a day.)
- earning quite good money (Say how much.)
- meeting different sorts of people (Say who.)
- having a wonderful time (Say why.)

Unit 3, Grammar 1 Exercise 4, p.33

Student A

Unit 7, Grammar 1 Exercise 4, p.83

Student A

1 a dishwasher
2 a dictionary
3 a supermarket
4 a rose
5 a grandmother

Unit 10, Reading 1 Exercise 5, p.121

Answers to the IQ puzzles on p.190

1 a) T b) F c) F d) T e) F f) F; 2 – 64; 3 –16;
4 Eight ladies and 14 cats; 5 a)

Unit 12, Listening 2 Exercise 1, p.147

1 Tommy Lee Jones and Will Smith.
2 They're law enforcement officers (protecting people against aliens).
3 To protect them from an alien light which would make them lose their memory.
4 Tommy Lee Jones retires.

Unit 13, Listening Exercise 5, p.158

Student A: You are going to interview the famous conservationist, Jane Goodall. Ask her these questions.
1 How did you become interested in animals?
2 How did you get involved in working with animals?
3 How many years did you spend in the wild?
4 What was your biggest challenge?
5 What was the most exciting thing you found?
6 What was your worst experience?
7 What dangers do the animals face now?
8 What is being done to help them?

Unit 14, Reading 1 Exercise 4, p.167

Group A

Rowan saves up enough money and sets off on her travels. She finds that the world is bigger and lonelier than she had expected, and that her image of the romance of travel does not match up to reality. When she finds herself alone in Sydney, without money or friends, she feels like giving up and going home. But then she finds a job, meets a young Australian man, and decides to stay.

Unit 13, Speaking 1 Exercise 1, p.156

1 Robbie Williams: Rottweiler
2 Leonardo DiCaprio: bearded dragon
3 George Clooney: potbellied pig

Unit 1, Grammar 2 Exercise 4, p.12

Student B
You've just come back from holiday. You've been …
- staying with your cousin, who lives in another country (Say where.)
- eating delicious food every day (Say what.)
- going out every evening (Say where.)
- meeting lots of people (Say who.)
- having a wonderful time (Say why.)

Unit 3, Grammar 3 Exercise 4, p.39

Unit 7, Grammar 1 Exercise 4, p.83

Student B
1 a dry cleaner's
2 February
3 a chimney
4 a telephone
5 a dentist

Unit 14, Reading 1 Exercise 4, p.167

Group B
Rowan stays in London dreaming of her travels, but stuck in her dead-end job. Then a friend helps her to get an interview for a job with a big international company which would give her the chance to travel through her work – but she would have to move to live in Australia. Rowan is offered the job and accepts, but then at the last minute she realises that everything she really cares about is back at home in Scotland, and she returns to the place she started from.

Unit 12, Reading 1 Exercise 4, p.142

After a long investigation, it is discovered that Rebecca made the holes herself as she had a fatal illness. Once Maxim de Winter has been cleared of her murder, he leaves England forever and goes to live abroad with his new wife.

Unit 12, Speaking Exercise 3, p.145

1 Mrs Amos was sentenced to 60 days' imprisonment, but this was reduced on appeal. She said her time in prison had not been pleasant, but had taught her a lesson.
2 Smith was sentenced to 20 months in prison, a $5,000 fine, community service and a ban on computer and Internet activity. US authorities said the punishment serves as a warning to would-be virus writers who think they can launch viruses on the Internet without paying a price.
3 Major Ingram and his wife each got an 18-month suspended sentence and were fined £25,000 including costs. The friend got a one-year suspended sentence and a fine of £17,500 including costs.
4 Nine of the men received jail sentences, the longest being for 12 months. The three others were given 200 hours of community service. One of the jail sentences was suspended for a year. Eleven of the men were banned from all football games in Britain and abroad for up to six years.
5 Richard Ure was banned from driving for 18 months. He was also sentenced to three months' detention.

Unit 13, Use of English 2 Exercise 1, p.164

Match the answers to the questions (they are in jumbled order). How many did you get right?
a) As long as there is no meteor impact – millions of years.
b) Only once in front of witnesses (in 1972). The chances of it happening are one in a billion.
c) Because the building changes the direction of the wind high up in the air, sending it down towards the ground.
d) They do at the edges, but the water in the middle doesn't because of the speed at which it is travelling.

Unit 3, Grammar 1 Exercise 4, p.33

Student B

Unit 13, Listening Exercise 5, p.158

Student B: You are Jane Goodall, a famous conservationist. Read through the information below, then answer the interviewer's questions.

Childhood: Always interested in animals. Given a toy chimpanzee at age of two (still have it).

Early career: Worked as waitress to save up money to go to Africa. In Africa, was offered job studying group of chimpanzees in wild.

Time spent there: 26 years

Biggest challenge: Took a long time for chimpanzees to get used to me.

Most exciting discovery: Chimpanzees use sticks as tools to catch insects. (Before that, people thought only humans could make and use tools.)

Worst experience: Death of favourite chimpanzee, David Greybeard, through illness.

Dangers faced by the chimpanzees: Loss of their homes – forests being cut down as firewood. Hunters kill the animals for meat or capture them to sell as pets.

Conservation activity: Educating people to be aware of problems – feel that hope lies with young people.

Unit 8, Speaking 1 Exercise 3, p.94

Scoring

Box A

Friends think you're quiet and deep.

There's more to you than meets the eye – the people who know you well realise they can really depend on you. You're happier being with friends you know well rather than getting to know new people. But remember that strangers are just good friends you don't know yet!

Box B

Friends think you're lively.

You're the life and soul of the party – which is why people who meet you never forget you! You've always got something to say or a funny story to tell. The only trouble is that you sometimes try to hide shyness by going over the top – relax and people will like you just the same.

Box C

Friends think you're confident.

When people first meet you, they either love you or they don't! But that's fine – it isn't a problem for you. You've got the confidence to be yourself and you would never put on an act. You don't depend on others and that's why you've got such a good set of friends. But don't forget that other people may be less sure of themselves than you are.

Unit 8, Grammar 1 Exercise 1, p.95

Dear Aggie

As soon as I met Stephanie, I wanted her (1) .... (*be*) my best friend. I didn't have that many other friends – and I was pleased (2) .... (*have*) someone to do things with. We were both interested in (3) .... (*do*) all the same things – like watching football. We promised (4)............ (*support*) each other – and I really meant (5) .... (*keep*) my promise.

But now I've got the chance (6) .... (*move*) abroad (7) .... (*work*) for an international company, and I'd really like (8) .... (*accept*) the job. But I'm afraid Stephanie won't let me (9) .... (*go*) without getting upset about the idea. I'm really keen on (10) .... (*take*) the opportunity, though.

How can I tell her it's time for me (11) .... (*move on*)?

Marc

189

Unit 10, Reading 1 Exercise 5, p.121

1 True or false?
a) If Tuesday is the first day of the month, then the following Sunday is the sixth day of the month.
b) Maria's grandmother's son could be Maria's daughter's brother.
c) All my friends play football. Bruce plays football, therefore Bruce is my friend.
d) If you turn a right-handed glove inside out, it will fit on your left hand.
e) If a clock is placed upside down when the time is 12.45, the minute hand will point to the right.
f) Baz is taller than Gaz. Don is shorter than Baz. Therefore Gaz is the tallest.

2 What is the next number in this series?
144 … 121 … 100 … 81 … ?

3 Carlotta is four years old. Her big sister Amy is three times as old as Carlotta. How old will Amy be when she is twice as old as Carlotta?

4 A group of old ladies meet for an afternoon tea party. They bring all their cats. In all, there are 22 heads and 72 feet. How many old ladies and how many cats are in the room?

5 What would the next picture be in this series? Choose from a–e.

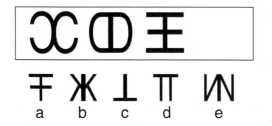

a b c d e

Turn to page 187 for the answers. How well did you do?

Unit 14, Reading 1 Exercise 4, p.167

Group C
Rowan saves up enough money to set off on her travels. She is ready to leave when her flatmate in London steals all her things and goes travelling instead, leaving behind her baby. Rowan has to take responsibility for the baby and this changes her whole life. Returning to the small town in Scotland where her family live, Rowan begins to see that her home could be the place where she'll find what she was looking for.

Unit 11, Speaking 1 Exercise 2, p.130

SCORING

☆ **Are you a 'people person'?** (Questions 1 and 2)

10 marks You would probably be happiest working alone – you could be self-employed. But you'll still need to work on those people skills!

15-20 marks You're clearly a people person with good communication skills. You might be suited to a career which involves meeting people and talking on the phone.

25-30 marks You are obviously an outgoing, sociable soul. Many jobs in the music business and in advertising require confident go-getters like you.

☆ **Are you a leader or a team player?** (Questions 3 and 4)

10 marks You probably like to blend in with the crowd. But you need to come out a bit, because the ability to work in a team and share ideas is one of the best skills you can have.

15-20 marks You're probably happy working in a team and sharing responsibilities. You would be suited to a job that needs good team skills, such as nursing.

25-30 marks You are clearly a natural leader and are willing to make that extra bit of effort to improve a situation. Have you ever thought of becoming a manager? A good leader works well in a team, encourages others and carries responsibility well.

☆ **How do you feel about change?** (Questions 5 and 6)

10 marks You might be a bit unsure about moving away from home to study or work just yet. That's OK – there's no hurry!

15-20 marks You have a healthy attitude to change and you don't mind trying new things.

25-30 marks You treat new things as a challenge. You might be suited to a job that involves lots of travel and meeting new people every day. Models, entertainers and tour guides need these qualities.

☆ **What motivates you?** (Question 7)

5 marks You might be quite money motivated or interested in a job that's high on glamour. You might be good at setting up your own business or working in fashion.

10 marks You're probably more active and fun loving. A career that involves meeting people and spending lots of time outdoors might suit you.

15 marks You are more motivated by creative fulfilment. A career that allows you to develop your creative potential would suit you.

Grammar reference

1 Adjectives ending in -ed and -ing

1.1 Adjectives ending in -ed

Adjectives ending in -ed or have the same form as the past participle of a verb, e.g. *amazed, relieved, terrified, thrilled*. We often use them to describe people's feelings. They normally follow *be, feel, seem, look*, etc.
*I was **amazed** to hear I'd won the prize.*
*What's the matter? You seem a bit **annoyed**.*

1.2 Adjectives ending in -ing

We use these adjectives to describe the effect that experiences or events have on us. They can be used before the noun or after *be* and other linking verbs.
*That was a **terrifying** experience.*
*The explanation was rather **confusing**.*

2 Adverbs

2.1 Formation of adverbs from adjectives

1 Many adverbs are formed by adding -ly to the adjective form of the word, e.g. *clear – clearly*.
For adjectives ending in -y, drop the y and add -ily, e.g. *happy, happily*.
For adjectives ending in -le, drop the e and add -y, e.g. *gentle, gently*.
For adjectives ending in -ic, add -ally, e.g. *automatic, automatically*.

2 Some words ending in -ly are adjectives only, not adverbs, e.g. *cowardly, friendly, silly*. If an adverb is needed, a phrase must be used.
*They greeted us **in a friendly way/manner**.*

3 Some words ending in -ly can be used both as adjectives and adverbs, e.g. *hourly, daily, nightly*.
*Take the medicine twice **daily** (adv.).*
*There is a **daily** (adj.) flight to the island.*

4 Some adverbs have the same form as adjectives, e.g. *early, fast, hard, still, straight; better, best, worse, worst.*
*He's got a **fast** (adj.) car and he drives it **fast** (adv.).*
*She has **straight** (adj.) hair. He looked **straight** (adv.) at me.*

5 Some adverbs have two forms, one like the adjective and the other form ending in -ly, e.g. *clear, close, direct, easy, free, hard, high, late*. There is usually a difference in meaning.
*Stand **clear** of the doors. (= keep away)*
*Try to speak more **clearly**. (= so we can understand)*
*He works very **hard**. (= he makes a lot of effort)*
*He had **hardly** any petrol left. (= almost none)*
*The balloon was **high** up in the sky. (= a long way up)*
*They think very **highly** of you. (= have a good opinion)*
*Children under 12 travel **free**. (= they don't have to pay)*
*You can walk **freely** in the hotel grounds. (= without restrictions)*
*The train arrived **late**. He's not been very well **lately**. (= recently)*

2.2 Comparison of adverbs

The comparison of adverbs is similar to that of adjectives. See 4.5.

2.3 Adverbs of manner

These adverbs are used to say how the action of the verb is carried out.
1 Common adverbs of manner include: *accurately, badly, carefully, patiently, straight, well*.

They usually come in the middle of the sentence, after the main verb. If the verb has an object, the adverb comes after the object.
He spoke (the words) **clearly***.*
She went **straight** *to the house.*

2 Prepositional phrases may also be used adverbially to answer the question *How?*
I ordered the book **over the Internet***.*
He shouted **in a loud voice***.*

2.4 Adverbs of indefinite frequency

1 These adverbs are used to talk about how often we do things. We can put them in order from most often to least often like this:

always   most often
almost always
generally/normally/regularly/usually
frequently/often
sometimes
occasionally
almost never/hardly ever/rarely/seldom
not ... ever/never   least often

2 In statements and questions, these adverbs come:
• after *be* when it is the only verb in the sentence
  I am **always** *a bit depressed in winter.*
• after the first auxiliary verb when there is more than one verb
  I have **often** *seen her walking here.*
• before the main verb when there is only one verb
  We **sometimes** *watch a video on Friday evenings.*
• in questions, after the subject
  Don't you **usually** *work with Jenny?*

3 In negative sentences, *not* comes before *always, generally, normally, often, regularly* and *usually.*
  We **don't often** *see him nowadays.*

4 *Always* and *never* come at the beginning with imperatives.
  Always *look on the bright side of life.*
  Never *refuse an opportunity.*

2.5 Adverbs of definite frequency

1 These are common adverbs of definite frequency:
  once
  twice   ⎫
  five times   ⎬ *a day/week/month/year*
  several times ⎭
  every day/week/month/morning/afternoon/evening
  every three/couple of/few years
  on Monday/Wednesday/weekdays, etc.

2 These adverbs usually come at the end of the sentence:
  I phone my sister several **times a day***.*
  He goes jogging **every morning***.*
  They go abroad **every few years***.*
  They may come at the beginning for emphasis.
  Several times a month *I go to the cinema.*

2.6 Sentence adverbs

Sentence adverbs do not modify the verb, but express the speaker's opinion or attitude.

1 The following adverbs explain how he/she is speaking: *honestly, personally, seriously,* etc.
  Personally, *I think it's wrong to hunt animals.*
  Seriously, *this is an important question.*

2 The following adverbs comment on how likely something is: *actually, certainly, clearly, definitely, maybe, obviously, perhaps, possibly, probably, surely,* etc.
  Perhaps/Maybe *it will rain tomorrow.*
  Surely *he is going to come?*
  We'll **probably** *be late.*

3 The following adverbs explain the speaker's reaction to some event: *annoyingly, hopefully, luckily, naturally, surprisingly, understandably,* etc.
  Hopefully, *we'll win the match.*

4 Sentence adverbs usually come at the beginning of the sentence. However, the adverbs *certainly, definitely, possibly* and *probably* usually come in the middle of the sentence, after the verb *be,* before the main verb, or after the first auxiliary verb.
  He is **definitely** *not a friend of mine.*
  I'll **certainly** *be seeing her tomorrow.*

2.7 Intensifiers: almost, barely, hardly, nearly, scarcely

These adverbs have a negative meaning. They come in the middle of the sentence.
I **almost/nearly** *missed the train.*
We could **barely** *hear the speaker.*
She **hardly** *knew anyone at the party.*

3 Articles

3.1 The definite article: the

We use the definite article *the:*
• when the person or thing referred to is unique
  The sun *came out and soon we were dry.*
  The President *is giving a speech tonight.*
  the London Marathon*,* **the Olympic Games**
• to talk about specific things when the context makes it clear what we are referring to
  Your shoes are in **the cupboard***.*
  Your dinner's in **the fridge***.*
• to talk about previously mentioned things
  A man and a woman walked into the room. **The man** *was wearing sunglasses.*
• with superlatives
  He's **the bravest person** *in the team.*
• to talk about a generic class of things
  The bicycle *was invented about 200 years ago.*
  The tiger *is in danger of becoming extinct.*
• with oceans, seas, rivers and deserts
  He's sailed across **the Atlantic** *and* **the Pacific***.*
  We went by canoe up **the Orinoco***.*
  She said she'd driven across **the Sahara***.*

- with plural mountain ranges and island groups
  Are **the Andes** as high as **the Himalayas**?
  The British Isles include **the Isle of Wight** and **the Isle of Man**.
- with continents and countries whose name includes a common noun
  He's from **the Czech Republic**, but he's living in **the United States**.
- areas
  There is a range of mountains in **the north**.
- with hotels, cinemas, theatres
  They had afternoon tea at **the Ritz**.
  That new Polish film is on at **the Odeon**.
- with newspapers
  The Times, The Guardian, The Independent
- with national groups
  The English are a mixed race.

3.2 The indefinite article: a/an

Use the indefinite article *a/an*:
- with (singular) jobs, etc.
  She's **an architect**.
  Is your sister **a football fan**, too?
- with singular countable nouns (mentioned for the first time or when it doesn't matter which one)
  I'd like **a sandwich** and **a glass of orange juice**.
  What you need is **a rest**.
- with these numbers: 100, 1,000, 1,000,000
  There were over **a hundred** people at the wedding.
  He made **a million** dollars in one year.
- in exclamations about singular countable nouns
  What **an amazing view**!

3.3 The zero article

1 We use no article (the zero article) when talking about:
- uncountable, plural and abstract nouns used in their general sense
  We had awful **weather** on holiday.
  Happiness isn't the only thing in life.
- continents and countries
  They are going to visit **Africa**.
  Have you been to **Nepal**?
- mountains and lakes
  They are going to climb **Mount Everest**.
  Is **Lake Titicaca** in Peru?
- villages, towns and cities
  San Marco is a pleasant little fishing village.
  Saffron Walden is a small market town near Cambridge.
  Auckland is the biggest city in New Zealand.
- streets, roads, etc.
  In London, there are some good shops on **Oxford Street**.
- magazines
  Do you read **Time** magazine?
- illnesses
  I've got **flu** and Sue's got **indigestion**.
  Watch Out! I've got **a headache** and I think I'm getting **a cold**.

2 Also use no article in the following expressions:
to/at/from school/university/college
at home
go home
in/to class
to/in/into/from church
to/in/into/out of prison/hospital/bed
to/at/from work
for/at/to breakfast/lunch/dinner
by car/bus/bicycle/plane/train/tube/boat
on foot
by accident/chance

4 Comparison

4.1 Types of comparison

There are three types of comparison:
1 to a higher degree (comparative form + *than*)
  Mountain climbing is **more dangerous than** windsurfing.
  The Andes mountains are **higher than** the Alps.
2 to the same degree (*as ... as*)
  Hiring a car would cost just **as much as** getting a taxi.
  I don't enjoy swimming **as much as** I used to.
3 to a lower degree (with *less* + *than* and *the least*)
  I am **less keen** on taking risks **than** I used to be.
  Antarctica is **the least** densely populated continent.

4.2 Comparative and superlative forms of adjectives

1 One-syllable adjectives
  Add *-er* and *-est* to form the comparative and superlative of one-syllable adjectives.
  Which is the high**est** mountain in the world?
  For one-syllable adjectives ending in a vowel + a consonant, double the consonant, e.g. *hot – hotter – hottest*.
  For one-syllable adjectives ending in *-e*, add *-r* and *-st*, e.g. *fine – finer – finest*.
2 Two-syllable adjectives ending in *-y* and *-ow*
  For two-syllable adjectives ending in *-y* after a consonant, drop the *-y* and add *-ier* and *-iest*.
  Childhood is the happ**iest** time of your life.
  For two-syllable adjectives ending in *-ow*, add *-er* and *-est*.
  The road became narrow**er** as we went along.
For other two-syllable adjectives see 4.3 below.

4.3 more and most + adjective

Use *more* and *most* with:
- two-syllable adjectives (except for those listed in 4.2)
  Walking at high altitudes is **more tiring** than at sea level.
  It was the **most boring** magazine I'd ever read.
- adjectives with three or more syllables
  This exam was **more difficult** than the last one.
  This is the **most interesting** book I've read.

4.4 Irregular comparative and superlative adjectives

These are the most common irregular forms:
good – better – best
bad – worse – worst
little – less – least
much – more – most
far – further/farther – furthest/farthest
Jim is a **better** player than I am, but John is **the best.**
It's the **worst** game I've ever seen. It's even **worse** than their last one.
You live **further** from the station than I do, but Pedro lives **the furthest** away.

4.5 Comparing adverbs

1 Most adverbs of manner have two or more syllables. Therefore they form their comparatives and superlatives with *more* and *most*.
   If you speak **more clearly**, everyone will be able to hear you.
   Sami works **the most quickly**.

2 Adverbs with the same form as adjectives form their comparatives with *-er* and *-est*.
   I can run **fast**, but Toni can run even **faster**.
   We were **the earliest** people to get to the party.
   He'll need to work much **harder** if he's going to pass the exam.
   It'll take much **longer** if we walk – let's get the bus.
   Who's **the quickest** at mental arithmetic?
   We'll get there **sooner** if we walk.

4.6 Irregular comparative adverbs

1 *badly* and *well* use the same comparative and superlative forms as *bad* and *good*.
   I did **worse** in Maths than I'd expected, but **better** in English.

2 Other irregular forms include: *late – later – latest, much – more – most, little – less – least*
   Tom arrived **later** than Peter, but Mary arrived **last.**
   I don't go to the cinema **much**, but I go **more** than I used to.
   She likes Howard **less** than Dean, but she likes Sylvester **least** of all.

4.7 Modifying comparisons

We can use the following words to modify comparatives:
far / much / a lot cheaper/less expensive
very much bigger/better
rather harder
a bit / slightly / a little faster
no worse than
not any quicker
just as good as
almost / not quite as expensive as
not nearly as cheap
Watch Out! You cannot use *very* with comparatives.

5 Conditionals

5.1 Conditional linking words and punctuation

Common conditional conjunctions are: *if, as/so long as, unless, even if, providing, provided (that), on condition that, no matter how/who/what/where/when*
When the clause with the conditional linking word (*if, unless,* etc.) is at the beginning of the sentence, there is a comma. When the main clause begins the sentence, there is no comma.
If you give me your number, I'll phone you tomorrow.
As long as you take your mobile, I can phone you any time.
I won't go **unless you come with me**. (= if you don't come with me)
We're going on the walk **even if it rains**.
I'll help you **on condition that you don't tell**.
No matter how many times you ask me to, I won't do it.
Note: *in case* is used to describe things we do as precautions against what might happen.
I'll take the mobile **in case** I need to phone you.

5.2 General truths

FORM: *If* + present simple + present simple in the main clause
USE: to describe a general truth
If there **is** life on other planets, we **are not** alone.
Unless lions **are** frightened or hungry, they**'re not** very dangerous.

5.3 Possibility/likelihood in the present or future

FORM: *If*, etc. + present simple/present continuous/present perfect + present continuous, future or imperative in the main clause
USE: to describe what is possible or likely in the present or future
You **won't get** an interview **unless you've filled** in an application form.
Ask Tom to buy the land **no matter** how much it costs.
If you**'re watching** TV, you **will see** him presenting the news.

5.4 Unlikely or contrary to present fact

FORM: *If* + past simple/continuous + *would/could* etc. + past participle in the main clause
USE:
1 To talk about something:
* that is contrary to the present facts, or seen as very unlikely to happen
   If I **was/were** twenty years younger, I**'d emigrate**.
   If I **was/were** Prime Minister, I**'d make** health care free.
* which is very unlikely to happen in the future
   No matter how safe it **was**, I **wouldn't want** to travel in space.
   I **wouldn't apply** for that job **unless** I **thought** I had a good chance of getting it.

2 To give advice.
   I**'d write** it out again **if I were you**.

5.5 contrary to fact in the past

FORM: *If* + past perfect + *would/could* etc. *have* + past participle in the main clause
USE: to describe something in the past that could have happened but didn't, or that shouldn't have happened but did
I **wouldn't have told** her that **if I'd known** she'd tell everyone else.
She **could have got** there on time **if she'd not missed** the bus.

5.6 Modal verbs in conditional sentences

Modal verbs *can, could, might,* etc. can be used in all types of conditional sentences.
I **might send** him an email **if** I **can find** his address.
If she **had** someone to look after the children, she **could go out** to work.
If they **had told** us about the danger, we **might never have gone** there.

5.7 Mixed conditionals

It is possible to have sentences that mix conditionals:
- an *if* clause referring to the past with a main clause referring to the present or future
  If I **had invested** in that company ten years ago, I **would be** rich now.
  If we **hadn't been given** all that homework, we **could go** swimming.
- an *if* clause referring to the present or future with a main clause referring to the past
  If you **don't like** sweet things, you **shouldn't have ordered** that dessert.
  If you**'ve got** an exam tomorrow, you **ought to have started** revising by now.

5.8 Polite expressions

1 *would* can be used after *if* in polite expressions.
   If you **wouldn't mind** waiting here, I'll find someone to look after you.
2 *If* + *should* is common in formal letters.
   If you **should** require any further information, please do not hesitate to contact us.
   For even greater formality, *if* can be omitted, and *should* can begin the sentence.
   Should you wish to contact me, I can be reached at the above address.

6 Countable and uncountable nouns

6.1 Uncountable nouns

These have no plural. The following are common nouns that are usually uncountable:
accommodation, advice, behaviour, bread, copper (and all other metals), *meat, sugar, English,* (and all other languages), *furniture, health, information, knowledge, luggage, maths* (and other school subjects), *news, progress, research, rice* (and all other grains and cereals), *salt,* (and all other condiments, e.g. pepper), *scenery, spaghetti, traffic, transport, travel, trouble, water* (and all other liquids), *weather, work.*
Note: Use *a slice, a lump* and *a piece* with uncountable nouns for food.
Just **one lump** of sugar, please.
I'll just have **a small slice** of cake.
Would you like **another piece** of toast?

6.2 Nouns which can be countable or uncountable

1 Nouns we can think of as a single thing or substance, e.g. *chicken, chocolate, egg, hair, iron, paper, stone*
   There are only **two chocolates** left in the box.
   You've got **chocolate** on your T-shirt.
   We'll have to buy **a new iron**.
   Green vegetables are rich in **iron**.
   Have you read today's **paper**?
   I need to go and buy **some paper** for the printer.
   There's **a hair** in my soup.
   She's got short dark **hair**.
   The house is built of **stone**. (= rock)
   The necklace is made of semi-precious **stones**. (= gems)
2 Nouns which are used to refer to particular varieties, e.g. *wine, country*
   Would you like **some wine**? This is **a very good wine**.
   I'd like to have a house **in the country**. He's worked in **five different countries**.
3 Words for some drinks, e.g. *coffee, beer*. The countable noun means *a glass of, a cup of, a bottle of,* etc.
   Coffee is produced in Africa and South America.
   Shall we have **a coffee** and a piece of cake?
4 *time, space, room*
   There's **no time** to talk – we have to rush!
   I didn't have **a very good time** at the party.
   There's **no space** left. You'll have to get another bag.
   Fill in the **spaces** with the correct preposition.
   There's **room** for seven people in this car.
   This is my favourite **room** in the whole house.

6.3 Uncountable nouns ending in -s

Some nouns ending in *-s* are uncountable and followed by a singular verb, e.g. *maths, physics, genetics, aerobics, athletics, news.*
The **news is** bad, I'm afraid.

6.4 Nouns ending in -s that are always plural

Some nouns are always plural and are followed by a plural verb, e.g. *clothes, glasses, jeans, trousers; pliers, scissors.*
These **trousers don't fit** me.
To refer to a single item, use *a pair of.*
I need **a new pair of glasses**.

6.5 Irregular plural forms

Some nouns have the same form in the singular and plural, e.g. *aircraft, crossroads, series, sheep, species*.
*There are many different **species** of dogs. This **species** is very rare.*

6.6 Collective nouns

Some nouns can be used with a singular verb if we see them as a single unit, or a plural verb if we are referring to members of the group, e.g. *the army, the family, the government, the media, the press*.
***My family** is very big. All **my family are coming** to the wedding.*
These nouns only take a plural verb: *cattle, the people, the police*

6.7 Determiners used with countable and uncountable nouns

1 *lots/a lot of* + plural countable and uncountable nouns (informal)
   *I've got **lots/a lot of** homework, so I can't go out.*
   *I've got **lots/a lot of** brothers and sisters.*
2 *much* + uncountable nouns
   *We don't have **much homework**.*
   ***How much money** do you need?*
3 *many* + plural countable nouns
   *How **many** bags have you got?*
   *There are **many** interesting places in the world.*
4 *little, a little, a bit of* + uncountable nouns
a) *a little, a bit of* means *at least some*
   *Just **a little rice**, please – not too much.*
   *I've got **a bit of money**, but not enough to get a taxi.*
b) *little* without *a* means *almost none*. This can be emphasised with *very*.
   *The government has done **very little** to improve the situation.*
5 *few, a few* + plural countable nouns (= some but not many)
a) Before *few* you can use:
   • the indefinite article *a*
     *There were quite **a few people** in the room.*
     *There were only **a few people** staying at the hotel.*
   • *the last, the first, the next, every*
     *Over **the next few weeks**, we have a lot to get ready.*
     *For **the first few minutes**, you may feel a bit nervous.*
     *I phone her **every few days**.*
b) When *few* is used without *a*, it means *almost no*. This can be emphasised with *very*.
   *(Very) **few** people know the secret.*
6 *some* + uncountable nouns and plural nouns (= between *a little* and *a lot*)
   *There's **some** useful **information** on that website.*
   *There are **some** good **scenes** in that film.*
   Note: If *some* is stressed in speaking, it often means *not many*.
   *I suppose he's written **some** good books.*

7 *hardly any* + uncountable nouns and plural countable nouns
   *There were **hardly any customers** in the shop.*
8 *no, not any* + uncountable nouns and plural countable nouns
   *There was **no milk** left./There was**n't any milk** left.*
   *There were **no students** on the bus./There were**n't any students** on the bus.*

7 Emphasis with *what*

This structure is a relative clause introduced by a *wh-* word. We use it to put emphasis on key information in a sentence. It is more common in spoken English, but is also used in writing.
Many people do not realise that these accidents can be avoided.
***What many people do not realise IS** that these accidents can be avoided.*
The authorities are collecting as much information as possible.
***What the authorities are doing IS** collecting as much information as possible.*
You should learn to say no.
***What you should learn to do IS** say no.*

8 Gerunds and infinitives

8.1 The gerund form -ing

The gerund form *-ing* is used:
● after some main verbs (see 8.2)
● after an adjective, verb or noun followed by a preposition
  *She's really good at **swimming**.*
  *He apologised for **arriving** late.*
  *I quite like the thought of **working** in a travel agency.*
● in some fixed expressions
  *I **can't bear listening** to people who complain.*
  *I **can't help feeling** that he's cheating us.*
  *That book is not **worth reading**.*

8.2 Common verbs followed by the gerund form -ing

admit, appreciate, consider, delay, deny, detest, dislike, enjoy, escape, face, feel like, finish, forgive, give up, imagine, involve, mention, mind, miss, postpone, practise, prefer, put off, recommend, resent, risk, suggest, understand
*I **don't recommend** going to that restaurant.*

8.3 The infinitive with to

The infinitive with *to* is used:
● after some main verbs (see 8.4 and 8.5)
● after some adjectives
  *I was **happy to see** her.*
  *They were **wrong to refuse**.*
● after some nouns
  *She never regretted her **decision to be** a teacher.*
  *It's **time to leave**.*
  *He has no **wish to become** involved in the matter.*
● to express purpose
  *I went to London **to see** my aunt.*

8.4 Common verbs followed by the infinitive with to

afford, agree, appear, arrange, ask, attempt, bear, begin, care, choose, consent, decide, determine, expect, fail, forget, happen, hate, help, hesitate, hope, intend, learn, like, love, manage, mean, offer, prefer, prepare, pretend, promise, propose, refuse, remember, seem, start, swear, try, want, wish

I can't **afford to eat** in that restaurant.

8.5 Common verbs followed by object + infinitive with to

advise, allow, ask, cause, command, encourage, expect, forbid, force, get, hate, help, instruct, intend, invite, leave, like, mean, need, oblige, order, permit, persuade, prefer, press, recommend, remind, request, teach, tell, tempt, trouble, want, warn, wish

He **asked me to help** him.
Her parents **forbade her to see** Tom again.

8.6 The infinitive without to

The infinitive without to is used:
- after some main verbs (see 8.7)
- after modal verbs
  You **must leave** now.
- after would rather/had better
  You**'d better come** in now.

8.7 Common verbs followed by an object + infinitive without to

let, make, hear, help, see
He **made me repeat** the exercise.
Her parents **won't let her stay** out late.
I **heard her play** in Milan.

Watch Out! In passive sentences make, hear, help are followed by an infinitive with to.
He was made to report to the police.
Let cannot be used in the passive form. Instead, allowed must be used.
My parents **let** me **stay out** late.
I **am allowed to stay out** late by my parents.

8.8 Verbs followed by a gerund or to-infinitive with a difference in meaning

1 can't bear/stand, hate, like, love, prefer
   When these verbs are used with the infinitive, they refer to more specific situations. When they are used with the gerund, they refer to more general situations. The difference in meaning is very slight.
   I **prefer to work** on a computer than to write by hand.
   I **can't bear** listening to her complaining all the time.
2 remember, forget, regret, stop, try
- remember/forget + -ing refers to an action that happened before the moment of remembering/forgetting; + infinitive refers to an action after the moment of remembering/forgetting
   I **remember seeing** you somewhere before. (= that I have seen you)

Did you **remember to lock** the door?
She had completely **forgotten telling** him about her brother.
I **forgot to give** Sally the book.
- regret + -ing means be sorry about an action in the past; + infinitive means be sorry about a present action
   I **regret going** to the party last night.
   I **regret to have to tell** you that your car has been stolen. (formal)
- stop + -ing means stop something you do; + infinitive with to means stop in order to do something
   I **stopped drinking** coffee because it kept me awake at night.
   We **stopped to have** a coffee on the way home.
- try + -ing means do an experiment – doing the action may not be successful; + infinitive means make an effort – the action may be difficult or impossible to do
   Try studying at a different time of day – it might suit you better.
   Try to study at regular times.

9 Habit

9.1 Past habit: used to

FORM:
Positive statements
used to + infinitive
Negative statements
did/didn't + use to + infinitive
Questions
Did you/she/they, etc. use to + infinitive
USE:
We use used to to talk about past habits and states that do not occur now or no longer exist.
We **used to be** driven to school, but now we walk.
What **did** people **use to do** before electricity was invented?
Ken **used to be shy**, but he's more confident since he met Cindy.
Watch Out!
1 used to is not used to say how often things happened or how long they took.
2 Be careful not to confuse used to with be/get used to + noun/gerund. This means be/become accustomed to something because you have been doing it for a while.
   I**'m used to** making my own meals.
   I can't **get used to** the cold winters.
   Do you think we'll ever **get used to** eating dinner at six o'clock?

9.2 Past habit: would

Would is also used to talk about past habits and repeated actions but **not** about past states.
When I was little, I **would/used to** play with my brother's model cars.
NOT: We ~~would~~ live in a small village.

9.3 Past habit: past simple

This can also be used to describe past habits and states.
*When I **was** a child, I **walked** to school every day.*

9.4 Present habit: present simple or continuous

To talk about present habits we can use:
- present simple, often with a frequency adverb
  *I **generally park** outside the library.*
- present continuous + *always*
  *He's **always going** abroad on conferences.*
  This often suggests an annoying habit.
  *My sister **is always borrowing** my clothes.*

10 *have/get something done*

FORM: *have* + object + past participle (the most common form)
get + object + past participle (also possible when people are speaking informally)
USE: to say that someone else did something for you because you wanted them to
*He **had his hair cut** specially for the interview.*
*He's got such big feet he **has to have** his shoes specially **made**.*
*Where can I **get these papers photocopied**?*
*He decided to **get the photograph enlarged**.*

We also use *have something done* to say that someone else did something to you even though you didn't want them to.
*He **had to have a kidney removed**.*
*She said she'd **had her necklace stolen**.*

11 Hypothetical meaning

11.1 wish

1 We use *wish* + past simple to express a wish that has not come true in the present or to talk about wishes that might come true in the future. We use this structure when we want our own situation (or the situation of the person who is doing the wishing) to be different.
   *I **wish** Eleanor **liked** me.*
   ***Don't you wish** you **had** a big car?*
   *I **wish** she **was/were** going out with me.*
   ***We all wish** the weather **wasn't/weren't** so bad.*

2 We use *wish* + *would* and *could* to refer to general wishes for the future.
   *I **wish** the sun **would shine**.*
   *I **wish** I **could be** in the basketball team.*

3 *wish* + *would* is used to talk about wishes we have for other people.
   *I **wish** my sister **would** stop smoking.*
   *I **wish** he **wouldn't** chew gum all the time.*
   Watch Out! This form is not often used with *I* or *we*. To talk about wishes we have for ourselves we use *could*.
   *I **wish** I **could** have a holiday.*

4 We use *wish* + past perfect to refer to things we are sorry about in the past.
   *I **wish** I **had been invited** to the party.*
   *She **wishes** she **hadn't told** him about Carlo.*

11.2 If only

If only is used with the same verb forms as *wish*, and is used when your feelings are stronger. It is often used with an exclamation mark (*!*). It is often used with *would/wouldn't* to criticise someone else's behaviour.
If only I could find the answer!
If only they would stop talking!
If only I had never met him!

11.3 It's time

It's time is used with the past simple to talk about the present or future. We mean that the action should have been done before. For emphasis, we can also say *It's about time* and *It's high time*.
It's (about) time you started revising for the exam.
It's (high) time we set off. The train leaves in half an hour.

11.4 would rather

1 We use *would rather* + past simple to say what we want someone or something else to do in the present or future.
   I'd rather you didn't tell anyone about all this.
   Would you rather I asked someone else?
   I'd rather we didn't discuss that, if you don't mind.

2 We use *would rather* + past perfect to say what we wanted to happen in the past.
   I'd rather you hadn't told her that.
   I'd rather you had asked me first.
   Note: *would rather* + infinitive without *to* is used to talk about our or other people's preferences in the present or future.
   I'd rather go to the concert than to the opera.
   They'd rather go on foot.

11.5 suppose/what if?

Suppose means *What if ...?* It is used with:
1 the present simple to describe something that may possibly happen or may have happened.
   Suppose someone sees her with us.
   Suppose someone hears you coming in.

2 the past simple to talk about something that is just imagination or which is unlikely to happen in the future.
   Suppose Eleanor knew you loved her. What would you do?
   Suppose you won the prize. How would you feel?

3 the past perfect to talk about something that could have happened in the past but didn't.
   Suppose we hadn't told her. Do you think she would have found out?
   Suppose you had married Carlos. Would you have been happy together?

11.6 as if/as though

As if and as though can be followed by a present tense to talk about something that is likely to be true. When followed by the past tense, the implication is that the situation is unlikely.

You look **as if you are** hungry. (likely)
He talks **as if he knew** all about it. (unlikely)

12 Indirect speech, reporting verbs

12.1 Indirect speech

This is when we report something that has been said or written.

1 If the report is after the time the thing was said or written, the verb form generally changes as follows:

Direct speech	Reported speech
Present simple/continuous →	Past simple/continuous

'I **like** your shoes, Kate,' **said** Jack.
Jack **said** he **liked** Kate's shoes.

Past simple/continuous →	Past simple/continuous or past perfect simple/continuous

'I **saw** them advertised on TV,' said Kate.
Kate said she **saw/had seen** them advertised on TV.

Present perfect simple/ continuous →	Past perfect simple/ continuous

'I**'ve bought** a hat,' Helen told me.
Helen told me (that) she **had bought** a hat.

will →	would

'I**'ll** take you there if you want,' she said.
She said she **would** take me there if I wanted.

must (obligation) →	had to

'You **must** buy a ticket,' he said.
He said that we **had to** buy a ticket.

can →	could

'I **can** speak Spanish well,' said Mel.
Mel said he **could** speak Spanish well.

2 The verb form does not need to change when:

- the situation being reported is unchanged
'Bananas **are** good for energy,' said the doctor.
The doctor told us that bananas **are** good for energy.
'The castle **is** 800 years old,' said the guide.
The guide told us that the castle **is** 800 years old.

- the thing reported contains the modals would, could, might, ought to and should or must for logical deduction
'I **ought to** buy a new car,' she said.
She said she **ought to** buy a new car.
'I think he **must** be coming,' she said.
She said she thought he **must** be coming.

- the thing being reported contains the past perfect
'He **had** already **been given** a prize,' she said.
She said he **had** already **been given** a prize.

3 Other changes that occur in reported speech are:

Direct speech	Reported speech
tomorrow	the next day, the day after, the following day
yesterday	the day before, the previous day
last week	the week before
here	there
this morning	that morning
today	that day
next Friday	the following Friday
ago	before

12.2 Reported statements

FORM: verb (+ that) + clause
'He works in television,' she said.
She **said (that) he worked** in television.
'I took the money,' she admitted.
She **admitted (that) she had taken** the money.

12.3 Reported questions

1 Reported Yes/No questions
FORM: When there is no question word in the direct speech question, we use if/whether. Word order is the same as in the statement. The verb tense and other changes are the same as for other types of reported speech.
'Could I borrow your bike?' she asked.
She asked **if/whether** she could borrow my bike.

2 Reported wh- questions
FORM: The wh- word is followed by statement word order (subject followed by verb). All tense and other changes are the same as for other types of reported speech.
'Why did you leave that job?' she asked him.
She asked him **why he had left that job.**
'Where is the swimming pool?' he asked her.
He asked her **where the swimming pool was.**

12.4 Reported orders

FORM: verb + object + infinitive with to
'Please open your suitcase', said the customs official.
The customs official **told/ordered** me to open my suitcase.

12.5 Reported recommendations

FORM: recommend + (that) + clause; recommend + -ing
'I'd buy the red coat,' my friend said.
My friend recommended **buying/(that) I buy** the red coat.

12.6 Reported suggestions

FORM: suggest + -ing
suggest + that + past simple
suggest + that + (should) + infinitive without to
'Let's pay half each,' she said.
She **suggested paying half each.**
She **suggested we paid half each.**
She **suggested that we should pay half each.**
Watch Out! We can't say: She suggested ~~to pay/~~ ~~suggested us to pay~~ half each.

12.7 Reporting verbs

1 Verb + infinitive with *to*
   agree, decide, offer, promise, refuse, threaten
   We **agreed to go** to the meeting.

2 Verb + object + infinitive with *to*
   advise, beg, encourage, invite, order, persuade, remind, tell, warn
   She **asked me to tell** the truth.

3 Verb (+ *that*) + clause
   accept, admit, claim, explain, promise, recommend, say, suggest
   She **says (that) we should be repaid the money.**

4 Verb + object (+ *that*) + clause
   promise, remind, tell, warn
   He **told us (that) he would be on time.**

5 Verb + gerund *-ing*
   admit, deny, recommend, suggest
   He **admitted taking** the money.

6 Verb + preposition + gerund *-ing*
   apologise for, insist on
   She **apologised for being** late.

7 Verb + object + preposition + gerund
   accuse (of), blame (for), congratulate (on), discourage (from), forgive (for)
   She **discouraged me from going** in for the competition.

8 Verb + *wh-* word + infinitive
   describe, explain, know, wonder
   She **explained what to do.**

9 Verb + object + *wh-* word + infinitive
   ask, remind, tell
   They **told us who to see.**

13 *it is, there is*

1 We use *There is/There are* to begin a sentence describing whether or not something exists. It is often followed by an indefinite noun.
   There is a little house at the foot of the hill.
   There are some trees growing along the side of the road.
   There's no point in worrying about it.

2 We use *It is/was*, etc. to begin a sentence giving information about time, weather and distance.
   It is a bright, sunny day.
   It was half past six in the morning.
   It's just over 10 km to the nearest town.

3 We use *It is* as the subject of a sentence to refer forwards to a later clause with *that*, an infinitive or an *-ing* form.
   It is a pity that no one can help.
   It's good to see you again.
   It's no use crying over spilt milk.

14 Modal verbs and expressions with similar meanings

14.1 Ability

1 We use *can/could* to express general ability and typical behaviour of people or things.
   Temperatures **can rise** to over 30°C in the summer.
   Employers **can be** unwilling to employ people over 50.
   My father **could be** very generous. (past)

2 We use *can/be able to* for present and future ability.
   I **can** use a word processor but I **can't** type very well.
   Will your parents **be able to** help you?
   I like **being able to** cook my own meals.

3 We use *can* for the future where there is a sense of opportunity.
   I **can come** tomorrow if you like.
   You **can practise** your French when you go to Paris.

4 We use *could/couldn't* to talk about general past ability.
   I **could swim** before I **could** walk.
   Andrew's father **couldn't get** a job.

5 We use *was/wasn't able to* to talk about past ability in a specific situation.
   Fortunately, he **was able to** swim to the shore.

6 We use *could/couldn't* + perfect infinitive to talk about unfulfilled ability in the past.
   I **could have gone** to university, but I decided not to.
   I **couldn't have been** a ballet dancer. I was too tall.

7 Other expressions for ability:
   Do you **know how to** type?
   He **succeeded in becoming** a professional footballer at 18.
   We **managed to** find our way home. (suggests difficulty)

14.2 Possibility

1 We use *can* or *could* for theoretical possibility.
   Can there be life on Mars?
   Can that be Peter over there?
   The weather **could be** better tomorrow. (it's possible)

2 We use *may, might, could* + infinitive to talk about likelihood in the present or future.
   He **may be** in a meeting. (quite likely to be true)
   She **might/could be** here already. (less likely)

3 We use *could/may/might* + *have* + past participle (perfect infinitive) to talk about the possibility that past events happened.
   His face was familiar. We **may have met** somewhere before.
   He's not in the office. He **might have finished** work early.
   She **could have been** at the party, but I didn't see her.

14.3 Certainty (deduction)

1 We use *must* to say that we are sure about something in the present or past.
   You **must be** pleased with your exam results. (present)
   He **must have touched up** the photograph. (past)

2 We use *can't* or *couldn't*, not *mustn't*, in negative sentences.
*That **can't be** Nicole Kidman. She's not young enough.* (present)
*They **can't have got lost**. They know the area really well.* (past)
*It **couldn't have been** Tom that I saw.* (past)

14.4 Strong obligation and necessity

1 We use *must/mustn't* to talk about present and future obligations/prohibitions imposed by the speaker, often on him/herself.
*Payment **must** be made in cash.*
*I **must** get some new shoes.*
*You **must** read that book – it's excellent!* (= recommendation)
***Must** I really go now?*
*You **mustn't** park here.* (= prohibition)
*You **mustn't** eat so much.* (= strong advice)

2 We use *have to/have got to* to talk about present and future obligations that are imposed by someone other than the speaker.
Note: *have got to* is more common in British than American English.
*I **have (got) to take** my holiday in February.*
*Do we **have to pay** to go in?*

3 We use *had to* to talk about past and reported obligations of all kinds.
*They told us we **had to** leave our bags in the cloakroom.*
*We **had to** stand up when the teacher came in.*
*I knew I **had to** make a decision.*

4 We can also use *need to* to talk about obligation and necessity.
*Do we **need to** type our work?*

14.5 Obligation and advice: should *and* ought to, be supposed to

1 We use *ought to* and *should* to talk about obligations and duties in the future, present and past, or to give advice.
*You **ought to/should speak** English in class.*
***Shouldn't we tell** someone about the accident?*
***Oughtn't we to have invited** Mandy?*

2 We can use *be supposed to* when saying what someone should or should not do according to rules or regulations.
*You**'re not supposed to** park here.*

3 *Should + have + past participle* is often used to criticise your own or other people's behaviour.
*I **should have told** you before.*
*You **shouldn't have promised** that.*

4 Other phrases for advice:
*It is **advisable/wise** to keep documents in a safe place.*
*You **should remember** that …*
*Travellers **are reminded that** banks close on Saturdays.*
*Guests **are recommended to** keep documents in a safe place.*

14.6 Lack of obligation or necessity

1 We use *needn't, don't need to, don't have to* to talk about a lack of obligation in the present or future.
*You **don't need to/needn't meet** me at the station.*
*We **don't have to wait**. We can go straight in.*

2 We use *needn't + have + past participle* to say that somebody did something, but that it was unnecessary.
*You **needn't have gone** to all that trouble.*

3 We use *didn't need to + infinitive* to say that something wasn't necessary without saying whether the person did it or not.
*You **didn't need to bring** any extra money.*

14.7 Asking for and giving permission

1 We use *can* to ask for and give permission.
***Can I borrow** your calculator for a few minutes?*
*Yes, you **can stay up** and watch the late night film.*
*You **can't wait** here. It's private.* (= not allowed to)

2 We use *could* to ask for permission when we are not sure what the answer will be.
A: ***Could I** open the window?*
B: *Yes, of course you **can**.*
Watch Out! *could* is **not** used for **giving** permission.

3 We use *may* to ask for or give permission in formal situations.
***May** I take that chair? You **may** use pen or pencil.*

15 Modifiers and intensifiers

USE: We can use adverbs to make adjectives, other adverbs and verbs stronger or weaker.

1 We can use these adverbs before gradable adjectives (i.e. adjectives that can be used in the comparative) and adverbs:
- *very, extremely, really, particularly, terribly* (emphatic)
- *quite, pretty, fairly, rather* (weaker than *very*)
- *a bit*
*I felt **terribly upset** when I heard the news.*
*He drives **rather fast**.*
*I thought the story was **a bit silly**.*
Watch Out! *quite* has two meanings.
*The picture was **quite** good.* (= good but not very good)
*Her cooking was **quite** wonderful.* (= very, very good)

2 Extreme or absolute (non-gradable) adjectives include: *amazing, boiling, disastrous, fantastic, freezing, impossible, marvellous, superb, wonderful*. We can use the following adverbs with extreme adjectives: *absolutely, really, utterly*.
*The special effects were **utterly amazing**.*

3 We can use these adverbs to emphasise adjectives and verbs: *just, completely, totally* (= in every way).
*I **completely/totally** forgot about your birthday.*
*It's **completely impossible** to finish in time.*
*You look **just fantastic**.*

16 Participle clauses

USE: We can use a participle clause to make our writing more economical.

16.1 -ing *participle clauses*

An *-ing* participle clause has an active meaning. It can replace relative clauses which have an active verb.
This is the road **leading** *to the school. (which leads …)*
There was a huge lamp **hanging** *from the ceiling. (which hung …)*

16.2 -ed *participle clause*

An *-ed* participle clause has a passive meaning. It can replace relative clauses which have a passive verb.
The cathedral, **built** *in the Middle Ages and recently* **restored***, is well worth a visit. (which was built … which has recently been restored)*

17 Passives

FORM: appropriate tense of *be* + past participle

Present simple:	*Most phone calls* **are made** *on mobile phones.*
Present continuous:	*Calls* **are being made** *every day.*
Past simple:	*The first email* **was sent** *in the 20th century.*
Past continuous:	*I thought I* **was being asked** *to help.*
Present perfect:	*Millions of text messages* **have been sent***.*
Past perfect:	*Once personal computers* **had been invented***, they spread quickly.*
Future *will***:**	*She***'ll be given** *her own room.*
Future perfect:	*The arrangements* **will have been made** *by the end of the week.*
*going to***:**	*The event* **is going to be organised** *by the manager.*
Modals:	*The machine* **must have been** *left switched on.* *Messages* **may not be delivered** *immediately.*
Gerund (-*ing* **form):**	*Our dog doesn't like* **being left** *on his own.*
Present infinitive:	*They hope* **to be chosen** *to take part.*
Perfect infinitive:	*I was happy* **to have been selected** *for the team.*

Notes:

1 Verbs that do not take an object (e.g. *ache, arrive, sit down*) do not have passive forms. It is not possible to say: *I was ached.*

2 For verbs with two objects, one of them a person, the passive sentence usually begins with the person.
Someone gave Mary a present.
Mary was given *a present.*
NOT: *A present was given to Mary.*

3 The verbs *make, hear, see, help* are followed by the infinitive with *to* in active sentences, but the infinitive without *to* in passive sentences.
They **made** *him* **go** *home. >* *He* **was** *made* **to go** *home.*

4 *Let* does not have a passive form. We use *be allowed to* in the passive.
They don't **let** *us talk in class. We* **are not allowed to** *talk in class.*

USE: the passive is used:

• to talk about actions, events and processes when the action, event or process is seen as more important than the agent. This is often the case in formal or scientific writing.
The equipment **was checked** *carefully.*
Rats **have been trained** *to open boxes.*

• to put new information later in the sentence
Hamlet **was written** *by Shakespeare.*

17.1 by + *agent*

When we are interested in the agent, we use the preposition *by*.
He was saved **by** *his mobile phone.*
The team were guided **by** *a local climber.*

17.2 Impersonal passive structures

We often use reporting verbs such as *believe, claim, report, say, think* in the following passive structures when we don't know or don't wish to specify the subject.

• It + *be* + verb + *that*
It is thought that *the criminal is a local man.* (present)
It was claimed that *the minister had been involved.* (past)

• Subject + *be* + reporting verb + infinitive
The criminal is thought to be *a local man.* (present)
The minister was claimed to have been involved. (past)

18 Relative clauses and pronouns

18.1 Relative pronouns

The most common relative pronouns are:
who (subject), **whom** (object): to refer to people
which: to refer to things
that: to refer to either people or things
whose: the possessive of *who* and *which*
when: used after nouns referring to time
where: used after nouns referring to place
why: used to refer to reasons
Note: *what* is not a relative pronoun.
Watch Out! The relative pronoun replaces the subject or the object.
People **who** *(they) live in glass houses shouldn't throw stones.*
The vase, **which** *I bought (it) years ago, is very valuable.*

18.2 Defining relative clauses

In defining relative clauses:
1 the relative clause defines or identifies the person, thing, time, place or reason.
   *Chris is the son of a woman **who works in television**.*
   *That's the man **whose son is an actor**.*
   *Winter was the time **when people tended to get insufficient fresh food**.*
   *I know the place **where the play is set**.*
   *I can't imagine **why he would want to leave you**.*
2 *that* can be used instead of *who* or *which*.
   *The girl **that (who) lives next door** rides a motorbike.*
   *The sports centre **that (which) is opening soon** will offer great new facilities.*
3 the relative pronoun can be left out if it is the object of the verb in the relative clause.
   *The person **(who/that)** I spoke to yesterday said it would be free.*
   *Sue bought the watch **(which/that)** she'd seen.*
4 no commas are used before and after the relative clause.

18.3 Non-defining relative clauses

The relative clause gives extra information which **can** be omitted. Commas are used before and after the relative clause. The pronoun *that* **cannot** be used instead of *who* or *which*.
*The museum**, where you can see Roman pottery**, is free.*
*The witness**, who refused to be named**, said the police had acted unwisely.*

18.4 Prepositions in relative clauses

Prepositions can come before the relative pronoun or at the end of the relative clause, depending on whether the sentence is formal or informal.
*The person **to whom I spoke** told me the hotel was fully booked.* (formal)
*John**, who I bought my car from**, has gone abroad.* (informal)

19 Verb tenses

19.1 Present simple

We use the present simple:
1 for routine or regular repeated actions (often with adverbs of frequency like *always, usually, often, sometimes, never, every Saturday morning, twice every week*).
   *We **go** running **every evening**.*
   *She **doesn't do** any work **at weekends**.*
   *I **never get** home before eight o'clock in the evening.*
2 when we are talking about permanent situations.
   *She **comes from** South America.*
   *They **live** in London.*
3 with scientific facts.
   *Water **freezes** at 0°C.*

4 with stative verbs (verbs which are not normally used in continuous forms): *be, have, depend, know, think, understand, disagree, like, want, hear, love, see, smell, taste*.
   *They **don't have** a car.*
   ***Does** she **understand**?*
   *I'm sorry, but I **disagree** completely.*
   *That perfume **smells** too strong.*
5 when we are talking about the future as expressed in timetables, regulations and programmes.
   *The plane **leaves** at 8.45.*
   *When **do** the holidays **begin**?*
6 in time clauses with a future meaning after *as soon as, if, until, when*.
   *I'll see her **when/as soon as** she's free.*
   *Give this to Susie **if** you see her.*
   *Tom can't apply for the job **until** he gets the right qualifications.*

19.2 Present continuous

We use the present continuous when we use dynamic (action) verbs to talk about:
1 actions happening now.
   *I think **he's watching** TV.*
2 changing/developing situations.
   *My broken leg **is getting** better.*
3 temporary situations.
   *I **am staying** in this hotel for two weeks.*
4 annoying or surprising habits with *always*.
   *She's **always losing** her keys.*
   *He's **always buying** her flowers.*
5 plans and arrangements in the future.
   ***Are** you **going out** this evening?*

19.3 Present perfect simple

We use the present perfect simple:
1 to talk about states, single or repeated actions over a long period of time up to the present (often with *ever/never, often/always*).
   *I**'ve always wanted** to be an actor.*
   ***Have** you **ever been** to Australia?*
   *I**'ve only used** my mobile phone **once** since I bought it.*
   *She**'s read** that book **at least ten times.***
   *That's the first time I**'ve ever eaten** octopus.*
   *It's the worst concert I**'ve ever been** to.*
2 to talk about recent single actions with a present result (often with *just, already, yet*).
   *I**'ve already seen** that film and I don't want to see it again.*
   ***Have you finished** your essay **yet**?*
   *Our friends **have just arrived**.*

Note: In American English, it is acceptable to use the past simple in sentences like these.
I didn't have breakfast yet.
I already saw that film.

3 to talk about an unfinished period of time up to the present (often with *for/since, this week/month/year*).
*Tomoko **has lived** in England **for five years**.*
*I**'ve been** in love with Stella **since 2002**.*
*I**'ve loved** travelling **all my life**.*
*I**'ve disliked** bananas **since I was a child**.*
*We **haven't had** a holiday **this year**.*

19.4 Present perfect continuous

We use the present perfect continuous:
1 to talk about a recent activity when the effects of that activity can still be seen.
A: *Why are you out of breath?* B: *I**'ve been running**.*

2 to emphasise how long an action has been going on for, or that it has been repeated many times.
*I**'ve been replying** to emails all morning.*
*I**'ve been cleaning** the house all day.*

3 to suggest that an activity is temporary.
*I**'ve been living** here for five years but I'm going to move soon.*

4 to suggest that an action is not complete.
*I**'ve been reading** War and Peace, but I haven't finished it yet.*

Watch Out! We don't use verbs that refer to a state (e.g. *be, know, love*) in the continuous form.

19.5 Past simple

We use the past simple:
1 to talk about a finished event that happened at a specific time in the past.
*I **saw** Paul **last night**.*
*I **went** to Brazil five years **ago**.*

2 to describe a sequence of finished events in chronological order.
*I **took** out my key, **opened** the door and **walked** in.*

3 to talk about habits in the past.
***Did** your parents **read** to you when you were younger?*

4 to talk about states in the past.
*When I **was** a child, I didn't enjoy watching TV at all.*
*The house **belonged** to my father from 1990 to 2000.*

5 in reported speech.
*She **said** she **didn't want** to join us.*

19.6 Past continuous

We use the past continuous:
1 to describe an action in progress in the past, often to set the scene for a particular event.
*I **was sitting** in the garden, reading a book.*

2 to talk about temporary situations in the past.
*Rodolfo **was living** in South America at the time.*

3 to talk about an event that was in progress in the past and was interrupted.
*I **was going** out of the house when I heard a noise.*

4 to talk about actions in progress at the same time in the past.
***While** I **was painting**, you were watching TV.*

5 to talk about anticipated events that did not happen.
*We **were going** to Greece for a holiday, but then I broke my leg.*

19.7 Past perfect

We use the past perfect:
1 to refer to a time earlier than another past time, when this is needed to make the order of events clear.
*The bird's wings **had been clipped** so I didn't think it could fly.*
*By the time the fire engine arrived, the house **had** completely **burned down**.*

Watch Out! Be careful not to overuse the past perfect. It is not necessary with *before/after*, which make the sequence of events clear. Once we have established the time sequence, we can revert to the past simple.

2 in reported speech.
*They said they **had met** before.*

19.8 The future

FORMS:
shall/will + infinitive
going to + infinitive
Present continuous (see 19.2)
Present simple (see 19.1)
Future continuous (*will + be + -ing* form)
Future perfect (*will + have +* past participle)

1 We use *will* + infinitive:
• for predicting something based on our belief or our knowledge of characteristic behaviour
*This medicine **will make** you feel sleepy.*
*You**'ll feel better** when you've had a good night's rest.*
Watch Out! We cannot use the present continuous in this case.

• for promises, threats, offers and requests
If you tell anyone, I'll kill you!
I promise I'll pay the money back.
I'll meet you at the station if you want.
Shall I meet you at the station?
Will you do the washing-up for me?
Watch Out! We cannot use *going to* in this case.

2 We use *going to* or the present continuous to talk about things that have already been decided.
*She's decided she's **going to** lose 10 kilos.*
*Where **are** you **going to have** the wedding reception?*
Watch Out! We cannot use *will/shall* + infinitive in this case.

3 We use *going to* to talk about things that are certain to happen because there is present evidence.
*I've got a terrible sense of direction – I know I**'m going to get** lost.*
*Look out – you**'re going to fall**!*
Watch Out! We cannot use *will/shall* + infinitive or the present continuous in this case.

4 We use *will/shall* + infinitive to talk about future actions decided at the time of speaking.
I think I'll give up smoking.
I'll wear my black dress.

5 We use the future continuous (*will/shall* + *be* + *-ing*) to say that an action will be in progress at a definite time in the future.
I'll be living a normal life by this time next year.

6 We use the future perfect (*will/shall* + *have* + past participle) to describe something that will be completed before a definite time in the future.
By the end of the month I'll have been at this school for a year.

20 Words that cause confusion

20.1 like

1 *like* can be a preposition, meaning *similar to* or *in the same way as*.
Do you look like your sister?
Like John, I hate cooking.

2 We use the question *What … like?* when we are asking for a description of a person, place or thing.
'What's the restaurant like?' 'Oh, really good.'

3 *like* can mean *such as/for example*.
Let's buy him something nice like/such as a CD.

4 *feel like* + object/*-ing* is used to talk about something that we want or want to do.
I feel like (eating) some crisps.

5 *seem/sound/look like* + object is used to introduce an idea we may not be completely sure about.
It seems like a good idea.

6 *like* is not used before an adjective on its own.
They seem happy. It feels cold.

20.2 as

1 *as* can be a preposition, coming before the name of a job or a role, or to describe the purpose of something.
She works as a sales manager.
As your father, I can't allow you to do this.
We use the loft as a play room for the kids.
I think of her as my best friend.

2 *as* can be a conjunction, followed by subject + verb.
You should do as your parents say.
I'll do as we agreed earlier.

Watch Out! In colloquial English *like* is also used as a conjunction in this way, but this is regarded as incorrect by some people, and is not used in formal writing.
Like I said, he's a really nice guy. (colloquial)
I want you to do like I tell you. (colloquial)

20.3 as if/as though

As if/as though are conjunctions followed by subject + verb. They are followed by the present or present perfect tense when referring to something likely.
It looks as if it's going to be a nice day.
He looks as if he has just won a prize!

To show that something is imaginary or unlikely, they can be followed by the past tense.
He looks as if he had seen a ghost!
He behaves as if he knew more than us.
(See also 11.6.)

Watch Out! In colloquial English *like* is often used instead of *as if/though*.
You look like you're worried. (colloquial)
It looks like we're going to win. (colloquial)

20.4 so/such/too/enough/very

1 *so* and *such*
FORM:
• *so* + adjective/adverb/determiner (+ noun) (+ *that* clause)
The journey was so dangerous that they gave up.
He has travelled so widely that he's forgotten what home is like.
I had so little information that I couldn't make a sensible suggestion.
It was so hot! (emphatic)
• *such* + (adjective) + noun (+ *that* clause)
The taxi took such a long time to come that I decided to walk instead.
He had such fun at the party that he didn't want to go home.
We had such a good time! (emphatic)
USE: *so* and *such* are used to introduce a clause of result, or for emphasis

2 *too*
FORM: *too* + adjective/adverb/determiner (+ noun) (+ *to* infinitive)
USE: *too* has a negative meaning – the speaker is not happy about the situation
It was too hot to sleep.
You're speaking too quickly – I can't understand.
That's too much (money). I can't afford it.

3 *enough*
FORM:
• adjective/adverb + *enough* (+ *to* infinitive)
He's rich enough to buy up the whole town.
You're not doing that work carefully enough.
• *enough* + noun (+ *to* infinitive / + *for* + noun)
Have you got enough money to get a taxi?
USE: *enough* has a positive meaning – the speaker regards the situation as possible

4 *very*
FORM: *very* + adjective/adverb/determiner (+ noun)
USE: *very* is used for emphasis in either a positive or negative statement. It is sometimes used when we wish to avoid using a negative word.
It's very difficult, but I think I can do it.
He's working very hard – he's bound to pass.
Very few people agree with her.

Writing reference (Paper 2)

Contents

Checklist

When writing the answer to any task, check that you have paid attention to the following points.

Answering the question
Have you
- answered all parts of the question?
- included all the necessary information?
- written the required number of words?
- organised your ideas appropriately, using paragraphs where necessary?
- written clearly so that it is easy to read?

Accuracy
Are there any mistakes in grammar, vocabulary, spelling or punctuation?

Range
Have you used
- a variety of grammatical structures?
- a range of interesting vocabulary?
- a range of linking words?

Style
- Is your language appropriate for the type of writing? (Remember to think about **who** you are writing for.)
- Is your answer interesting for the reader, and would it have a positive effect?

Formal transactional letter (Part 1)

(For work on formal letters, see pages 28, 64 and 140.)

Task

You recently had a short holiday in a large city which you booked through a company called Citibreaks. You were very disappointed with the holiday. Read the CitiBreak advertisement for the holiday you booked and the notes you have made. Then write a letter to CitiBreaks, explaining what the problems were and telling them what you want them to do.

Citibreaks

Enjoy a short holiday in the capital city.

We offer two nights' accommodation in a four-star hotel in a central location.

> Not central – long way out!

All rooms have their own bathrooms, and a view of the river.

> View not river – only car park

The price of £150 per person includes all meals as well as a ticket for a show of your choice in one of the city's leading theatres.

> Dinner cost extra

> No choice of show

This will be a real holiday to remember!

> Refund – half cost?

Write a **letter** of between **120** and **180** words in an appropriate style. Do not write any postal addresses.

Model answer

Dear Sir,

I am writing to complain about a short holiday I had recently, which was organised by Citibreaks. I was dissatisfied with several things.

First, your advertisement promised a hotel in a central location, whereas in fact the hotel was a long way from the city centre. You also said that all the rooms would have a river view, but my window just looked over the car park, which was very noisy. I also had to pay extra for dinner, although the advertisement had stated that it was included in the price. To make matters worse, I had no choice of which show to go to. I had wanted to go to a new musical, but the only ticket offered to me was for one which I had seen already.

I had been looking forward to my holiday very much, but it was completely ruined by these problems. I therefore feel that you should refund half the cost of the holiday in compensation for my disappointment.

I look forward to hearing from you soon.

Yours faithfully,

Ursine Schmidt

Ursine Schmidt

(173 words)

DO begin by saying why you are writing. DON'T begin by saying who you are.

DO list your complaints clearly, using linking words to connect your actual complaint with the details.

If you begin your letter *Dear Sir/Madam*, end with *Yours faithfully*. If you begin *Dear Ms* (or *Mr, Mrs, Miss*), end it *Yours sincerely*.

DO make a clear connection between your letter and the task input. DON'T repeat the exact words in the task input.

If you expect a reply to your letter, DO finish with this sentence on a separate line.

Sign and print your full name.

Useful language

Complaining

- *I am writing to you about* (several problems related to my city break in June).
- *I have been waiting for* (two weeks for a reply to my letter).
- *To make matters worse,* (we were informed that there was no record of our cheque being cashed).
- *I would be grateful if you could* (refund my deposit as soon as possible).

Requesting information

- *I am writing in response to* (your advertisement in The Daily Standard on July 20th).
- *I would be grateful if you could* (send me further details about the position).
- *I am writing to enquire whether* (you could let me have further details about the holiday).
- *I would like to know more about* (the arrangements for the evening meal).

Giving information/Responding to requests for information

- *In response to your query, I would like to inform you that* (I passed the FCE in June).
- *With reference to your letter of* ... (I enclose details of my qualifications).
- *You asked me to tell you about* (my travel plans and I enclose further details).

Story

(For work on stories, see pages 40 and 152.)

Task

Your teacher has asked you to write a story for the school's English language magazine. It must begin with the following words:

I wanted to do my best, but more than that I wanted the team to win.

Write your **story**. (You should write between **120–180** words.)

Useful language

- **We had been** (talking about John) **just before** (he phoned).
- **It wasn't until** (I read the letter) **that** (I realised how dangerous the situation was).
- **While** (I was waiting for my friends, I saw someone go into the house opposite).
- **As soon as** (my friends arrived, we went to have a look).
- **I was just about to** (open the door), **when** (I heard a noise downstairs).
- **By the time** (I got back to the house, there was no one to be seen).
- **After** wait**ing** (for a few minutes, I decided to climb in through the window).
- **A few seconds later,** (the lights went out).
- **Eventually/After a while,** (my friends arrived).
- **At last** (I knew what I had to do).

Model answer

> DO use phrases to show when things happened in your story (e.g. *It was the last football game of the season. When the second half started …*).

> DON'T make mistakes with narrative tenses.

> DO use direct speech because it makes the story more interesting to read.

> DO try to create some suspense.

> DO try to have a dramatic end.

I wanted to do my best, but more than that I wanted the team to win. It was the last football game of the season, and if we won, we would be the champions. As we ran onto the pitch, I couldn't help feeling nervous. The crowd was cheering, but the opposition looked strong. It wasn't going to be easy.

The game started. I got the ball and raced towards the goal. 'Go on!' roared the crowd, but I kicked it straight into the hands of the goalkeeper. 'Never mind,' yelled my team-mate Joe. 'Good try!' We played hard, but at half-time the score was 0–0.

When the second half started, it was raining heavily. Our chance of winning the championship was slipping away. We struggled to get the ball through the defence, but time after time they stopped us. Now there were only two minutes left. Suddenly I had the ball. I passed it to Joe, who headed it straight into the goal, just as the referee blew his whistle. The crowd went crazy. We were the champions!

> DON'T write about a topic if you don't know some specific vocabulary related to it (e.g. *score, goalkeeper, goal, pitch*). DO use interesting vocabulary (e.g. *raced, roared*).

> DO add extra detail to add to the atmosphere of the story.

(179 words)

Informal letter

(For work on informal letters, see pages 16 and 164.)

Task

You have received a letter from your pen friend inviting you for a visit in July. Write a letter to your pen friend, accepting the invitation, suggesting something you would like to do and asking what you should bring with you.

Write your **letter**. Do not write any postal addresses. (You should write between **120–180** words.)

Model answer

Useful language

Beginning the letter
- *Many thanks for your letter* (– *it was really nice to hear from you again*).
- *I thought I'd better write* (*and give you some more details about …*)
- *It's been such a long time since we wrote to each other.*
- *How are you and your family?*
- *How are things with you?*
- *How was* (*your holiday*)?

Introducing the topic
- *I know you're longing to hear all about* (*my holiday*).
- *You remember I told you in my last letter* (*that I was going to …*)

Ending the letter
- *Once again,* (*thanks very much for all your help*).
- *Give my love/regards to* (*your family*).
- *Please write/drop me a line soon.*
- *I look forward to* (*meeting up again soon*).

DO invent a name. Don't write *Dear Pen friend.*

DO mention a letter you have received from the person you are writing to, or refer to a shared experience.

DO say what you've been doing recently.

DO think of some specific details to include in each paragraph – this will make your letter more interesting.

DO mention the next time you will see the person you are writing to.

DO use an appropriate informal phrase to end your letter, e.g. *Love, All the best, Best wishes.* DON'T finish your letter with *Yours sincerely/faithfully.*

Dear Carla,

Thanks for your letter – it was great to hear from you. I'm sorry I haven't written for ages, but I've been really busy preparing for my exams. It's really good news that you've passed your driving test. Congratulations!

Thank you so much for your invitation to stay with you for a week in July – I'd love to come. I know that you have a wonderful beach near your house, and I'd really enjoy spending some time there. I expect that the weather will be hot, so I hope we can go swimming.

You said that I don't need to bring much with me. What sort of clothes should I pack? Casual or formal? Would you like me to bring anything for you? I would like to bring something special for you and your family from my country.

I'd better stop now and get on with my studying. I hope you're enjoying driving your car, and I'm looking forward to seeing you in July!

Thanks again for the invitation.

All the best,

Irene

(169 words)

Report

(For work on reports, see pages 78 and 114.)

Task

The school where you study English has decided to spend some money on **either** buying more computers **or** improving the library. You have been asked to write a report for the school director describing the benefits to the school of both these things, and saying which one you think should be chosen and why.

Write your **report**. (You should write between **120–180** words.)

Model answer

DON'T begin and end your report with *Dear Sir/Madam*, like a letter.

DO use headings because this makes it easier for the reader to find the main information.

DO include two or three points under each heading.

DO use numbering or bullet points to highlight main points.

DO use formal language.

Useful language

Introduction
- *The aim of this report is to ...*
- *This report is intended to ...*

Reporting results
- *Most people seem to feel that ...*
- *Several people said/told me/suggested/thought that ...*

Presenting a list
- *They gave/suggested the following reasons:*
- *They made the following points:*
  - *1   ...*
  - *2   ...*

Making recommendations
- *I would therefore recommend* (that we expand the library/installing a new coffee machine).
- *It would seem that* (banning mobile phones) *is the best idea.*

Use of money for school improvements

Introduction
The aim of this report is to compare the advantages of additional computers and of improving the library, and to suggest which of these would be best. I interviewed a number of students to find out their views.

Buying more computers
Some of the students thought that this was a good idea, saying computers were useful for:
- practising writing
- using the Internet
- playing games.

However, other students said that they preferred to use their own computers at home.

Improving the library
Most of the students preferred this suggestion, giving the following reasons:
1 Many students do not have a quiet place to study at home. The library would be a good place for private study, but at present there are not enough tables and chairs there.
2 They feel that up-to-date dictionaries and reference books are needed.
3 They want to be able to read modern books written for young people.

Recommendations
Both ideas have benefits, but the majority of students felt that improving the library would be more useful. I would therefore recommend this.

(179 words)

DO say how you collected the information.

DO use a range of specific vocabulary or set phrases e.g. *Some thought this was a good idea .../other students said they preferred ...*, but DON'T use lots of adjectives and dramatic language as you do in a story. A report gives factual information.

DON'T include irrelevant details or description.

DO express opinions impersonally. DON'T express recommendations or opinions until the conclusion.

Article

(For work on articles, see pages 52, 102 and 126.)

Task

You see this advertisement in a local English language newspaper.

> **Hey!** *magazine is looking for articles about celebrations around the world.*
> Write us an article about a celebration that is important in your country, explaining why the celebration is important and describing what people do. If your article is chosen for the magazine, you will win a weekend in a city of your choice.

Write your **article.** (You should write between **120–180** words.)

Model answer

Useful language

Involving the reader
- *Are you thinking of* (getting married in the near future)?
- *I'm sure you'll agree* (it was a great idea).

Developing your points
- *Let's start with* (why it is so important to take plenty of exercise).
- *Another advantage* (of using a computer is that …)
- *On top of that,* …

Giving your own opinion
- *I think that/In my opinion* (traditional celebrations are very important).
- *It seems to me that* (people are much more aware of the importance of a good diet nowadays).

DO think of an interesting title. DON'T start and finish your article in the same way as a letter.

Olinda's carnival – something for everyone

When most people think of Carnival, they think of Rio de Janeiro. But Rio isn't the only city in Brazil that knows how to have parties. I live in Olinda, a lovely city in the north-east of Brazil. What can we say about the carnival at Olinda? Just that it's the best in the world!

DO try to involve your readers, e.g. by using a question.

Carnival has its origins in ancient Egyptian and Roman festivals. It was introduced to Brazil by the Portuguese, and was influenced by African rhythms and Indian costumes. Now it's a big national celebration.

Once Carnival starts, the whole town goes crazy! Everyone's singing and dancing. Parades of people wearing costumes typical of our north-eastern folklore dance through the streets. I love the giant street dolls, both the traditional ones such as 'the man of midnight' and the new ones that appear each year.

DO use informal language to involve the reader.

DON'T forget to express your opinion.

The best thing about our carnival is that no one has to pay and there are no big stars. Everyone takes part, rich and poor, old and young, residents and tourists. If you come, I promise you'll never forget it!

DO finish your article by summarising your main point and giving your opinion or expressing your feelings.

(179 words)

Letter of application

(For work on writing applications, see page 140.)

Task

You see this advertisement in a local English language newspaper.

> **We are looking for students of English to spend two mornings a week helping in the local tourist office.**
>
> *Good pay and conditions for the right applicants.*
>
> Write to us, giving information about your level of English, and explaining why you would be suitable for the job.

Write your **application**. Do not write any postal addresses. (You should write between **120–180** words.)

Useful language

- *I have always been interested in* (using English in my work).
- *One of the main reasons I am applying for this job is that* (I want to work in England).
- *I have a lot of experience of* (dealing with the public).
- *I am available to start work* (at any time/from the end of the month).
- *Thank you for considering my application.*
- *I would be grateful if you would* (send me further details of the job).
- *I can be contacted* (on 0849 58 48 43) *at any time.*
- *I can be contacted* (at the above address).
- *I look forward to hearing from you soon.*

Model answer

Dear Sir/Madam,

I am writing to apply for one of the positions helping in the local tourist office which were advertised in 'Kent Weekly' on August 23rd.

I am 19 years old and come from Switzerland. German is my mother tongue and I have been learning English and French for five years at a comprehensive school. At the moment I'm a student at English International, studying for the FCE.

I have always been interested in working with people. As I have already spent three months in England, I know the local tourist attractions quite well. I would also say that I have a good knowledge of history and old places, because I have read a lot about the subject recently. In the near future, I would like to continue studying English, and so the job in your tourist office would be a great opportunity for me to improve my speaking.

I am available for interview at any time. I can be contacted on 0795 51 32 41 after 6 p.m. every evening.

Thank you for considering my application. I look forward to hearing from you.

Yours faithfully,

Gabriella Daniels

Gabriella Daniels

(183 words)

DO say which job you are applying for and where and when you saw it advertised. You can invent a newspaper and date if you need to.

DO organise your application so that you mention each of the areas in the advertisement.

DON'T make mistakes with time expressions and tenses.

DON'T forget to mention why you think you are suitable.

DO say when and how you can be contacted.

DO begin and end your letter as you would other formal letters.

Composition

(For work on compositions, see pages 90 and 176.)

Task

You have been doing a class project on technology. Your teacher has asked you to write a composition giving your opinion on the following statement:

People in the modern world depend too much on computers.

Write your **composition**. (You should write between **120–180** words.)

Model answer

DO restate the question in your first sentence.

DON'T start by saying *I agree with this* – your composition should present your own argument.

In today's world, nearly every aspect of life is affected by computer technology. Computers are used for business, public services, education and entertainment.

Some people are concerned by this development. They fear that vital skills are being lost as computer technology replaces traditional ways of working in a wide variety of areas, from art and design to banking and commerce. They point out the chaos that can occur when computer systems fail, leading to the breakdown of essential services such as transport, law and order.

DO include supporting detail for the points in each paragraph.

DO use linking expressions to introduce points.

However, people could not continue to enjoy their present standard of living without computer technology. There are now far more people in the world than there were a generation ago. The fact that there is enough food for them, that they can travel safely from one place to another, and that they can be provided with medical care, is largely due to computer technology.

DON'T forget to express your opinion in the conclusion.

In my opinion, therefore, we have to accept our dependence on computers, but at the same time we should work to find ways of making this dependence less dangerous.

(178 words)

Set book

About the exam: In Question 5, you answer one of two questions based on your reading of one of the set books. You may be asked to write a composition, an article, a report or a letter.

You do not have to answer Question 5. If you do, make sure that you know the book well enough to be able to answer the question properly. Here is a suggested **procedure** for writing about the set text.

1 Read the book all the way through, to get a general idea of the story and the characters – and to enjoy it!

2 Read the book again, this time more carefully. Make notes under the following headings.

Plot: include the main events and the order they come in the story.

Characters: include information about what they are like and how important they are in the story.

Relationships: include information about who likes/dislikes who, and the things that affect their relationships.

Places: include quick descriptions of the most important places.

Your own reactions: write down your feelings about the book, with some reasons for your opinion.

3 Make a list of the kind of questions you might be asked to write about, and discuss them with other students. Here are some ideas:

• What makes the book interesting/ exciting? Describe an exciting or memorable moment in the book.
• Choose the most interesting character. Describe him/her. Is this your favourite character?
• Is the title a good one for the book? Why?
• Does the book have a good ending? Explain why/why not.
• Do you think the book would make a good film? Explain your reasons.
• Would you recommend the book to a friend? Say why/why not.

Task

(a)

An international student magazine is running a series of articles on interesting characters in fiction, and has asked readers to send in their suggestions. Write an **article** on the character you found most interesting in the book you have read, saying who the character is and why you think they are so interesting.

(b)

Your friend is going on holiday and wants to take a book to read on the journey. Write a **letter** to your friend, recommending the book you have read and giving reasons why you think they will enjoy it.

Model answer (article)

> ### A lady with no name
>
> It seems strange to experience a story through the eyes of a nameless person – but this is the case in 'Rebecca', by Daphne du Maurier. Rebecca is the name of the first wife of Maxim de Winter. She dies before the story begins, and the novel is narrated by Maxim's second wife, whose name we never learn, but who is to me the most interesting character in the book. As we read, we learn of her feelings for Maxim, and of what she discovers about his past life and the wife she has replaced.
>
> So why do I think the narrator is such an interesting character? Although she is nameless, she has a strong personality. She is emotional and her problems and feelings are vividly described, so that you feel sorry for her. She has not had an easy life, and you want her to be happy, in spite of the strange things that happen after her marriage.
>
> All in all, her lack of an identity makes her all the more memorable – and perhaps that is why I find her so fascinating.
>
> (182 words)

DO focus on what you have been asked to do. DON'T just tell the story of the book.

DO make links between paragraphs clear.

DO describe a characteristic and then say why you like it so much.

Useful language

• **The book is really exciting because** (it starts with a murder).
• **The best moment is when** (the murderer is revealed).
• **The book tells the story of** (a family who have been separated).
• **The first thing that happens is** (Sarah leaves home).
• **The main character,** (Marian, is a teenager who …)
• **The most interesting character is** (Joe, the young man who lives …)
• **The title is really good, because** (it is mysterious and it makes you want to find out what it really means).
• **The story takes place in** (the South of France).
• **Events revolve around** (a robbery).
• **The ending is very exciting because** (it is completely unexpected).
• **It would make** (a really good film), **because** (it is such an exciting story).
• **The best thing about the book is that** (the characters are so interesting).
• **I would recommend this book because** (it is easy to read).

Useful linking words and phrases

Time sequencers

before, after, after a while, eventually, later, then, finally, as soon as, at first, at last, when, while

*I immediately phoned the police. **While** I was waiting for them to arrive, I watched the house.*

***At first**, no one got out of the car, but **after a while** the driver's door opened.*

*And **then** I **finally** found what I was looking for.*

Listing points

first, firstly, first of all, to begin with, secondly, thirdly, finally

*Our holiday was spoiled, **firstly** because the hotel was uncomfortable and **secondly** because the weather was bad.*

Adding information/emphasising points

as well as (that), in addition (to), moreover, furthermore, not only … (but also) …, what's more, on top of that, to make matters worse, in fact, as a matter of fact

*The hotel was miles from the beach. **On top of that**, the view from our bedroom window was terrible.*

***Not only** was the hotel miles from the beach, **but** the view from our bedroom window was terrible too!*

***In fact**, everyone is different when it comes to personal taste.*

Giving examples

for example, for instance, such as

*I like pop groups **such as** The Backstreet Boys.*

*My town has a lot of things for young people to do. **For example**, there are three cinemas.*

Reasons, causes and results

as a result, because, because of (this), so, therefore

*I have visited Britain several times and, **as a result**, my English is quite good.*

*By the end of the day, you haven't managed to find anything that you like. **So**, you go home frustrated.*

Contrast

1 *but*

   But links two contrasting ideas. It is not normally used at the beginning of the sentence.

   *Many people argue that TV is bad for you, **but** I disagree with this.*

2 *however*

   However can come at the beginning or end of a sentence. It must be separated off by commas.

   *The advert claimed that there were huge discounts for students. **However,** the discount was only 5%.*

*I love travelling. I don't enjoy long flights, **however**.*

3 *although, even though, though*

   These expressions introduce a subordinate clause of contrast. If the subordinate clause comes first, it is separated from the main clause by a comma.

   ***Although** he practised every day, he didn't manage to improve.*

   *I walked home **even though** it took me two hours.*

   Note: *though* can be used after a comma at the end of a separate sentence that expresses something surprising.

   *We lived in the middle of a city. We still had a large garden**, though.***

4 *whereas, while*

   Whereas and while are used to compare two things and show how they are different.

   *She likes football **whereas** I prefer tennis.*

   *My sister is very like my father **while** I take after my mother.*

   While is also used in the same way as although.

   ***While** computers are important, we shouldn't let them rule our lives.*

5 *in spite of (the fact that), despite (the fact that)*

   These expressions must be followed by a noun or -ing form. *Despite* is slightly more formal.

   ***In spite of** the fact that they are expensive, many people want to buy designer clothes.*

   ***Despite** all the research that has been done, we still haven't found a cure for cancer.*

6 *in fact, the fact of the matter is*

   This is used when you are saying what the real truth of a situation is.

   *According to the brochure, the service is free for students. **In fact,** students are charged at the same rate as everyone else.*

7 *On (the) one hand …. On the other hand …*

   These expressions are used to introduce an opposite point in a discussion.

   ***(On the one hand,)** if I take the job in Milan, I'll be able to go to the opera. **On the other hand,** if I take the job in Barcelona, I'll be able to go to the beach.*

8 *otherwise*

   This is used to say what will happen if something else does not happen first.

   *You have to choose your holiday carefully. **Otherwise,** you could be disappointed.*

Sample answers

The following scripts were written by students. Read the Paper 2 general marking guidelines on the inside back cover, and use them to help you evaluate each answer and decide on its strong and weak points. Then read the comments given and the suggested band score, and compare your ideas.

Formal transactional letter
(Part 1)

Task

You recently entered a competition for learners of English, and have just received a letter from the organisers of the competition. You have made some notes on the letter.

Congratulations! You have won first prize in our competition – a two-week trip to Vancouver or San Francisco.

Your prize includes —————— **Direct flight?**
* FREE return flight to the city of your choice
* FREE two-week course at the Vancouver or San Francisco School of International English —————— **Hours? Morning/afternoon?**
* Two week's FREE accommodation with a family —————— **Distance from school? Meals?**

We need to know your choice of city, your preferred dates, and if you would like us to make any special arrangements for you. —————— **Stay an extra week?**
We look forward to hearing from you. Once we have the information we will send you your tickets and further details.

Yours sincerely

Jacky Thompson

Jacky Thompson
Competition Manager

Write a **letter** of between **120** and **180** words in an appropriate style. Do not write any postal addresses.

Sample answer

Dear Mrs Thompson,

Thank you very much for the letter which I received yesterday. I am very pleased that I've won the prize. I would like to go to San Francisco because I have never been to the USA before. However, there are several questions I would like to ask.

First of all, I would like to know whether the return flight is a direct flight or not. I would like to book a direct flight because it is much more comfortable.

Secondly, I would like to know how long we are being teached every day and if there are classes in the morning or the afternoon. Is there a difference between Vancouver and San Francisco concerning this point?

You wrote about a free accommodation with a family. Are the meals included and/or do I have the opportunity to cook by myself? Please let me also know the distance from the school.

Finally, I would like to ask you if it is possible to stay at school for an extra week. If it is possible please let me know the price I have to pay.

I like to thank you in advance for your assistance and I look forward to hearing from you soon.

Yours sincerely,

Lennart Moser

Comments

This is rather long, but there is no irrelevant information and the student answers all parts of the question. He makes a couple of grammatical mistakes (e.g. *we are being _teached_; ~~a~~ free accommodation*), but these don't cause problems in understanding the meaning. He uses quite a wide range of structures, although he tends to repeat *I would like to know*. Vocabulary is appropriate and ideas are organised in clear paragraphs. The style is sometimes too formal (e.g. *concerning this point*) but the letter would have a very positive effect on the reader.

Band 5

Story

Task

Your teacher has asked you to write a short story for the school's English language magazine. Your story must begin with the following words:

It was not easy, but Carol knew she had to do it.

Write your **story**.

Sample answers

A

It was not easy, but Carol knew she had to do it. In front of her there was this big river, with water that was running very fast, and this rubber dinghy. Behind her she could hear the guide explaining that the water is only about 8C warm. Furthermore, he told to Carol's group that there are some dangerous places, where they have to take special care. After that, the guide smiled and cried: 'Let's go!' For one moment, Carol was thinking of an escape. But this river-rafting tour was her birthday present from her friends, and they were all there. She was the last one who got into the boat, and sat down at the back of it. She tried to smile and join the others pleasure, however, she wasn't very successful. She closed her eyes and the boat set off. After a while, Carol began to enjoy the trip. In fact, it was great fun, and at the end, when they arrived, Carol decided to book a next trip two weeks later.

B

It was not easy, but Carol knew she had to do it. She was in Trieste, Italy. She came there to visit her friend. His name is Stefano who she met in their language school in England. Actually she didn't know about Italy until she met him. So she couldn't speak Italian, was not good at Italian geography.

As the first mistake, she thought that Trieste was close to his house, but it was his fault. He lived in Trento, near Verona. She should have used a different airport. Trieste airport was quite small. She wasn't able to find a person who can speak English.

As the biggest mistake, she couldn't call him!! She usually contacted with him by emails, so she didn't know how to call.

She tried to communicated with Italian people with body language many times. She didn't give up. If she gave up, she couldn't meet him. One hour past ... and she learned how to call him!! Eventually she was able to talk with him.

Three hours later Stefano come to her at the airport. She shouted for joy "Stefano!! I missed you!!"

Comments

A This answers the question and gives some detail, and there is a clear beginning, middle and end. There is some good accurate use of language (*Behind her she could hear the guide explaining; After a while, Carol began to enjoy the trip*) but there are several mistakes with reported speech (e.g. *he told ~~to~~ Carol's group that there <u>are</u> some dangerous places*) and other mistakes (e.g. ~~an~~ *escape; a <u>next</u> trip*). There is some use of direct speech to add interest and there is quite a good range of vocabulary, but the student has not divided the story into paragraphs. It has a positive effect on the reader.
Band 4

B This is a lively story. There are quite a lot of grammar mistakes (e.g. *who she met* instead of *and she had met him, she tried to communicate~~d~~ with*). However, the student also uses a range of structures accurately (e.g. *She should have used; She didn't give up.*) There are some mistakes in vocabulary so that the meaning is not always clear (e.g. *it was his fault* instead of *He'd made a mistake; she learned how* instead of *she found out how*). Linking of ideas and sentences is not always clear. However, there is good use of direct speech and a strong ending which has a positive effect on the reader.
Band 4 (low)

Informal letter

Task

You have received a letter from a pen friend who is planning to visit you in July. Write a letter to your pen friend, describing the activities you have planned for his/her visit. Give them advice on what to bring and ask about any special requests.

Write your **letter**. Do not write any postal addresses.

Sample answers

A

Dear Carria,

Nice to hear from you. I'm so surprised that you are on your way to come here this summer. I have to say that you've made a good decision.

First of all, I would like to recommend you some places where you shouldn't miss such as Sentosa island. You can have different activities there. For example, if you would like having sunbathing. I think 'Sun World' is the best choice to relax. Don't forget to bring swimwear. I don't think Bird Park is a good place to visit. It's quite boring I have to be honest to say that. However if you are really interesting in visiting there I could show you around.

Secondly, it's the best time come here if you enjoy the shopping. We have big on sale in July. Therefore, I can arrange the shopping table for you. I will be very please to show you how interesting on big sale in here!

I don't think you need to bring any special stuff. That's because you can buy them here. Don't forget to prepare some more empty suitcase for your shopping.

If you have any question just ask me. I'll do my best to solve them.

I'm looking forward to hearing from you again!

Best wishes,

Carel

B

Dear Diego,

Hi! How are you? Thank you for your letter! I'm very happy about your plan! OK! If you let me know your arrival time, I will come to you, at Narita airport. I've thought about our plan in Japan. I know you really like football! So, how about visiting stadiums of the World Cup? You can visit a locker room in Yokohama International Stadium where the final was held, and you can see autographs of Brazilian national team members.

In July, Japan is very hot, but sometimes there is a heavy rain so you have to bring an umbrella. And there are lots of mosquitoes, you must bring a medical cream to protect yourself against them.

Do you have any special requests? If you have any, please let me know. I'll try to do it!

I'm looking forward to your reply and to meeting you in July!

Lots of love,

Yuka

Comments

A This is a full answer to the question, with a fairly good range of grammar, but there are quite a few grammatical problems (e.g. *recommend you some places where you* instead of *recommend some places to you which; interesting in* instead of *interested in*). Vocabulary problems sometimes make the meaning unclear (e.g. *I can arrange the shopping table for you*). Paragraphs and connecting words are well used and the style is generally suitable for a letter from a friend. It has a satisfactory effect on the reader.
Band 3

B All parts of the question are dealt with, in an informal style. There are some grammatical mistakes (e.g. *there is a̶ heavy rain*) and problems in pronoun use (e.g. *I'll try to do it!*) but the student uses tenses accurately and shows a good range of vocabulary, and the paragraphs are clear and well constructed. The letter has a positive effect on the reader.
Band 4

Composition

Task

You have had a class discussion on what people do in their free time. Your teacher has now asked you to write a composition, giving your opinions on the following statement:

Shopping has little value as a leisure activity.

Write your **composition**.

Sample answers

A

Does shopping have little value as a leisure activity? I think most people are really keen on shopping but is it really useful?

For example, if we ask students what they're going to do in a big city, the answers are almost always 'shopping', and they don't think about going to museums and sight-seeing. Most tourists go shopping sometime instead of to see the famous places and so they don't learn about places they visit.

However, people who enjoy shopping like every stage about shopping, from window shopping, trying clothes on, thinking if they should buy or not, to buying. The final stage is to be satisfied with seeing what they have bought in their house or wearing it in front of their mirror like a fashion show.

This activity is proved to be a complete leisure activity. Indeed, I read an article in a newspaper called 'Shopping is a way to relax'. We should all use this nice relaxation and not feel guilty. Don't you think so?

B

I believe that shopping can be one of the important things people do, like eating and sleeping, and for some shopping is their chance to do their favourite things like walking and meeting friends.

On the one hand, I think that is true that shopping has no value in some lifestyles. People think of shopping only as a chance to do whatever they want, and then it is an escape from doing things they should do. I mean people go shopping instead of do work.

However, others think of it as a chance to meet some friends who you only see from time to time. In addition, it is useful time to discuss every day problems - for example, if you have got some problems, in that shopping time you might listen to others problems and think that yours are nothing compared to theirs. It can make a break from every day work pressure and so it is valuable for some who have a hard job and lifestyle.

In conclusion, it's true that buying things has little value, but people are different, which means that shopping will be priceless for some.

Comments

These answers are both **Band 4**, for different reasons.

A This has clear organisation, with paragraphs giving points for and against the statement. However, the first sentence just repeats the task. There are some good expressions (e.g. *if we ask … the answers are almost always 'shopping'*) but also some grammatical mistakes (e.g. *go shopping <u>sometime</u> instead of <u>to see</u>*). There is quite a good range of topic-related vocabulary, but the style is too informal in places (e.g. *Don't you think so?*). It has a positive effect on the reader.

B This answers the question clearly and uses a wide range of vocabulary and some good expressions (e.g. *think that yours are nothing compared to theirs*). However, there are grammatical mistakes (e.g. *instead of do work*). The style is appropriate. The conclusion clearly returns to the question and gives a nice summary of the writer's opinion. It has a positive effect on the reader.

Report

Task

The owner of the school where you study English has decided to make some changes to the school classrooms. He has asked for ideas from students about what should be done to make the classrooms better places to study in. Write a report making suggestions for how the classrooms could be improved.

Write your **report**.

Sample answer

<u>Introduction</u>
This report is to suggest what we need to make the classrooms better in our school. I asked students for their ideas.

<u>Background situation</u>
What it's need to be inside a good school classrooms is that they all have all the equipment students might need starting from the essential things like chair, blackboards, finishing with accessories like televisions.

<u>Suggestions</u>
I certainly believe that two things need to start our plan to improve the school classrooms, they are money and good management. My idea of improving the classrooms is to start with what we have and see what needs to be repared and what has to be thrown away and replaced with a new equipment and some computers that the students might need also having a massive liberrary is one of the more important things that students request. Heating and air conditioning are necessary to make the atmosphere in the classrooms cosy.

<u>Personal opinion</u>
In conclusion, the chance of having a good classrooms looks easy from a distance, in fact it isn't, and that we must try to find the balance between having a very good school and not spending too much.

Comments

This report makes some relevant points, but the style is more suitable for a composition than a report. It would be much better in bullet points.
It is not easy to identify the main suggestions because of problems with sentence linking and punctuation. *My idea of … is to start with what we have* is good. The problem is the sentence is too long and needs splitting up, e.g. *My idea of improving the classrooms is to start with what we have. Then we can see … .* There are some problems with passive forms (e.g. *what it's need* instead of *what is needed*) but also some good expressions (e.g. *to start with what we have; we must try to find the balance between*). The student has a good range of vocabulary although this is not always appropriately used (e.g. *massive; cosy*) and there are some spelling mistakes (e.g. *repared, liberrary*). It has a satisfactory effect on the reader.
Band 3

Article

Task

You have seen this advertisement in a magazine for young people.

Sample answer

> *I'd love to have ...*
>
> Write an article about something you would like to have, saying why you would like to have it and what difference it would make to your life.
>
> **The writer of the best article will win a lap-top computer.**

Write your **article**.

I'd love to have a lot of money although I think money is not a perfect solution. Of course not! However, if I had enough money, I could do a plenty of things which I want to do.

Above all, I want to study in other countries, because. It is a good chance to develop my abilities. In this case, I don't need to worry about the fee of education in my life. I can only concentrate on studying as long as I do my best.

Secondly, I would like to prepare a lovely house for my parents. Although they didn't say to me at all, I think the work of electric services is so hard to continue at their ages within 10 years. Therefore, I hope that I could make them relax and enjoy their life.

On the other hand, I can help the other people who are suffering from lack of food, illness and so on. When I saw a TV programme which announced those people's stories, I thought if I were them I would get really depressed.

Sometimes, money can be used in a bad way, but if I am a rich person, I will spend them on not only for me, but I also give an opportunity to others.

Comments

This answer gives relevant information and answers the question. There is quite a good range of structures and vocabulary but these are not always used very accurately (e.g. *If I am a rich person, I will spend them on not only for me* instead of *If I were rich, I wouldn't just spend the money on myself*). It is also difficult to understand exactly what she wants to say about her parents in the line *Although they didn't say to me at all, I think ...* . The paragraphs are well planned but there are mistakes with linking words (e.g. *On the other hand* instead of, e.g. *As well as that*) and with punctuation. There is a mixture of informal language (e.g. *Of course not!*) and formal language (e.g. *Therefore*). It has a satisfactory effect on the reader.

Band 3

Vocabulary reference

Page numbers indicate where you will see each item in *NEW First Certificate Gold*. The letter R means the phrase is in the recording.

The grammar of multi-word verbs

There are four main types of multi-word verbs.

1 **Verb + particle** (phrasal verbs)
  e.g. *break down, grow up*

  His marriage **broke down.**
  He **grew up** in the country.

  The verb and particle are inseparable. This type is intransitive (does not take an object).

2 **Verb + particle + object / Verb + object + particle** (phrasal verbs)
  e.g. *bring (sb.) up, take (sth.) up*

  My grandmother **brought** me **up.**
  I'd like to **take up** diving seriously.

  The verb and particle are separable. If the object is a pronoun (e.g. *me, it* etc.), it must come between the verb and particle.

3 **Verb + preposition + object** (prepositional verbs)
  e.g. *come across sb./sth., look after sb./sth.*

  I **came across** some old photos recently.
  We're **looking after** the neighbour's dog.

  The object must follow the preposition.

4 **Verb + particle + preposition + object** (prepositional verbs)
  e.g. *come up with sth., look down on sb.*

  We need to **come up with** some ideas for marketing the product.

  The object must follow the preposition.

break down p.134 stop working successfully: *His marriage* **broke down**.

break in/break into sth. p.145 enter a building by force: *He* **broke into** *a house.*

bring (sb.) up p.42 look after and educate a child: *Jamie Oliver was* **brought up** *in the country.*

bring (sth.) up p.168 mention a subject or start talking about it: *Working in a team can* **bring up** *new ideas.*

build (sth.) up p.25 increase: *They can* **build up** *their confidence gradually.*

carry on (with sth.) p.14R continue: *I wish I'd* **carried on** *with my education.*

carry (sth.) out p.46 do: *Scientists* **are carrying out** *experiments.*

catch on (to sth.) p.123 understand: *He* **catches on** *to new ideas quickly.*

come across sb./sth. p.37R find something by accident: *She* **came across** *a book she used to own.*

come through p.71 succeed after a difficult time: *I've had my share of problems, but I've* **come through**.

come up p.7R be mentioned or suggested: *Four names* **came up** *again and again.*

come up with sth. p.157 think of, invent: *The company has* **come up with** *a new gadget.*

cope with sth. p.80R manage to do something that is difficult: *It was difficult to* **cope with** *the lack of light.*

deal with sth. p.74 act to solve a problem: *It is washable, to* **deal with** *those inevitable kitchen spills.*

drop out p.14R stop an activity before you have finished it: *I* **dropped out** *in the first round.*

eat out p.131R eat in a café or restaurant: *I* **eat out** *most evenings.*

end up p.70 be in a particular situation that you did not intend to be in: *We might* **end up** *forgetting how to talk to one another.*

face up to sth. p.168 accept a difficult situation and try to deal with it: *You need to* **face up to** *problems.*

fall out (with sb.) p.169 quarrel with: *I* **fell out with** *my coach.*

find out (about sth.) p.7R discover information: *They were trying to* **find out about** *the most popular films of the 20th century.*

flick through sth. p.34R look quickly through the pages of something without reading carefully: *I* **flick through** *celebrity magazines.*

gather (sth.) up p.108 collect things into one place: *I* **gathered up** *my books.*

get (sth.) across p.123 explain, communicate: *He* **gets** *new ideas* **across** *to the students.*

get down to sth. p.123 start doing something seriously: *She couldn't* **get down to** *her homework.*

get on p.168 make progress, succeed: *To* **get on** *in life, you need clear goals.*

get on (with sb.) p.95 have a good relationship: *At first Marc and I* **got on** *really well.*

get up p.42 get out of bed: *Jamie* **got up** *very early on his wedding day.*

give (sth.) away p.56 donate for free: *The shop **gave away** free samples.*

give (sth.) up p.18 stop doing something: *I **gave up** my job.*

go ahead p.93 start to do something: *I got the backing of a TV company and **went ahead**.*

go in for sth. p.37R entered: *I **went in for** a competition.*

go on p.109R happen: *I didn't know what was **going on** in my flat.*

go on (doing sth.) p.193 continue: *I **went on** trying.*

go out (with sb.) p.43 have a romantic relationship with someone: *He started **going out with** Jools.*

grow up p.43R become an adult: *He **grew up** in a restaurant.*

hit on sth. p.150 think of: *He **hit on** a new idea.*

keep on (-ing) p.71 continue: *We'll **keep on** fighting till the end.*

keep up (with sth.) p.34R stay up to date: *I want to **keep up with** events in the music world.*

knock (sth.) down p.111 deliberately destroy: *The shopping centre has been **knocked down**.*

let (sb.) down p.98 disappoint someone, especially by not doing what you promised: *Maria will never **let** you **down**.*

live on sth. p.145 eat only a particular kind of food: *He **lived on** Pepsi and dog biscuits.*

look after sb./sth. p.23 take care of: *You need to **look after** yourself.*

look down on sb. p.33 feel you are superior to: *He **looks down on** everyone else.*

look forward to sth./-ing p.9 be excited and happy about something that is going to happen: *I am **looking forward** to the challenge.*

look into sth. p.32 try to find out about something: *The authorities are **looking into** the cause of the fire.*

look out for sb./sth. p.33 try to find or notice someone or something: ***Look out for** Steve at the party.*

look up to sb. p.33 admire and respect: *He **looks up to** his grandfather.*

made up of sth. p.43R consisting of: *a band **made up of** Jamie and his high school friends*

make (sb./sth.) out p.171 be only just able to see: *I can't **make out** much detail in the dim light.*

make (sth.) up p.116 invent: *Dominic **makes up** stories to help him remember things.*

pick (sth.) up p.25 learn: *I climbed by instinct, just **picking it up** as I went along.*

put off (by sth.) p.34 discouraged: *I try not to be **put off by** difficult books.*

run out of sth. p.100 have no more left: *The car stopped because it had **run out of** petrol.*

save up for sth./to do sth. p.12 keep money so you can use it later: *He's **saving up** to go to Canada.*

set off p.18 begin: *You **set off** on a journey.*

shoot up p.19R go up quickly: *I **shoot up** to the surface again.*

show (sb.) around p.169R go around a place with someone to show them what is interesting: *He **showed** me **around** the air base.*

show (sth.) off p.57 to let people see things you are proud of so they will admire you: *Most of us like to **show off** what we can afford.*

shut up/shut (sb.) up p.98 be quiet, stop talking: *When Pietro starts talking, I can't **shut** him **up**.*

sneak out p.145R leave without anyone noticing you: *She was trying to **sneak out** without paying.*

switch (sth.) off p.88R turn off a machine: *I **switched off** the TV.*

take (sth.) in p.123 understand, concentrate on: *I can't **take in** what he's saying.*

take off 1 p.25 start to fly: *I started by **taking off** from small hills.*
2 p.42R start to be successful: *That was when his career really **took off**.*

take (sth.) on p.19R start doing something or being responsible for something: *There's no way I could **take on** a dive like that on my own.*

take to sb./sth. p.19R start to like something or someone: *I **took to** free diving immediately.*

take (sth.) up p.19R begin to do something regularly: *My teacher encouraged me to **take up** diving seriously.*

throw (sth.) away/out p.37R get rid of: *They meant to **throw** the papers **away**.*

touch (sth.) up p.69R improve something by making small changes to it: *The photograph was **touched up** to make her look thinner and more beautiful.*

trip over (sth.) p.145R hit something with your foot and fall as you are walking: *She **tripped over** a child.*

turn (sth.) off p.78 make a machine stop working: ***Turn off** your mobile phones in class.*

turn (sth.) on p.14 make a machine start working: *You **turn on** the radio.*

turn out p.7R happen in a particular way, have a particular result: *It **turned out** that the most popular films were those set in the future.*

turn up p.19R arrive: *When I **turned up** for the class, I was the only woman there.*

wake up p.31 stop sleeping: *It must be a dream – I expect I'll **wake up** soon.*

wear off p.131 gradually disappear: *The novelty's **worn off**.*

work (sth.) out p.105 tell or calculate something: *It's hard to **work out** anything from his face.*

Nouns, adjectives, verbs and expressions followed by prepositions

+ about

to complain p.14
concerned p.24
encouraging p.19
enthusiastic p.45
happy p.44
nervous p.37
single-minded p.167
to think twice p.23
unrealistic p.167
upset p.154
worried p.96

+ as

to act p.174
to emerge p.149
ideal p.58
identified p.174
known p.43R
to make your name p.42R
to serve p.20
to train p.43R
treated p.111
to work p.42

+ against

to campaign p.56
to compete p.54
a struggle p.7
to succeed (against all the odds) p.11

+ at

to gaze p.32
good p.33
to look p.7R
to stare p.31
successful p.138R
surprised p.60R

+ for

an advertisement p.64
to apologise p.61
to apply p.137

to arrange p.145
bad p.120
to blame sb. p.61
to come in handy p.58
convenient p.58
to despise sb. p.111
to forgive sb. p.61
to get a feel p.24
ideal p.58
implications p.85
to pay p.10
perfect p.58
to plan sth. p.124
possible p.171
prepare p.23
a prize p.122
to provide p.133
a reason p.23
a replacement p.25
responsible p.43
to search p.139
to stand p.7R
to study p.158
a substitute p.120
a talent p.43
useful p.58
to vote p.10

+ from

to benefit p.120
different p.24
to disappear p.160
to escape p.34
to prevent sb./sth. p.45

+ in

active p.96
to believe p.23
a career p.23
a change p.120
common p.155
an experiment p.80R
high (in cholesterol) p.42
an increase p.84
interested p.19
involved p.24
low p.45
no point p.30
rich (in vitamins) p.42
a rise p.120

set p.7R
to specialise p.83
to succeed p.23
to take part p.14
to take pride p.174
vital p.93

+ into

to change p.137
to convert p.111
to do research p.45
to translate p.157

+ of

to accuse sb. p.61
afraid p.43
aware p.145
capable p.19R
a collection p.62
a danger p.19R
to dream p.11
the experience p.123
the fault p.145
frightened p.19
full p.142
to gain understanding p.45
a glimpse p.30
to hear p.37R
the origin p.148
sign p.30
a source (of protein) p.42
a stroke (of luck) p.43R
a study p.44
supportive p.96
a symbol p.148
to think p.11R
a waste (of time) p.34

+ on

based p.92
to concentrate p.133
to congratulate sb. p.61
to depend p.14R
an influence p.160R
keen p.95
to make an impression p.88R
to pass something (on to sb.) p.92
to spend (money) p.85
to waste (money) p.137

+ over

to fall p.145
to fight p.139
power p.57
to reach a compromise p.76
to trip p.31

+ to

acceptable p.105
addicted p.23
an answer p.149
to appeal p.43
to apply p.158R
an approach p.55
attached p.155
to belong p.8
close p.43R
connected p.92
exposed p.120
an introduction p.25
a key p.120
sympathetic p.167
valuable p.96

+ with

annoyed p.19
associated p.139
bored p.167
to communicate p.158R
content p.43R
a contract p.10
fitted p.157
friendly p.39
friends p.9
frustrated p.19
to help p.133
to interact p.120
to interfere p.125
to lose touch p.11R
to mix p.25
to share (a flat) p.12